T0305184

Promoting Competition in Global Markets

Promoting Competition in Global Markets

A Multi-National Approach

P.J. Lloyd
Ritchie Professor of Economics and Director, Asian Economics Centre, University of Melbourne, Australia

Kerrin M. Vautier
Research Economist, Auckland, New Zealand

Edward Elgar
Cheltenham, UK • Northampton, MA, USA

Published by
Edward Elgar Publishing Limited
Glensanda House
Montpellier Parade
Cheltenham
Glos GL50 1UA
UK

Edward Elgar Publishing, Inc.
6 Market Street
Northampton
Massachusetts 01060
USA

A catalogue record for this book
is available from the British Library

Library of Congress Cataloguing in Publication Data

Lloyd, P.J. (Peter John)
    Promoting competition in global markets: a multi-national
approach / Peter J. Lloyd, Kerrin M. Vautier.
    Includes bibliographical references.
      1. International trade. 2. Competition, International.
   3. Foreign trade promotion. I. Vautier, Kerrin M. II. Title.
HF1379.L594 1999
382.'.3—dc21   98–53418
                                                                     CIP

ISBN 1 85898 803 9

Printed and bound in Great Britain by Bookcraft (Bath) Ltd.

Contents

Figures and Tables

Figures

Tables

Acknowledgements

First and foremost we are indebted to the Institute of Policy Studies at Victoria University of Wellington, and particularly to its former Director Professor Gary Hawke, for supporting our initial research which culminated in our 1997 publication *International Trade and Competition Policy: CER, APEC and the WTO.* The Institute's willingness to waive copyright so that we could use that work freely in the development of a much more comprehensive presentation of wider international interest is gratifying. Parts of Chapter 2 have drawn on an article, Lloyd (1998b), published in *The World Economy.*

Mark Toner, solicitor, wrote Chapter 3. We are grateful to him and we acknowledge the support of his employer, Bell Gully Buddle Weir.

We are grateful to the European Commission (Alexis Jacquemin and Robert Meiklejohn); the OECD (Darryl Biggar, Crawford Falconer, Marie-Pierre Faudemay, Gary Hewitt, Bernard Phillips and Mark Warner); the WTO (Robert Anderson, Jill Courtenay, Henrik Horn and Patrick Low); and the OAS (Barbara Kotschwar, Maryse Robert and Jose Tavares) for participating in discussions.

Others, in New Zealand, including Justice David Baragwanath, Pare Keiha, Chris Noonan, Robert Scollay, Rudd Watts & Stone Librarians, Ministry of Commerce, Ministry of Foreign Affairs and Trade, the Australian Consulate and the USIS, responded generously to various information requests.

We also acknowledge the contributions of seminar participants at the University of Strathclyde, the European Institute for Advanced Studies in Management, Brussels and the Economic Policy Research Unit of the Copenhagen Business School; and input by Rod Falvey of the University of Nottingham's Economics Department. The support of the University of Auckland, University of Melbourne and University of Nottingham, while the authors wrote this book, is appreciated.

Special PECC meetings on PECC's competition principles project were also very instructive as our research developed. Paris-based members of PECC's Associate Member Committee French Pacific Territories (Dr Jacques Gravereau and Professor Jean-Luc Le Bideau) were also helpful as was Dr François Souty of the Conseil de la Concurrence.

Once again we are indebted to Elayne Pownall for her diligent and untiring efforts on the manuscript.

P.J. LLOYD
KERRIN M. VAUTIER
July 1998

Abbreviations

ABA	American Bar Association
ABA	Australian Broadcasting Authority
ABAC	APEC Business Advisory Committee
ACCC	Australian Competition and Consumer Commission
ACS	Australian Customs Service
ADA	Anti-dumping Authority (Australia)
AFTA	ASEAN Free Trade Area
ANZBC	Australia New Zealand Business Council
ANZCERTA	Australia New Zealand Closer Economic Relations Trade Agreement
APEC	Asia-Pacific Economic Cooperation
ASEAN	Association of South-East Asia Nations
CACM	Central American Common Market
CAP	Collective Action Plan (APEC)
CARICOM	Caribbean Community and Common Market
CEC	Commission of the European Communities
CEEC	Central and East European Countries
CEPR	Centre for Economic Policy Research (London)
CER	Closer Economic Relations Agreement
CITT	Canadian International Trade Tribunal
CTI	Committee on Trade and Investment (APEC)
DGIV	Directorate-General IV (EU)
DOC	Department of Commerce (US)
DOJ	Department of Justice (US)
EBRD	European Bank for Reconstruction and Development
ECOSOC	United Nations Economic and Social Council
EEA	European Economic Area
EFTA	European Free Trade Association
EU	European Union
EVSL	Early Voluntary Sector Liberalization (APEC)
FDI	Foreign Direct Investment
FTAA	Free Trade Area of the Americas
FTC	Federal Trade Commission (US)
GATS	General Agreement on Trade in Services
GATT	General Agreement on Tariffs and Trade
IAEAA	International Anti-trust Enforcement Assistance Act

IAP	Individual Action Plan (APEC)
IPR	Intellectual Property Rights
ITC	International Trade Commission (US)
ITO	International Trade Organization
JFTC	Japan's Fair Trade Commission
MAPA	Manila Action Plan for APEC
MERCOSUR	Common Market of the Southern Cone
MFN	Most Favoured Nation
MITI	Ministry of International Trade and Industry (Japan)
MLAT	Mutual Legal Assistance Treaty
MOU	Memorandum of Understanding
MTO	Multilateral Trade Organization
NAFTA	North America Free Trade Area
NTM	Non-tariff Measures
OAS	Organization of American States
OECD	Organization for Economic Cooperation and Development
PECC	Pacific Economic Cooperation Council
SAR	Special Administration Region (of China)
SME	Small and Medium-sized Enterprises
STE	State Trading Enterprise
TNC	Trade Negotiations Committee (FTAA)
TRIMS	Trade-related Investment Measures
TRIPS	Trade-related Aspects of Intellectual Property Rights
UN	United Nations
UNCTAD	United Nations Conference on Trade and Development
UNCTC	United Nations Commission on Transnational Corporations
USIS	United States Information Service
USTR	United States Trade Representative
VER	Voluntary Export Restraint
WTO	World Trade Organization
WTO Working Group	WTO Working Group on the Interaction between International Trade and Competition

1. Introduction

A growing international interest in policies to promote or defend competition is accompanying globalization of markets. This reflects in part the increased market orientation of government policies — as these are substituted for government planning and intervention — and the growing recognition of the key role that competition plays in efficient markets.

'Competition policy' has been defined variously but it has become the shorthand label for a set of competition issues and the related research and policy work in numerous international agencies (including the OECD, WTO and UNCTAD) and country groupings (including EU, CER, APEC and the FTAA). It is not surprising that the WTO in its 1997 Annual Report (WTO, 1997a, Chapter 4) and UNCTAD in its World Investment Report for 1997 (UNCTAD, 1997, Part 2) chose as their themes the relationship between competition policies and, respectively, international trade and foreign direct investment. The international surge of research pertaining to an array of competition issues and policy responses has enormous education value and is contributing to a better understanding of the issues and their implications for business and consumers.

This book is about the promotion of competition in globalizing markets and the role of inter-government cooperation in setting the policy environment for competition. In large part it focuses on concerns about cross-border private business transactions that could interfere with the competitive process as markets are enlarged, but no chapter attempts a review of national or regional laws. This focus reflects the state-of-play internationally and the extensive efforts being made, particularly by international agencies, to address the perceived risk that competition-reducing private conduct could undermine competition-inducing government actions (including trade liberalization and deregulation).

In large part, as a result of US advocacy and the importance attached to competition law in the context of EU membership, there has been a significant adoption of national laws which target anti-competitive business conduct and acquisitions. Many national governments, regional groupings and international agencies see competition law as the principal or ultimate guardian of the competitive process.

When it comes to the international dimensions of 'competition policy' there is a diversity of view among countries. The United States leads the debate but it takes a comparatively narrow view. Itself under attack for its extraterritorial use of anti-trust and its threats of unilateral trade remedies, it has unquestionably helped focus international attention on the potential for cross-border business transactions to interfere with the competitive process.

The US strongly advocates a culture of sound national anti-trust enforcement and, to that end, promotes the sharing of anti-trust experiences, bilateral cooperation/coordination between national anti-trust agencies, and technical assistance for developing economies. The European Union, on the other hand, has been much more inclined to recommend the development of multilateral options. Some economies, notably Singapore and Hong Kong, SAR, are arguing in international fora that a comprehensive national competition law is not an essential feature of an effective consumer-driven competition policy, although limited and flexible regulation in non-tradable sectors may be. Such a policy should, first and foremost, apply competition principles to government actions (including trade remedies and domestic regulations). Markets should be open to all modes of supply.

Competition law is a complex area of policy. It involves decisions on policy objectives and the desired degree of market freedom; the principles to be applied; decisions on the substantive rules and the extent of *per se* prohibitions; decisions on the type and severity of deterrents; and, increasingly, consideration of cross-border business transactions and enforcement. While not every country (developed or developing) has or believes it needs a general law to govern the structure and conduct of commercial activity, proponents of competition law argue that convergence in this policy area will help to harmonize (and keep surveillance of) business conditions in markets that are no longer defined by national or jurisdictional boundaries.

The growing interest in competition law sanctions is something of a paradox in the context of markets becoming more competitive through liberalization of trade and foreign direct investment, deregulation and privatization in many economies, and the development of information technology. Although access to individual economies and foreign consumers has increased, significant barriers to competition in markets clearly remain. It is interesting that the literature largely ignores this paradox. Rather, it tends to take for granted that guardianship of markets via competition law is a necessary accompaniment to trade and investment liberalization and deregulation; and that the risk of anti-competitive business conduct will justify this legal response.

Business, however, as it constantly reorganizes and seeks efficient ways of pursuing opportunities provided by more open and expanding markets, has a legitimate concern that interventions from over-zealous regulators will impede rather than enhance the competitive process, especially in an era of dramatic technological change and speed of change. But increased adoption of the language and principles of *competition* law itself signals a more positive approach to the promotion or defence of competition as traditional trade and other barriers fall. A focus on the promotion of competition — not as an end in itself, but as a means of promoting efficiency — leads to a wider scoping of so-called competition policy. This is clearly desirable.

Internationalizing pro-competition principles necessarily encompasses government as well as private actions affecting competition and efficiency in markets. The private sector is not the only influence on the competitive process and therefore should not be the sole target of so-called competition policy. Governments themselves are engaged in commercial activities, and governments are primarily responsible for the remaining regulations and barriers affecting market entry and effective merit-based competition. Thus, enhancement of competition and efficiency in regional and global markets requires a combination of policy measures to strengthen the overall competitive process and yield efficient and welfare-enhancing outcomes. This requirement becomes the basis for developing a more coherent competition-based framework to guide market-related policy deliberations in both national and multi-national fora and to guide the resolution of economic policy conflict both within and between governments.

We make a significant departure from the common proposition that 'competition policy' warrants attention because it is a new trade-related issue. Our research shows that this proposition is confusing the issues. There is a stand-alone case for policies to promote competition, and widely applied competition principles would make a positive contribution to the development of a policy framework for promoting competition. The objective of so-called competition policy is not to increase or maximize trade without regard to competition, efficiency and welfare outcomes.

It is no coincidence that the title of this book does not contain the terms 'trade', 'competition law' or 'competition policy'. (Indeed, the authors avoid the term "competition policy" unless it has been explicitly used by others.) This reflects the following propositions: (i) competition issues are not simply trade-related; (ii) objectives relating to increased market access for a country's exports, or to increased market share for a country's exports, are not appropriate substitutes for a goal of global welfare via efficient competition in enlarging markets; (iii) considerable confusion surrounds the term 'competition policy': to some it includes a general competition law, to others the term simply equates with competition law, and, to a few, it need not include competition law; (iv) a culture of *competition* needs to be pervasive in policy formation if competition is to fulfil its role as an efficient mechanism for allocating resources; (v) it is just as important that there is a competition dimension in other government policies that impact on markets, as there is in regulation of private business conduct.

Our earlier book was entitled *International Trade and Competition Policy: CER, APEC and the WTO*. It reviewed the reasons for and the issues arising from the growing prominence of 'competition policy' as a 'new trade-related issue'. This book builds on that research and draws from much new material. It significantly expands coverage of the competition dimension of trade liberalizing groups beyond CER, APEC and the WTO by adding the EU, NAFTA and other economic arrangements that are developing in the Americas. It examines more fully the contributions to debate by the OECD and UNCTAD.

Part One provides an overall analytical framework. Parts Two to Five
review and analyse the principal mechanisms for addressing 'competition
policy' — bilateral, regional, plurilateral and multilateral. Part Six, entitled
'Emerging Patterns and Principles', assesses the potential of the different
mechanisms for shaping a multi-national policy framework governed by
sound competition principles. The economic and social desirability of a
comprehensive and coherent policy framework for the promotion of
competition in enlarging markets is a central theme of this book.

PART ONE

Competition in Global Markets

2. The Framework for Policy Analysis

The growing attention to cross-border competition problems is part of a general increase in attention around the world to competition in globalizing markets. Governments are adopting more pro-competitive policies in areas such as deregulation, privatization, and foreign direct investment. They recognize that, however these policies are labelled, they can impact on competition and efficiency in national as well as internationalizing markets. These trends reflect the convergence of views around the world towards governments putting more emphasis on market mechanisms and competition in markets as a means of improving efficiency in individual economies.

For example, in many countries public utilities were deregulated and, in most cases, privatized during the 1980s and 1990s. Deregulation had a similar effect to trade liberalization; the partial freeing up of markets revealed the need for further policy actions to make sure that the maximum benefits were derived from liberalization. These effects are particularly notable in East European countries which are dismantling state control of all industries (see Estrin and Holmes, 1998) but they are observable in many other developed and developing countries.

The number of countries with competition laws increased rapidly in the 1990s. All OECD countries have competition laws. Many non-OECD countries do not have a general competition law directed at anti-competitive business conduct. Thirty countries adopted competition laws in the 1990s and over 20 had them under preparation as at mid-1996 (UNCTAD, 1997, Annex Table A.22). All of these in both categories were developing countries or countries in transition with a sole exception. The exception is Italy which adopted competition law in 1990. In most countries which have had competition law, the scope is tending to widen to cover more sectors and government commercial practices. A recent comprehensive review of the scope of competition laws in OECD countries is provided by the Hawk study (OECD, 1996a).

Modes of Supply and Competition in Global Markets

The problems of developing policies which promote competition have become much greater due to the globalization of markets. More markets for products are now global markets. In a few cases, individual producers now sell in virtually every nation; this is true, for example, of producers of internet services or computer hardware and software, telecommunications,

7

civil aviation services and Coca Cola.

Evidence of increased cross-border sales in markets is provided by the statistics compiled annually by the WTO. In the latest period, from 1990 to 1996, the volume of world merchandise trade increased at an average compound rate of 6.0 per cent per year whereas the volume of world merchandise output increased by only 1.5 per cent per year. Thus, more of the world's output is being traded internationally. (The value of world trade in services is increasing at about the same rate as the value of trade in goods but there are no estimates of service trade in real terms.)

One form of integrated international production is the manufacture of products in a sequence of stages which are distributed across several countries with manufacturers now sourcing inputs from the cheapest country. This has increased the focus on vertical restraints on trade such as vertical mergers or foreclosures or restrictions on the sales of products to downstream producers if they reduce competition.

Another form involves intellectual property rights. These have greatly expanded in recent years, especially in knowledge-intensive industries, and are an important adjunct to competition law. Intellectual property rights can be a factor in the establishment of monopolies or the abuse of dominance in global markets for goods or services; for example, in some countries copyright and trademark laws have been used to ban parallel imports from other than authorized dealers.

New business practices have emerged in globalized markets; for example, new forms of cross-border alliances in addition to the traditional forms (joint ventures, licensing, franchising, etc.) have emerged in recent years and grown very rapidly. These include R&D alliances and strategic production alliances (see UNCTAD, 1997, Chapter V).

The dominant influence in the creation of global markets has been the cumulative effect of liberalization of border barriers to international trade in goods and services in the 1980s and 1990s. Unilateral, regional and multilateral actions have reduced substantially the average levels of these border barriers to trade. The multilateral reductions under the Uruguay Round Agreements will continue until they are fully implemented in 2005. Of particular value in the Uruguay Round is the tariffication of many non-tariff barriers.[1] Quantitative restrictions have much greater effects on the degree of competition in markets where they apply than tariffs because they also limit the volume of supply and the number of competitors. In the present context, trade liberalization has increased the market access of exporters to many economies and thereby increased sources of competition in these economies. Indeed, an increase in competition within and between economies is one of the major benefits of trade liberalization. A second factor which has helped create global markets has been the development of information technology and electronic commerce in particular.

The globalization of markets emphasizes the connection of national markets that has come about through reductions of barriers to cross-border trade and investments. More producers, both national and multinational firms, recognize that competition is increasingly global. This leads naturally to consideration of the ways in which national markets are connected.

Typically those who write about the multinational corporation identify two modes of supply (excluding non-equity arrangements). The first is the mode of supply through production of the commodity in the home country and export to the foreign country. This is the traditional mode and the basis of the rules of the world trading system over the last 50 years. The second is the establishment of an affiliate corporation in the foreign country in which the buyers are located. The choice between these two modes of supply is the basis of the modern theory of the multinational firm and the derivative theory of foreign direct investment (see Ethier, 1994, and Markusen, 1995, for surveys of this theory).

The second mode is sometimes called international production: 'International production is defined as that production which is located in one country but controlled by a multinational corporation (MC) based in another country' (Cantwell, 1994, p. 303). With this terminology, the two modes of supply to foreign markets are international trade and international production.

There is in fact a third, and increasingly important, mode of supply, namely supply by establishing an affiliate in a foreign country and exporting from that country. This mode could be regarded as a variant of the first and second modes as it combines both international trade and international production in a triangle of countries. (In some cases, the outputs of foreign investors are exported to the home country of the foreign investor. There are then only two countries but the flows are two-way.)

The second (and third) mode has become more important because increased competition through access to product markets across national borders has been accompanied by the liberalization of cross-border movements of capital. For some years the United Nations Conference on Trade and Development (UNCTAD) has estimated the sales of foreign affiliates worldwide by extrapolating the sales of foreign affiliates of France, Germany, Italy, Japan and the US on the basis of their share in world outward foreign direct investment. These estimates indicate that the sales of foreign affiliates have exceeded world exports of goods and non-factor services in every year since the series began in 1984. For 1994, the latest year available, sales of foreign affiliates were 1.30 times the value of imports of goods and non-factor services (UNCTAD, 1997, Table I.3). On the basis of a survey of transnational corporation (TNC) managers, UNCTAD predicts that the proportion of total sales accounted for by international production will continue to rise (UNCTAD, 1997, pp. 36—8).

The multiple modes are combined in the notion of contestability of markets which has recently been applied to cross-border competition in work sponsored by the OECD Trade Committee (OECD, 1996b; Lawrence, 1996; Zampetti and Sauvé, 1996). A contestable market is one in which firms can enter and exit. It is, therefore, potentially competitive or 'contestable', even if the actual distribution of firms is concentrated. This use of the notion of contestability has been adopted from industrial organization theory where it was first applied to policies relating to natural monopolies and oligopolies, ignoring competition across national borders. (The classic study is Baumol, Panzer and Willig, 1980.) In this multicountry application, less emphasis is put on exit of firms from national markets as the exit of a foreign producer from one national market may merely mean shifting its production to another country and supplying from this country rather than exiting the market.

Contestability clarifies the relationship between international trade and competition. Market access is not sufficient for foreign suppliers to contest a market. A market may be contested by exports or by entry into the local market from another country. Therefore, a contestable market spanning more than one country also requires the absence of restrictions on foreign investment and national treatment for foreign investors. National treatment of foreign firms covers a wide range of policies such as government procurement, essential facilities, standards and tax policies.

Hence, questions of contestability in global markets involve a broad approach to the promotion of competition. Foreign investment policy is particularly important because entry into global markets may come from the mode of supply involving foreign direct investment. Similarly, multimodal supply indicates the importance of deregulation within national economies.

The increasing prominence on international agendas being given to so-called 'competition policy' gives rise to definitional problems: what should or should not be included in international discussions and agreements on competition policy? A broad definition of 'competition policy' could be adopted. It could be defined as all government policies aimed directly at promoting competition among producers, but this would mean that policies relating to such areas as international trade and intellectual property would be included in competition policy when they are amended deliberately to promote competition. On the other hand, many have adopted a narrow definition so that only competition law/anti-trust is covered. This omits many policies which have the purpose or effect of promoting competition in markets. We do not think it is productive to continue this debate. Rather than trying to reach agreement on what should or should not be included in a definition of 'competition policy', it is better to consider all those policy instruments relevant to the promotion of efficient competition in markets. A range of policy instruments is clearly relevant to this objective even if not explicitly labelled as 'competition policy'. Barriers to competition arise from numerous sources, including both public and private actions.

We shall, therefore, use the term 'competition policy' only when referring to one or more policies that others have described as 'competition policy'. Our concern is the influence of an overall competition framework on competition and efficiency in markets. Figure 2.1 sets out the major areas of government policy and business conduct which affect competition

in markets. Multilateral policies with respect to freeing international trade
and direct foreign investment are well developed and are under constant
review, and policies with respect to deregulation and privatization are
regarded as matters for national governments only.

Government policies	Business conduct (public & private)

- market access for
  trade in goods
- market access for services
- trade remedies
- FDI
- government procurement
- IPR
- standards
- regulation
- privatization
- competition law

- unilateral conduct
- collusive conduct
- mergers & takeovers

Figure 2.1: A policy framework for promoting competition

The term competition law does not present the same definitional
problem. It refers to the body of law which addresses specifically
competition issues arising from business conduct or structures. Such law
may be accompanied by other laws or regulations, such as trade law and
intellectual property law, which can also affect business conduct and
structures. This category of laws may be termed competition-related law.

International dimensions of competition law are becoming much more
important. There is, however, no generally accepted definition of the
'international' dimensions of a national competition law or its enforcement.
Ideally, one would like a measure of the incidence of conduct which raised
questions of cross-border anti-competitive behaviour, that is, the potential
cases which might be investigated and pursued if legal means were available.
In practice, one will be confined to actual cases which have been
investigated under existing laws. The main international dimension in these
cases should be whether relevant conduct under examination in one
jurisdiction occurred in a foreign jurisdiction(s) or whether consumers or
buyers in another jurisdiction(s) were affected by the conduct within the
home jurisdiction. The international dimensions should also include

whether a foreign government has been approached for assistance in collecting evidence or taking action in the case.

Given the lack of convention on the definition, there are no statistics compiled on the international dimensions. In a communication to the newly created WTO Working Group on the Interaction between Trade and Competition Policy, the US Government stated:

> we do know that US antitrust enforcement work of all sorts is becoming more international in terms of the firms involved, the location of relevant evidence, and the enforcement interests of other countries, among other factors. For example, in 1997, nearly 30 per cent of DOJ's [Department of Justice's] criminal antitrust investigations had substantial international aspects (up from 10 per cent in 1993) and involved firms based in over 20 countries. Routinely, about 50 per cent of the FTC's [Federal Trade Commission's] pending merger investigations involve matters in which the FTC has been in contact with foreign enforcement authorities because one or both of the parties, relevant assets, or significant third-party information is located abroad. (WTO, 1998a)

These figures indicate clearly the growth of the international dimensions of US anti-trust law. In terms of the products, they cover a wide range of manufactured products. Services are under-represented compared to their share of GDP, probably because a lower proportion of services is traded internationally, but a few individual service industries have an important international competition dimension, most notably telecommunications.

There is an important question as to whether international competition law would be needed at all if all national markets were completely open to international trade in goods *and* services *and* capital. Completely free trade would mean that all modes of supply were unrestricted across national borders. Both Hong Kong and Singapore, which are the only two economies at present with close to free trade in goods, services and capital, argue that they do not need comprehensive national competition laws because their trade is completely free (see Hong Kong Government, 1996, and Lall, 1996). This is the extreme form of the general argument that trade liberalization increases competition in markets. Hong Kong and Singapore have put these views forward in the debate in APEC concerning harmonization of 'competition policy' of the APEC member countries (see Vautier and Lloyd, 1997, Part IV) and in the WTO Working Group on the Interaction between International Trade and Competition.

The WTO (1997a, p. 51) rejected the view that free trade made competition law superfluous. It argued that there are natural barriers to international trade and firms may still seek to limit competition in ways other than restricting trade. The same applies to cross-border entry as there are natural and created barriers to entry. Unrestricted cross-border entry for exporters and foreign firms who seek to establish production in the markets may not make markets contestable if there are large sunk costs or restrictions within nations that inhibit supply. UNCTAD (1997, p. 203) reached the same conclusion.

In this context, it is notable that the relatively open and large markets of the US and the EU have the most active competition law; in the latter case an EU-level competition law was introduced specifically to ensure that the Common Market, with complete freedom of movement of labour and capital as well as goods and services, was not frustrated by private anti-competitive conduct. Even if all countries were to remove all barriers to cross-border movement of goods, services and capital, there would still be a need for some government measures to promote competition.

National Competition Laws in Global Markets

Fundamentally, it is the coexistence of *global* markets with *national* jurisdictions which causes the search for mechanisms to cover cross-border competition problems. National competition laws deal adequately with cross-border competition problems when the foreign corporation has a commercial presence within the jurisdiction, provided national treatment applies. Advocates of some form of international action in the area of competition law believe that national competition laws have a number of inherent shortcomings in dealing with cross-border competition problems when the foreign supplier does not have a commercial presence.

The primary concern is that the existing patchwork of national laws supplemented by bilateral, regional and international agreements fails to control some anti-competitive conduct which affects more than one country. There are additional concerns that the procedures available under existing extraterritoriality, comity and cooperation arrangements, when they address cross-border anti-competitive conduct, pose administrative problems. They are unnecessarily costly to administer; this is especially true of the examination of merger proposals which involve two or more jurisdictions (see Whish and Wood, 1994, and Campbell and Trebilcock, 1997). Some mechanisms, notably the use of extraterritoriality, create substantial conflicts between jurisdictions.

Viewing these problems of cross-border competition from the point of view of one nation, there are two types of *policy failure* to address cross-border anti-competitive conduct. First, national competition laws do not normally reach conduct which affects the national economy but which is taken in other jurisdictions. Secondly, national competition laws do not normally consider injury or costs imposed by the conduct of producers in their jurisdiction on the residents of other jurisdictions. These may be called Type 1 and Type 2 failures respectively (see Figure 2.2).

In the Type 2 failure, national competition laws do not address practices of enterprises within their jurisdictions which cause injury to or impose costs solely on the residents of other countries by raising prices or restricting competition in those countries. Similarly, when they cause injury to both the domestic and foreign residents and national competition authorities, they may not give equal weight to the injury caused to the foreign residents. Countries typically take a more lenient view of actions by their citizens which harm residents of other countries. For example, many countries exempt export cartels from national competition laws.

Coverage of the national law
- conduct in 'markets' in the jurisdiction
- some cross-border conduct with impact on 'markets' in the jurisdiction

Cross-border failures not covered by the national law
- Type I: Cross-border conduct originating in other countries and impacting on markets in the jurisdiction
- Type II: Cross-border conduct originating in the jurisdiction and impacting on 'markets' in other countries

---

Figure 2.2:   Business conduct covered by the competition law of one jurisdiction

Type 2 conduct by producers in one country which harms residents of a second country is, from the point of view of this other country, Type 1 conduct. The laws of nations presume that each nation state will look after the interests of its residents. If there is a failure of Type 2, the presumption is that it is the nation representing the party or parties whose interests have been harmed which will initiate an investigation. Comity and cooperation are designed to assist this nation within the rules laid down. However, we believe it is also important for the countries in which Type 2 conduct originates to consider whether a problem is best addressed in the source country.

As an example of Type 1, foreign producers may collude to share international markets or directly raise prices. Or a foreign enterprise may attempt to eliminate competition facing a subsidiary in the home jurisdiction; the parent company may supply the requirements of its foreign subsidiary at an artificially low price, thus enabling the subsidiary to engage in predatory behaviour in the market for its products. In some cases, such conduct cannot be dealt with adequately by national laws.

Some cartels are international and action against them may take place in more than one jurisdiction. Similarly, firms may be dominant in the markets of more than one country or even in global markets and consequently may be subject to examination by the competition authorities of more than one country.

A merger involving a domestically registered company and a foreign investor generally requires the separate approval of competition authorities in each jurisdiction. Cross-border mergers have been growing rapidly and accounting for a higher proportion of total mergers in many jurisdictions (see UNCTAD, 1997, Chapter V).

A particularly difficult manifestation of these international dimensions occurs when more than one foreign country is involved. This happens most frequently with merger proposals when the companies involved may be incorporated in several or even many different countries.

Another difficult variant of Type 1 occurs when two (or more) producers take action in two countries which has an adverse effect on a third country (or countries). This might be a market allocation agreement or cartel or a merger. (For an example of third-country effects of a merger, see UNCTAD, 1997, Box V.8.)

When the competition law of a country seeks to act against producers located in one or more foreign countries, there are major problems of enforcement. Restraints are often beyond the reach of national jurisdictions. This limitation results in the incurring of additional costs when the restraints or actions occur simultaneously in more than one foreign country.

Another concern is the difficulty for national competition authorities of obtaining information from producers located in another country. As an example, an enterprise in a particular country may call for tenders internationally. In response, members of an international cartel, all of whom may be located abroad without assets, subsidiaries or affiliates in the country concerned, may collude. It may be difficult in the first instance to prove collusion. Companies incorporated in other countries may avoid providing information. Under national laws, most competition authorities are not permitted to share information they have gathered with foreign authorities. The OECD Competition Law and Policy Committee has considered how information relating to market conduct in two or more countries can be shared between governments. UNCTAD (1997, p. 218) emphasizes this information problem, along with the difficulty of applying remedies outside the territories of each jurisdiction, as the reason for international cooperation.

Remedies which are used under national laws to deter persons from contravening the national law include measures such as injunctions, pecuniary penalties, damages, divestiture of assets and criminal sanctions. Obviously, attempts to apply any of these traditional remedies beyond national borders are fraught with legal and political difficulties.

One can see the issues of cross-border competition law by conducting the following thought experiment. Consider any conduct by a private party or parties which affects adversely producers or consumers/buyers in another country. It may not be actionable under the present national laws of the second country. Now suppose that these countries merged into one larger country with a single competition authority and law. Further, suppose that these two countries have identical laws in order to rule out the supplementary consideration of which country's laws prevail when they merge. The conduct would be actionable under the competition law of the single country.

This experiment highlights the conflicts between the interests of consumers and producers in separate countries and their different treatments under separate national jurisdictions. In the combined area, the interests of all consumers and producers in these situations could be considered and the law would be enforced uniformly in the combined territory.

There is a broad *in principle* case for a *multi-national* approach to such competition issues which stems from the internationalization or globalization of the world economy. The integration of markets across national borders means that competition problems have become increasingly internationalized. For the purposes of competition analysis, the relevant markets are international markets. The breakdown in the barriers to international trade in goods and services and FDI has broken down segmentation into national markets. For those services which require a commercial presence or the movement of persons to the country in which the service is consumed or used, trans-border market access and trans-border investment flows and aspects of competition such as access to networks cannot be separated.

The problem is, however, larger than enforcement across national borders. Many countries are opposed to the development of international rules relating to business conduct or the extraterritorial enforcement of national laws in other countries because they see these developments as an infringement of national sovereignty. Sometimes they will oppose these actions because they believe the action by the competition authority of another country may harm their own producers. Similarly, past attempts at international action by means of comity and cooperation have encountered difficulties when a nation whose assistance is requested perceives that its interests would be harmed.

The question of whether international action to combat conduct which adversely affects the interests of other nations does harm or benefit to the nation in which the conduct originates is a crucial question. It largely determines the attitude of the government of the country or countries whose producers are being examined. It also determines in part the gains and benefits to the world as a whole from such action.

Sometimes there will be a mutuality of interests between the nation initiating the action and other nations affected by the case and sometimes there will be a conflict of interests. Some cases are straightforward in their effects on individual nations. If the foreign country or countries in which the producers are located produce but do not consume the good, their producers will lose from the action. One nation may be solely a producer of the product(s) and the other a consumer; some export cartels and market allocation schemes are clear examples of this pattern. There is a clear conflict between the interests of the nation initiating the action and the foreign nation(s) affected by it. A reverse pattern of effects applies in the case of action against a foreign supplier who is subsidized by its own government; subsidies provided to national champions are an example. In this example, nations which buy but do not produce will clearly lose from international enforcement which eliminates subsidies to 'national champions' in high-technology industries and other nations which are major producers will gain.

In the last two years there have been two major instances of conflict between jurisdictions. In the Framework discussions between the US and Japan, the US has sought to improve the access of US producers to Japan for photographic film, automobiles and auto parts, insurance, telecommunications, medical equipment and other goods; in the US view, these access problems arise from anti-competitive actions within Japan. (We examine the *Kodak/Fuji* dispute in Chapter 11.) In this instance, there is a sharp conflict of interest between the US and Japan, as well as a difference of view as to why US producers have had such difficulty in penetrating Japanese markets. In the examination by the European Commission of the proposed merger between Boeing and McDonnell Douglas, both US firms, there was again a sharp conflict between two governments.

For nations which are affected by conduct originating outside their jurisdiction and which both produce and consume the product, it will be necessary to consider the effects of any international enforcement on both their producers and their consumers. Consider again the case where producers of two or more countries form a cartel or allocate markets or merge, with the result that the world price rises. In this case, the interests of producers in all countries coincide and those of consumers in all countries also coincide; the producers gain from the action and the consumers lose (see Levinsohn, 1996, and Lloyd, 1998a). Hence, any conduct which raises the seller's price will yield a gain to the producers of other competing countries and a loss to their consumers. If there are no efficiency effects on the costs of production, international trade theory indicates that a country gains or loses (according to the potential income criterion) from a price increase if it is a net exporter or net importer of a commodity (see, for example, Woodland, 1982, Chapter 9); that is, if the quantity of the good produced exceeds the quantity consumed, or the reverse. The enforcement across borders of the laws of one country (by, say, preventing a merger or breaking up an international cartel) will reverse these effects. Thus, a foreign nation gains or loses from competition law enforcement depending on the balance of producer and consumer effects. If there are efficiency effects on the costs of production, the analysis is more complex. There is an additional gain which might accrue to the country taking action or in other countries.

As background to the options for cross-border approaches to competition, the following section examines the means which are currently available under national competition laws to deal with cross-border aspects of business conduct.

A Classification of Mechanisms dealing with Cross-Border Conduct

The spread of the interests of national competition authorities across borders has given rise to a number of mechanisms to handle these dimensions.

One mechanism used by a few countries, notably the US and the EU, is the extraterritorial extension of their national laws. It is a unilateral act and does not involve cooperation with the government or competition authority of the foreign country or countries in which the conduct took place. Indeed, it is the antithesis of cooperation and has become the most controversial means of combating negative spillovers because national governments see it as an infringement of their national sovereignty and an attack on the interests of their residents.

Other mechanisms involve the cooperation or concerted action in some form of two or more governments. Distinctions are made between *bilateral, regional, plurilateral* and *multilateral* arrangements. Bilateral arrangements involve two countries (or a bloc of countries as one party, in the case of arrangements entered into by the EU with foreign governments). A regional arrangement relating to competition laws is an arrangement among the members of a regional trading agreement. A plurilateral agreement is an agreement which is not binding on the signatories.[2] In terms of both the number of countries involved and the binding nature of the agreement, a multilateral agreement is the most comprehensive form of international agreement.

Using this terminology, this book distinguishes between *multi-national* approaches to competition issues and a *multilateral* approach. Multi-national is the generic term to cover all possible options for multi-national arrangements: that is, bilateral, regional, plurilateral and multilateral. By contrast, a multilateral approach is the specific proposal to develop law in a binding multilateral agreement. Consequently, a multilateral approach to competition is only one of the multi-national approaches to competition issues.

These distinctions have been based on two criteria, namely, the number of countries involved in an agreement and the binding/non-binding nature of the agreement. There is a choice with regard to both criteria. Concerning the latter, it may be more useful to pose this choice as one between an arrangement or mechanism which coordinates the actions of different governments and one which centralizes them into a supranational authority with overriding powers.

There are other ways in which these arrangements may differ. We make a distinction between the following three concepts:

- principles;
- rules;
- standards.

These three terms are used frequently in the literature but the meanings are somewhat unclear. We take them to have the following meanings. *Principles* embody general characteristics or values which can be used to guide policy formation and its implementation: for example, non-discrimination, transparency and competitive neutrality. *Rules* are dictates as to what economic agents can or cannot do: for example, the Articles of the GATT (1994) are the rules of the world trading system, and a *per se* prohibition on 'hard-core' cartels. *Standards* reflect agreed levels of tolerance or acceptability on some scale: for example, a threshold of market dominance for determining a competition law breach and the level of the Hirschman/Herfindahl index which can be used to determine an unacceptable level of market concentration.

Bilateral, regional and plurilateral agreements have been evolving since the 1950s (see UNCTAD, 1997, Part II, and WTO, 1997a, Chapter 4.V, for surveys of the major developments).

The first multi-national agreement of any kind relating to competition was that of the 1957 Treaty of Rome which established the European Economic Community (which became the European Union after the Maastricht Treaty), principally Articles 85—92. Subsequently the EEC/EU rules have been extended to the new members of the EU, the European Economic Area (EEA), and the states associated with the EU in Central and Eastern Europe and the Mediterranean. This now involves a total of 33 countries (the 15 full members of the EU, the three remaining members of the EEA, the ten Central and East European countries, and the five Mediterranean countries). Six other regional trading agreements have incorporated some agreement relating to competition; these are: the 1990 extension to the Closer Economic Relations Agreement between Australia and New Zealand; the 1992 North American Free Trade Agreement among the US, Canada and Mexico; the 1991 Andean Community of five members; the 1996 MERCOSUR Agreement of four members; the Group of Three Treaty; and the Canada—Chile Free Trade Agreement. (Chapters 4, 5 and 6 discuss the EU, CER and the Americas respectively.) Thus, not double-counting those countries in more than one regional agreement, 49 countries were involved in regional competition agreements as at July 1998. Two of these agreements — the EU and the EEA — have created central supranational authorities, the Directorate General IV (DG IV) and the EFTA Surveillance Authority.

The first bilateral cooperation agreement was that between the US and Germany in 1976. Subsequently the US government has signed bilateral agreements with other OECD countries and a few other pairs of countries have signed similar agreements. (Chapter 3 discusses bilateral cooperation agreements.)

Plurilateral efforts to encourage cooperation in areas of competition began with the 1960 GATT Decision on Arrangements for Consultation on Restrictive Business Practices, 1967 OECD Recommendations Concerning Cooperation between Member States on Anticompetitive Practices

Affecting International Trade and the 1976 OECD Guidelines for Multinational Enterprises. In 1980 the UN adopted the Set of Multilaterally Agreed Equitable Principles and Rules for the Control of Restrictive Business Practices.

Thus, the coverage of countries involved in cross-border competition arrangements is piecemeal. Furthermore, this says nothing about the enforcement or effectiveness of these arrangements in practice.

These mechanisms can be usefully classified in terms of the Types 1 and Type 2 failures of cross-border competition law. Almost all of the mechanisms have been developed to deal with Type 1 failure only. Thus extraterritoriality, negative and positive comity and the bilateral and plurilateral agreements are designed to assist a national authority to carry out investigations and prosecutions in cases where the conduct took place outside the prosecuting jurisdiction. Only regional agreements look at the interests of the producers and consumers in the whole area. The straightforward explanation for the concentration on Type 1 failures is that Type 2 failures are regarded as the concern of the affected country.

The case for some form of multi-national competition mechanism is accepted by most countries which have comprehensive competition laws. After its review of trade and competition policy issues, the WTO (1997a, p. 85) concluded that: 'The large number of mechanisms for co-operation between governments in combating anti-competitive enterprise practices would seem to reflect a clear recognition of the need for intergovernmental co-operation.' The EU has concluded: 'Many countries or regions have implemented comprehensive competition policies but lack appropriate instruments to apply domestic competition rules to anti-competitive practices with an international dimension as well as to obtain relevant information outside their jurisdiction' (European Commission, 1996). Even the US, which is the least enthusiastic of the OECD countries for the development of multi-national competition law, has advised the WTO that: 'The US enforcement experience of recent years . . . has convinced the US antitrust agencies that they need to improve the ability to work with foreign counterparts in international investigations, on a basis of assured confidentiality and mutual benefit' (WTO, 1998a).

This case for some form of multi-national response leaves completely open the mechanism or mechanisms which might resolve these cross-border difficulties *in practice*. There is much disagreement among governments and individual writers on the advantages and disadvantages of each mechanism. The approach taken in this book is to view these choices as a problem of optimal policy choice and to use the economic theory of policymaking to elucidate the choice.

Elements of the Framework for Policy Analysis

Economists are accustomed to making a choice among alternative instruments by choosing the optimal instrument or set of instruments. This approach has been widely used in such area as taxation (the 'optimal tax' literature) and, closer to the concerns of competition law, to regulation of industries and to border trade policies (as in the 'optimal tariff' debate and more generally the 'free trade' debate[3]). The same approach can be used to elucidate the choice in the present context.

Any consideration of a choice problem in economics must follow a sequence of steps:

- specify the problem or problems;
- enumerate the policy options/instruments;
- specify the objective function;
- evaluate the effects of each option/instrument on the objective function.

Comparing the effects of each of the options on the objective function, the options can then be ranked and the best can be chosen.

First, the specification of the problem or problems comes, in the present context, to the specification of the markets and jurisdictions in which competition will be considered, and the conduct to be considered. We take it that it is desirable to cover markets for all goods and services and all business conduct which may affect competition in these markets.

Secondly, the multi-national options have been grouped in terms of the country scope of the mechanisms — bilateral, regional, plurilateral and multilateral. The multiple options for the development of a multi-national approach to competition also vary in terms of the coverage of anti-competitive conduct, the instruments, and their non-binding or binding nature. They range from non-binding bilateral cooperation to binding multilateral law. More details follow in later chapters.

Thirdly, in the analysis of a problem, the objective function specifies what is to be maximized: for example, the welfare of some group or the volume of exports or the degree of economic integration. To be precise, there are two aspects of the objective function, namely the variables and the choice of agents whose interests will be considered. Technically, this is the choice of the variables which enter into the function and the group of agents over which the variables are defined. For example, one might choose economic welfare as the variable to be maximized and the residents of a country as the group whose welfare is to be maximized.

Concerning the first aspect, the competition laws of different countries have different objectives or goals. (For reviews of the objectives of national competition laws, see UNCTAD, 1997, Chapter V.2, and references therein.) Some relate merely to the enforcement of competition. Some give more emphasis to a goal of 'efficiency', which can mean efficiency in production, and some to 'consumer welfare', and some have a 'national interest' provision which requires them to take account of the interest of both producers and consumers. Some refer to 'development' of the economy. Others have goals such as economic integration (the EU) or 'fair competition'. Moreover, all countries with competition laws have exemptions and exclusions which can be regarded as the application of other objectives; the exemptions apply to areas such as labour markets, government enterprises, media or agriculture, or small and medium enterprises (see OECD, 1996b). Thus, national competition law is sometimes required to consider objectives which are additional to the primary objectives. These supplementary objectives can override the primary objectives in the application of these laws:

> However, in the past decade, there has been a significant degree of convergence in the goals of competition policy as it is practised by many countries towards the core values of promoting economic efficiency and consumer welfare. (WTO, 1997a, p. 49; see also the OECD Interim Report of the Convergence in Competition Policies, OECD, 1994)

Indeed, efficient markets will contribute more to fairness in markets than attempts to build fairness or redistributive objectives into policy instruments aimed at the promotion of competition. Non-efficiency objectives are better pursued through more appropriately targeted policy instruments. The theory regarding the assignment of instruments to targets or objectives is well developed in economics.

Economists would regard efficiency in the general equilibrium sense of Pareto-efficiency, that is, loosely speaking, it is not possible to make some household(s) better off without making some other household(s) worse off. This provides a general goal which includes efficiency in consumption allocations as well as efficiency in production allocations, both being required for the maximization of the welfare of consumers. The Pareto criterion is concerned with the welfare ('utility') of all households and takes account of both price and income effects on households of each situation. In comparing situations where some individuals gain and some lose and in which the criterion is inconclusive, the criterion of potential gain via hypothetical lump-sum redistributions of income enables a choice to be decided. (In practice, potential gain is often approximated by the partial equilibrium single industry calculation of the sum of consumer surplus and producer profits.)

Free-trade and competitive economies are efficient (that is, Pareto-efficient). This is the First Fundamental Theorem of Welfare Economics.[4] It is this theorem which leads to the advocacy of competitive behaviour and of free international trade. Both free trade and competitive behaviour are desirable in themselves, though sometimes liberalizing trade will also have beneficial competition effects. There is empirical evidence that the freeing of cross-border trade generally increases competition (see European Commission Directorate-General IV, 1997, pp. 177—81, and Neven and Seabright, 1997). Conversely, promoting competition will sometimes increase trade. This is clearly the case when the means of limiting competition are trade restrictions.

The second aspect of the specification of an objective function, that is, the target group(s), raises the issue, for example, of whether national competition authorities should act in the interests of the residents of the nation only or should take account of the interests of residents of other nations. Assuming efficiency is the targeted variable, this is equivalent to whether their objective should be maximization of the welfare of the residents of the national economy or of all countries. As noted above, there will in some cases be a conflict between the interests of these two groups in a situation involving anti-competitive conduct. (The same issue arises in a regional approach to competition, though it would be natural if a regional competition agency pursued an objective of regional efficiency. (See Pelkmans, 1997, p. 185, for a discussion of the EU.)

The traditional advocacy of free trade, based on the principle of comparative advantage, maximizes global welfare through the efficient allocation of resources. By contrast, national competition laws almost invariably are concerned only with the welfare of residents of the nation and, therefore, exclude the welfare of all non-residents. In some circumstances, this is mitigated by consideration of comity among nations. (See, for example, the discussion of the comity analyses and procedures followed by the US Department of Justice in deciding whether to enforce anti-trust law extraterritorially in Chapter 6 below.) Comity is encouraged by the OECD Recommendations and by the 1960 GATT Decision on Arrangements for Consultation on Restrictive Business Practices. Some competition specialists have advocated that national authorities adopt a global welfare view (Crampton and Witterick, 1996, and Fox and Ordover, 1995 and 1997).

One aspect of the choice of objective has recently been developed in a most interesting way by Bacchetta, Horn and Mavroidis (1997) and the WTO (1997a, Chapter 4.III.2). Assuming that national competition authorities are concerned only with national welfare, there are gains from international cooperation on competition issues in so far as the cooperation leads to a higher global welfare than the uncooperative or uncoordinated independent actions of the national authorities. Consider two countries, the home country and the foreign country, and the national authority of the home country must choose between two competition law outcomes, A and B, in a competition law case. The outcomes differ in their effects on the welfare of the residents of the home and foreign countries, one maximizing the welfare of the residents of the home country and the other maximizing the welfare of the whole world. Clearly, there will be cases where this difference arises, as in cartels and market allocation agreements where one country is a net producer of the good and the other the net consumer.

The WTO (1997, Chapter 4.III.2) distinguishes between two effects of the decisions of national competition authorities: for example, a decision to block a merger or break up a cartel. These are *negative spillover effects* and *distortions*. Negative spillovers occur when the authority of one nation chooses an action which lowers the welfare of the foreign country's residents. By contrast, a distortion arises when the authority's choice is not the choice which would maximize global welfare. It emphazises that a choice may have negative spillovers but not be a distortion. This is a most important distinction. The analysis can clearly be extended to more than two countries and to encompass such cases as third-country effects.

The WTO (1997, Chapter 4.III.2) sees the existence of distortions to the world economy resulting from the actions of national competition authorities as a motive for international cooperation or coordinated action on a competition issue. This could be done at the bilateral, regional, plurilateral or multilateral level.

To eliminate distortions, competition law should act so as to maximize global welfare, not national welfare. At the national level, the interests of the country in which the producers are located and the interests of a second country whose consumers or buyers are adversely affected by the conduct sometimes coincide, as noted above. In these cases, action by a national authority is in the economic interests of both countries. In other cases, the interests of the two countries conflict. Falvey (1998) makes a useful distinction in this regard between effects which are merely redistributive in nature and those which have a net effect of increasing or decreasing world welfare. In the first category are effects which shift profit between companies located in different countries and terms of trade effects; a terms of trade gain of one country is necessarily a terms of trade loss of some other country (or countries). In the second category are efficiency effects such as the deadweight loss (gain) of consumer surplus when prices rise (fall) and the increase or decrease in aggregate profits. Redistributive effects may cause negative spillovers but they are not grounds for opposing a change which increases global welfare.

In the long run, each country would benefit from actions taken by other countries. As the long-run gains would be positive for the world as a whole, there is an expectation that positive spillover effects would outweigh negative spillover effects and all countries would gain by this cooperation.

The fourth stage of the analysis of choice of options is the evaluation of the relative effectiveness of the options. This will require a detailed analysis of each option. Only then will it be possible to rank options and choose the best. Each option will have advantages and disadvantages. For example, developing countries may have more limited options due to institutional capacity constraints. (This point is taken up in Chapter 3.)

This choice between bilateral, regional, plurilateral or multilateral mechanisms is a particularly difficult problem of policymaking. One set of problems is that of enforcement of any action required to promote competition across national borders. Here there is a choice between coordination of national actions and centralization in a supranational authority. There are several factors which will determine the costs and benefits of coordination or centralization of powers in each alternative. These include the extent of the powers to gather information and investigate and impose remedies, and the credibility of the authorities. There are considerations other than enforcement involved in these choices too. Mechanisms differ in coverage. The benefits will also depend upon the choice of objective function, one aspect of which is the danger of capture by producer interests in each option. The analysis by the competition authority is also important because of the greater complexity of analysis of competition problems when markets span multiple countries. In evaluating the *de Havilland* merger case, for example, the Canadian and European competition authorities agreed that the world was the relevant market but they differed in their analysis of the competition impacts of the merger.

An Example of Policy Analysis: Cross-Border Mergers

As the issues in the regulation of competition behaviour which spills over national borders are complex and many of the concepts are novel, an example may be helpful. The example chosen is that of merger proposals which may raise the prices in connected national markets. Mergers have been the most debated example in the small literature dealing with anti-competitive cross-border conduct (see Lloyd, 1998a, and Falvey, 1998, and the references therein). Moreover, the issues raised in this example are similar to those which arise in cartels and market allocation schemes which also raise prices in world markets.

Consider a merger between two (or more) firms. Suppose both countries have national competition laws which can deny approval of mergers. Under standard procedures, a merger involving firms from two (or more) countries has to be approved by the competition authorities of both countries. We want to see if the actions by national authorities operating in an uncoordinated fashion and in pursuit solely of the interests of the residents of the home jurisdictions will be in the interests of the two countries combined, that is, in the interests of the global economy. This enables us to compare the efficacy of the option of uncoordinated decisions by national competition authorities, which act to maximize national welfare, with that of the option of a global authority which acts to maximize global welfare, the sum of the profits and consumer surpluses in the two countries.

Falvey (1998) has the most appropriate model. It is a version of the cross-hauling model frequently used in oligopoly theory. In it, there is a market for a single homogeneous good and two countries. There are a number of firms producing the good in both countries. Competition is assumed to be Cournot: that is, each firm sets the quantities it sells in the market, assuming the quantities sold by its competitors. These firms have constant but different unit costs and the decisions to merge are endogenous, but subject to approval. Consider for the time being that the world market is a completely integrated market with a single price in the two countries.

A merger of two firms with different unit costs will result in the closure of the firm with the higher costs (the relatively inefficient firm). A merger between a low-cost producer and a high-cost producer which results in the abandonment of the high-cost firm's inefficient technology has an added benefit to offset the costs of the merger because of higher prices. The output of all remaining firms increases and this benefit will be distributed among them as higher profits. If low-cost producers are in the foreign country, the probability of this country having a net reduction in welfare is reduced.

The new equilibrium is simply that which would obtain in the absence of the closed firm. (Hence, the analysis is similar to other actions which reduce the number of firms.) As the number of firms is reduced, total output falls, the market price rises, and the profits of the remaining firms increase. Consumers in the market will lose and remaining producers will gain. Social welfare is the sum of consumer surplus and producer profits. The reduction in consumer surplus and in the loss of profits of the firm which closes are deadweight losses but these may be offset by the reduction in average unit costs and the associated increase in profits on this output. This introduces an 'efficiency' defence of a merger. In sum, such mergers have, therefore, both positive and negative welfare effects. (A similar effect is introduced if there are firm-level economies of scale due to, say, fixed costs. In this event a merger eliminates one set of fixed costs.)

There are two types of mergers. In one, the two merged firms are located in the same country, and in the second, they are in different countries. Our interest lies particularly in the distribution of these merger effects between countries. In the case of firms located in one country, there are spillover effects of mergers to the producers and consumers of the foreign country. The spillover effect on the producers of the foreign country will be positive and that on the consumers will be negative. The net spillover effect may be positive or negative. The national authority of this country is assumed to act in the interest of its residents only, and the national authority of the other country is assumed not to have a veto. Any national merger approved by the home country's competition authority will increase the welfare of this nation. Any national merger not approved by the home country's competition authority itself has spillover effects on the second country. These may be negative or positive. This authority may disallow some mergers that increase global welfare but not national welfare, and it may approve some mergers which are national-welfare-improving but decrease global welfare. In both cases, there is a distortion, to use the terminology of the WTO (1997).

Some of the effects of a merger merely redistribute income between the two countries and have a zero effect on global welfare. Falvey (1998) shows that the welfare effects of a merger can be expressed in four terms. Two of these, profit-shifting and terms of trade effects, merely distribute income between the two countries. The other two are the efficiency gain due to the closure of the high-cost firm and the deadweight loss to consumers. The two redistributive effects do not change aggregate global welfare but they are taken into the calculation of the national authorities. In particular, an increase in the price of an internationally traded good has a positive effect on national welfare if the country is a net exporter and a negative effect if it is a net importer. Thus, negative decisions may be against the world interest if the country is a net importer and positive decisions may be against the world interest if it is a net exporter. This holds because in each case the national authority takes account of an effect which is zero for the world as a whole.

Consider now the second case in which a merger is between two firms located in two different countries. A merger proposal must now be approved by both national authorities and the cost-efficiency effect and the profits associated with it will be distributed across both countries. If a merger lowers world welfare, it will lower the welfare of one country at least and, if it raises world welfare, it must raise the welfare of one country at least but it may reduce the welfare of one of the two countries. Consequently, an approach that gives a veto to both authorities will veto a globally undesirable merger but it will also disallow a globally desirable merger when the welfare gains to the other country exceed the loss to the country disallowing it.

This example illustrates the importance of all the aspects of the policy approach listed above. First, in general, uncoordinated decisions by national authorities can result in the non-approval of mergers which are in the interests of both countries combined or in the approval of a merger which is not in the interests of both combined. There are, therefore, gains from a global authority which acts in the global interest. If one of the nations does not have a competition law, it increases the risks that mergers which are against the global interest will be allowed; this will occur when the country which does not have a competition law is adversely affected by a merger. It also decreases the risk that mergers which are against the global interest will be disallowed.

This example also illustrates the importance of the objective function. The objective function has been assumed to be the welfare of interests in either a nation or in the two nations combined. National authorities might act in the interests of producers alone, ignoring the interests of consumers, either because of the objective written into national legislation or because the producer interests succeed in capturing the authority. In this case, the outcomes of decisions by merger authorities could go against the national interest. A producer orientation will increase the bias in favour of approving merger proposals that are against the interests of the nation and the world.

Conversely, the adoption of a global welfare objective by national authorities would achieve the global-welfare-maximizing decision without the creation of a global authority or coordination between national authorities, but this would involve national authorities sometimes acting against the national interest. For the same reason cooperation between independent national authorities under a bilateral cooperation agreement would be difficult in some cases.

The example also illustrates the importance of the analysis of the problem at hand. It has been assumed that the national authorities and a global authority can accurately discern the interests of the group whose welfare they are concerned with.

Tariffs may be introduced into the model. Tariffs have the effect of encouraging inefficient production in the tariff-imposing country. Trade liberalization, which reverses this effect, makes relatively inefficient firms in the formerly protected market more attractive as merger partners and hence generates cross-border merger activities. These need not be globally welfare improving.

All the above results also apply to the analysis of two firms from different countries within a regional trading arrangement which includes a common competition law. They reveal that a regional competition authority with powers to control mergers and acting in the interests of the residents of all countries in the region can overcome the problems of spillovers from the actions of the authorities of the individual member countries which do not take account of the interests of the residents of other member countries.

Finally, the model can be used to analyse the effects of extraterritorial application by one nation of its merger laws. In this case, the merger of two (or more) firms relates to firms located wholly outside another nation. Suppose the nation considers its interests to be damaged by the proposed merger and seeks to block it by the extraterritorial application of its laws. The enforcement of such actions are difficult, but suppose it succeeds. Analysis of the model shows that, if the gains from improved efficiency are sufficiently large, this country may block a merger which is in the interests of the world as a whole.

Application of the Framework

Parts Two, Three, Four and Five examine the bilateral, regional, plurilateral and multilateral approaches respectively to the promotion of cross-border competition. In each part, we apply the framework outlined above by considering the options applicable to each approach and, where appropriate, the objective function of the relevant laws or policy instruments and their effects on the objective function. We concentrate on the effectiveness of the option in enforcing policies across national borders. One of the central issues is the benefits and costs of coordination versus centralization of powers in each form of multi-national mechanism. We comment upon this issue where it is relevant to each option. Part Six draws together the key positive features and principal limitations of each multi-national mechanism.

It is possible that no one policy option will dominate the others. One option may be better for some countries but not for others. Or it may be optimal in some countries to proceed with more than one option.

Notes

1. Under the Uruguay Round Agreement on Textiles and Clothing the quotas, 'voluntary' export restraints, orderly marketing agreements and other quantitative restraints on trade in clothing and textile products will end. Under the Agreement on Agriculture, quotas and restrictions such as the variable levies under the Common Agricultural Policy of the European Union will be replaced by tariffs. Under the Agreement on Safeguards, many non-tariff barriers which were previously permitted have ceased to be permissible.

2. The Uruguay Round Agreement, which established the WTO, used the term 'plurilateral' in a different and special sense, namely, an agreement which members may opt to sign but which is binding on those who do sign. The Uruguay Round included four such plurilateral agreements in addition to the multilateral agreements. These plurilateral agreements have only been signed by those members who wished to sign, in contrast to the other Agreements where members had to sign all of them under the Single Undertaking. We shall refer to such agreement as WTO—plurilateral agreements. Some earlier multi-national agreements, such as the UN Set of Principles and the OECD Guidelines and the OECD Recommendations, are sometimes described as multilateral agreements but the terminology adopted here is sharper. Hence, they are referred to in this book as plurilateral agreements.

3. The distinction between these two, and their opposing policy choices, arises because the theory of optimal tariff views the optimization from the point of view of the nation whereas the theory of free trade views it from the point of view of the world. In the latter case, the freeing of trade will benefit the individual nations, though strictly this requires the payment of lump sums across nations.

4. This theorem also assumes zero externalities, such as pollution or public goods.

PART TWO

Bilateral Cooperation on Competition Law
Enforcement

3. Bilateral Cooperation Agreements

Introduction

International cooperation among competition authorities is one possible way to improve effective enforcement of competition law in international markets. A number of countries have formalized their cooperation in bilateral competition cooperation agreements. (See Table 3.1 for a selective list of bilateral competition cooperation agreements.[1])

The United States leads the call for increased bilateral agreements with an ambitious programme of competition cooperation. The US commitment to cooperation is shown both by agreements in place and by the passing of legislation specifically enabling the US to enter into anti-trust cooperation treaties.[2] The OECD recommends that 'closer cooperation between Member countries is needed to deal effectively with the anti-competitive practices operated by enterprises situated in Member countries' (OECD, 1995).

The purpose of this chapter is to evaluate bilateral competition cooperation agreements currently in place. It first summarizes the main provisions that are being incorporated into bilateral agreements. The second section makes observations about the bilateral agreements in practice. In the third section bilateral cooperation agreements are evaluated, and the advantages and concerns about the bilateral cooperation approach are outlined. Finally, several issues are raised that need to be addressed if bilateral competition cooperation agreements are to be an important multi-national option.

Key Provisions of Bilateral Agreements

There exist today several bilateral cooperation agreements between competition authorities (see Table 3.1). Traditionally they have taken the form of a memorandum of understanding or an international agreement. Recently, some have been in the form of a Mutual Legal Assistance Treaty (MLAT). Some of their key provisions are discussed below in general terms.

33

Table 3.1: Selective list of bilateral cooperation agreements on competition law enforcement

	Year	Notification – Policy	Notification – Enforcement action	Consultation	Cooperation	Exchange of non-confidential information	Coordination of investigation	Negative comity	Positive comity	Exchange of confidential information
MLAT										
US—Australia [a]	1997	✓	✓	✓	✓	✓	✓	✓	✓	✓
US—Canada [b]	1990	✓	✓	✓	✓	✓	✓	✓	✓	✓[b]
'SecondGeneration' Agreements										
US—EC	1998	✓	✓	✓	✓	✓	✓	✓	✓	X
US—EC [c]	1991	✓	✓	✓	✓	✓	✓	✓	✓	X
US—Canada [d]	1995	✓	✓	✓	✓	✓	✓	✓		X
NZ—Australia [e]	1994	✓	✓	✓	✓	✓	✓	✓	✓*	X
NZ—Chinese Taipei [f]	1997	✓	✓	✓	✓	✓	✓	✓	✓*	X
Australia—Chinese Taipei [g]	1996	✓	✓	✓	✓	✓	✓	✓	✓*	X
Traditional Agreements										
US—Australia [h]	1982	✓	X	✓	✓	✓	X	✓	X	X
US—Germany [i]	1976	✓	X	✓	✓	✓	X	✓	X	X

Notes

*   Despite Spier and Grimwade (1997) asserting these agreements provide for positive comity, examination of the text of the agreement does not reveal anything close to the positive comity provisions of the 1991 US—EC Agreement.

a   Agreement between the Government of the United States of America and the Government of Australia on Mutual Anti-trust Enforcement Assistance (April 1997).

b   Treaty between the Government of Canada and the Government of the United States of America on Mutual Legal Assistance in Criminal Matters S. Treaty Doc. No. 28, 100th Cong. (1988). Came into force on 14 January 1990. Provides for exchange of information on criminal anti-trust matters only.

c   Agreement between the Government of the United States of America and the Commission of the European Communities Regarding the Application of their Competition Laws (23 Sept 1991), reprinted at 4 Trade Reg. Rep. (CCH) 13,504.

d   Agreement between the Government of the United States of America and the Government of Canada Regarding the Application of their Competition and Deceptive Marketing Practices Laws (3 Aug 1995), reprinted at 4 Trade Reg. Rep. (CCH) 13,503.

e   Cooperation and Coordination Agreement between the Australian Trade Practices Commission and the New Zealand Commerce Commission. See Chapter 5 for reference to 1990 Agreement between Australia and New Zealand.

f   Cooperation and Coordination Agreement between the New Zealand Commerce and Industry Office and the Taipei Economic and Cultural Office Regarding the Application of the Competition and Fair Trading Laws (December 1997).

g   The Chairpersons of the ACCC and Taipei's Fair Trade Commission exchanged letters in September 1996 confirming the signing of an Arrangement between the two parties.

h   Agreement between the Government of the United States of America and the Government of Australia Relating to Cooperation on Antitrust Matters (29 June 1982), reprinted at 4 Trade Reg. Rep. (CCH) 13,502.

i   Agreement between the Government of the United States of America and the Government of the Federal Republic of Germany Relating to Mutual Cooperation Regarding Restrictive Business Practices (23 June 1976), reprinted at 4 Trade Reg. Rep. (CCH) 13,501.

Notification

Early bilateral agreements provided solely for 'policy' notification. One of the primary functions of recent bilateral agreements is to provide notification when a competition investigation is in progress in one country that may affect another jurisdiction. Notification provisions contemplate that each party will provide the other with information about planned country actions which may affect the other's important interests, the test of such important interest being laid down by the agreement. The provisions are aimed at preventing potential conflicts when a competition investigation affects the interests of another country. Some agreements enumerate specific procedures for the notification of relevant investigations, mergers, and acquisitions. Generally, however, notification must be sufficiently detailed so that the other party can make an informed assessment of the situation.

Consultation for purpose of conflict avoidance

Further to notification provisions, most agreements provide for consultation between competition authorities to resolve mutual or unilateral concerns, whether based on notified activities or otherwise. The consultation may occur between the heads of the respective authorities meeting on a scheduled basis, or through the staff of the authorities updating each other on progress. Importantly, consultation covers prospective remedies in situations where the interests of more than one country could be affected.

Cooperation

These provisions articulate the intentions of both parties to cooperate in matters of competition law enforcement, where such cooperation is feasible in both practical and legal terms. All specifically allow the requested party to take its own interest into account in determining whether, and to what extent, to provide the requested cooperation.

Exchanges of non-confidential information

Further to the notification procedures for specific matters, there is also provision in most agreements for the parties to meet throughout the year to exchange information on, for example, their current enforcement activities and priorities, their common fields of economic interest, general industry analysis and any policy changes. Furthermore, if one party receives a request from another party to provide information, it is to provide it where possible.

Coordination of investigations

The notification provisions of the agreements generally ensure that cases of common interest are identified at an early stage. Where significant issues for both sides are involved, parties may activate the coordination provisions in an agreement. For example, in the 1991 United States—European Community Agreement,[3] Article IV provides a 'who goes first' procedure, where one party may decide to hold back its enforcement activities until the other has reached a decision. If that decision also solves the former party's problems, that party may decide that it no longer needs to take independent action.

Negative comity

Negative comity provisions represent the traditional approach to limiting the extraterritorial application of another country's competition rules. In basic terms, negative comity is a doctrine of politeness and good manners between countries in an attempt to bring their respective positions and remedies closer to each other in order to avoid one country creating a harmful effect on the jurisdiction of the other. Each party agrees to refrain from enforcing competition laws where such enforcement would unduly interfere with the legitimate sovereign interests of the other signatory.

Bilateral competition cooperation agreements commonly articulate that each party is to take into account the important interests of the other party in its enforcement activities. More specifically, the interests of the other party ought to be considered in decisions as to whether or not to initiate an investigation or proceeding, the scope of an investigation or proceeding, and the nature of the remedies or penalties sought.

'Second Generation' Agreements

Some more recent bilateral agreements have provided for more elaborate mechanisms for cooperation that indicate a willingness to make the agreements something beyond just a means to avoid conflict. The 1991 US—EC Agreement was the first to contain positive comity provisions. In 1994 the US passed the International Antitrust Enforcement Assistance Act (IAEAA). This Act allows the US to enter new MLAT arrangements with various foreign governments for both criminal and civil competition law violations. The only important example of a MLAT concluded under this enactment is the 1997 MLAT agreement between US and Australia (see below).

Some have described the more recent agreements as indicating a 'modern era of cooperation' (Varney, 1995). The phrase 'second generation agreements' has also been used to describe these agreements, in particular those providing for positive comity. Certainly, now that the

OECD is recommending the provision for positive comity in cooperation agreements in the 1995 Revised Recommendations and the IAEAA is allowing the US to seek more cooperation agreements in the form of MLATs, a new generation of cooperation agreements may be in sight.

The positive comity upgrade

While traditional or negative comity requires an agency to take into account important interests of the other when enforcing competition laws, positive comity addresses the situation where the effects on one party's interests are the result of a country not taking action under its law. Positive comity in a competition cooperation agreement allows country A to notify country B where A believes anti-competitive activities carried out in the territory of B are adversely affecting A's significant interests. Importantly, it allows the affected party to request the other party's competition authorities to initiate appropriate enforcement activities. The provisions therefore have the ability to avert potential conflicts over jurisdictional issues — particularly where the requesting nation has the ability to exert its competition laws extraterritorially. Formally, current positive comity provisions only obligate the recipient of such a request to consider, and if possible, to act favourably upon a request.

Positive comity has its roots in a 1967 OECD Recommendation on Cooperation between Member Countries on Restrictive Business Practices Affecting International Trade. It first appeared in the 1991 US—EC agreement and later in the 1995 executive agreement between the US and Canada. Because positive comity is considered to require highly developed and efficient competition law regimes, similar substantive and procedural competition provisions and a considerable level of reciprocal trust between two authorities, the principle cannot yet commonly be found at an international level.

The positive comity provisions of the 1991 US—EC agreement have been strengthened with the recent 1998 signing of a further comity agreement between the two parties.[4] This agreement seeks to clarify the circumstances under which a party will refer cases of anti-competitive practices to each other under the doctrine of 'positive comity' and the obligations that the competition authorities should undertake in handling these cases.

The agreement also specifies that the requesting party will normally defer or suspend its enforcement activities aimed at anti-competitive activities in the other party's territory in favour of a positive comity referral to the other party. A deferral or suspension is envisaged either where the foreign anti-competitive activities do not directly harm the requesting party's consumers or where foreign anti-competitive activities occur principally in and are directed primarily towards the other party's territory, yet incidentally harm the requesting party's consumers.

Mutual Legal Assistance Treaty Agreements (MLATs)

Most bilateral competition cooperation agreements, including those providing for positive comity, remain non-binding. They do not allow for any derogation from the internal rules applicable in each country, in particular on the protection of confidential information. Whilst this is not always an obstacle to effective cooperation (for example, where the information requested is in the public domain), it has prevented competition authorities sharing much of the specific information collected from companies on the basis of the investigatory powers of the respective agencies (see Rakovsky, 1997).

A modern MLAT is seen as a way to strengthen the investigatory powers of participating competition agencies and authorize exchanges of otherwise protected confidential information. Most countries have MLATs to obtain assistance in respect of investigations in other areas. MLAT agreements between various OECD member governments cover areas of fraud, securities law and taxation and provide, for example, for one country to take evidence on behalf of another.

The crimes covered by the US—Canada MLAT[5] include anti-trust cases where it is a criminal offence in these countries. This agreement allows for the exchange of information between US and Canadian competition authorities and has been used with success in several recent US investigations.[6] Because certain anti-competitive conduct (for example, hard-core cartels) is prosecuted criminally in both countries, the MLAT permits cooperation in these types of competition matters. As a result, the MLAT permits the competition enforcement authority of one country to request the assistance of the other in order to obtain evidence regarding possible criminal offences. Because it is an international treaty, the exchange of confidential information is allowed to the same extent that disclosure can be made to national law enforcing bodies.

The US has sought to expand the types of confidential information that can be shared between competition authorities in both civil and criminal competition enforcement matters in the passing of the IAEAA. This act is across-the-board authorizing legislation which allows the US to negotiate and conclude bilateral cooperation agreements with trading partners which include the ability to share all forms of confidential information (subject to certain conditions) and the ability to use the compulsory process to obtain information for each other.

The first example of an agreement under this legislation was entered into between the US and Australia. The IAEAA is expected to foster similar agreements to allow for the reciprocal sharing of investigative information between the US and other countries. But prospective countries must have the basic legislative or parliamentary authorization to hold up their respective end of the bargain.[7] In particular, this includes the ability to share investigatory information with a foreign competition authority and adequately protect the confidentiality of any information received.

The Agreements in Practice

This section makes some general observations about the agreements in practice, and leads to an evaluation of bilateral cooperation agreements in the following section.

Increased dialogue

Bilateral cooperation agreements have increased the dialogue between parties to the agreements. Their formal mechanisms have encouraged agencies to manage better their differences, resulting in fewer competition issues becoming politicized. Both the US and the EU note a marked increase in communication between the two authorities following their 1991 agreement.[8] Communication and cooperation between parties to bilateral agreements are also considered more intensive and case oriented (Schaub, 1998). In addition to formal cooperation and communication, most agreements have encouraged competition authorities to exchange ideas about competition law enforcement with their counterparts around the world.

Such communication and cooperation must be judged in light of the tension previously created by the US and the extraterritorial application of its competition laws. Many countries report that the steady flow of communications between all levels of enforcement agencies under bilateral agreements assists in developing an atmosphere of mutual trust or spirit of cooperation. Officials have commented widely how they understand this to be having a positive influence on a convergence of approaches to competition law. With such effects it would seem that the potential for expanded cooperation may be greater between those parties to bilateral cooperation agreements (see Spier, 1997).

Incremental value

The value of the agreements must be assessed in terms of what they add to the ability of competition authorities to enforce competition law. Little empirical work exists in this area. Some countries may see an advantage in bilateral cooperation because of a possible reduction in unilateral actions by other countries.

While the bilateral agreements have been credited with the frequency and scope of cooperation between particular competition authorities, it must be remembered that many of the agreements have simply formalized the informal practices that had occurred for years prior to an agreement. Most of the incidents of cooperation still involve relatively routine notifications or requests for publicly available information.[9]

Most activities and communication undertaken under the agreements could legally have occurred without an agreement.[10] To some extent active cooperation occurred and continues to occur without bilateral agreements. Klein (1997b) of the US Department of Justice observes:

> What is probably less well-known is that in the last couple of years, the Division has sought and received assistance in cartel investigations, not only from our good friends in Canada, but from many other countries as well (including Japan, I should note) pursuant to both MLAT requests and more traditional letters rogatory. This assistance has included searches and seizures of documentary evidence, witness interviews, and statements as well.

Many countries have similar access to evidence in other countries without the need to enter reciprocal bilateral cooperation agreements.

Slow results

Despite bilateral cooperation agreements involving only two parties, which thus are presumed to be easier to negotiate, bilateral cooperation agreements are still limited to a relatively small number of countries; nor is it envisaged that the world will soon have a broad network of bilateral cooperation agreements. Lengthy negotiations do not seem to be a problem, if the ability of the US and EU to negotiate their 1991 agreement in a few months is any indication.[11] Instead, a lack of political will, or differences in the stage of economic development and competition law (if it exists) in many countries, may account for the small number of bilateral agreements presently in place.

In particular, progress with second generation MLATs with the US under the IAEAA has been slower than anticipated in 1994, when the US Senate rushed the bill through all stages in a record ten weeks. During four years only one agreement has resulted, with Australia. This has been attributed to a lack in most countries of mutual assistance legislation that would permit their governments to negotiate IAEAA-type agreements (see Klein, 1997b). However, even where a bilateral agreement has been concluded, some parties have been slow to utilize provisions for cooperation.

Absence of procedural cooperation

Despite the introduction of many bilateral agreements, there has been limited harmonization of procedural requirements in the treatment of mergers and acquisitions. Whilst it would involve some harmonization of time-frames and information requests, it is believed this could be done without the necessity to rewrite substantive merger laws.

With over 30 national systems of merger control having been established, the lack of procedural harmonization is increasingly being viewed as imposing unnecessary uncertainty, expense, and delay on legitimate business activities; for example, Gillette's acquisition of Wilkinson Sword was considered by 14 different agencies around the world. A large merger that affects many countries' markets may require ten or more filings at different stages in the process. Something simpler and better ought to exist which could see national agencies defer to each other or at least standardize their often burdensome requests for information.

Examples of Actual Cooperation under the Agreements

Boeing/McDonnell Douglas

One of the best-known examples of dual competition law enforcement cooperation under the 1991 US—EC agreement was the *Boeing/McDonnell Douglas* merger case. Staff and officials on both sides consulted fairly regularly on development in the case, sharing with each other how they were analysing the various markets at issue and what factors were relevant under their respective laws.

First, the EU requested the US to take on board important European interests before reaching any final decision, in particular the EU's concern over long-term exclusive contracts. At a later stage, the roles were reversed, with US authorities making a request for consultation with EU authorities, where the US requested the EU to take into account important US defence interests. Some success was achieved: the EU acknowledged important US interests in declining to take any action with respect to defence markets. The US, in turn, acknowledged EU concerns by announcing that Boeing's exclusive agreements with airlines were 'troubling' and by committing to monitor the anti-competitive effects of those and any future long-term exclusive contracts.

The end result saw the EU and the US reach famously different enforcement decisions in analysing the same market: the world-wide market for large commercial aircraft. Whilst the US decided not to oppose the merger, the EU concluded that the merger would increase Boeing's dominance to the detriment of Airbus and competition in the commercial aircraft market.

Intense political pressure from Washington, culminating in threats of a trade war, ultimately saw a compromise reached between Boeing and the EU authorities, and the merger was approved by the European Commission.

Microsoft

In 1994 the Microsoft investigation and its settlement was the first application of the 1991 US—EC agreement.[12] The charges were the result of close coordination between the Antitrust Division of the Department of Justice (DOJ) and the DG IV of the European Commission and marked the first coordinated effort of the two enforcement bodies in initiating and resolving a competition law enforcement action.

Importantly here, Microsoft consented to both US and EU authorities exchanging confidential information. The efficiency gains evidenced in this investigation would therefore not necessarily be present in cases where the parties do not consent. The case was finally settled through a negotiation between Microsoft and the two enforcement agencies together.

Nielsen

In 1996 the DOJ conducted an investigation of AC Nielsen, a US firm that provides services tracking retail sales, to determine whether Nielsen offered customers more favourable terms in countries where it had market power if those customers also used Nielsen in countries where it faced significant competition. The EU also investigated complaints about practices primarily implemented and having their greatest impact in Europe. There was close contact between staffs of both agencies. The US, upon being satisfied that the EU would take action to remedy the situation, allowed the DG IV to take the lead and US authorities closed their investigation once the European Commission had secured the necessary undertakings from Nielsen.

An Evaluation

This section is in three parts. First, the advantages of bilateral cooperation agreements are outlined. Secondly, the limitations of bilateral cooperation agreements are surveyed. Finally, some requirements for enhancing the effectiveness of future bilateral competition cooperation agreements are suggested.

Advantages

PRACTICAL AND ACHIEVABLE
In pragmatic terms, bilateral competition cooperation agreements are considered achievable and a practical way to address many of the international practices of concern. The US, placing high importance on the practical law enforcement value of such agreements, has cited the speed of being able to negotiate and put in place such agreements as a reason to favour a bilateral agreement approach. Furthermore, US officials claim that bilateral agreements provide more short-term value and certainty than an 'unwieldy and theoretical WTO exercise' (Klein, 1997b) to reach a multilateral consensus on minimum competition standards. The pragmatic approach has even seen US officials concede that they would be willing to enter cartel-only bilateral cooperation agreements where broader agreement does not seem possible (Klein, 1997b).

LOCAL ACCOUNTABILITY AND LEGAL STRUCTURES

The bilateral cooperation approach does not create any new institutions or substantive law. Rather, the agreements preserve the advantages of localized political and legal structures, while attempting to minimize the inefficiencies of multiple systems. All agreements keep intact a country's own competition laws. This avoids the friction created by promoting one set of competition laws as the basis of a universal competition law.

Because bilateral cooperation agreements do not address substantive law, they avoid the need to reconcile and compromise the differences in approaches and institutions. Localized law and institutions are important from a jurisprudential point of view as national laws often represent unique social and legal visions of that country: one country's law cannot easily be exported to other countries. Furthermore, there are different legal systems: some countries have legal systems based in common law, others have a civil code. In respect of competition law, some countries have developed it through judge-made law, interpreting judicial precedents and elaborating broadly worded statutes. Others have applied precise rules and have not been bound by precedent.

Keeping competition legislation at a national level also ensures national accountability and democratic legitimacy. Few countries are willing to give up competition rules they know in favour of rules that are entirely new to them. Countries which do not have competition laws may wish to build on their existing legal structures, rather than, or at least before, signing on to an international code. The great differences in stages of economic development, and the numerous political and other considerations that influence policy formation, may suggest that competition law is most suited to a national context. Bilateral cooperation has the advantage of allowing this, yet at the same time assisting in making the law more effective at the bilateral level.

TAILOR MADE

Negotiating and implementing international cooperation agreements at a bilateral level allows countries to ensure that an agreement is custom-made and incorporates refinements which may be important to particular country relationships. For example, bilateral agreements can address factors such as different levels of economic development, the strength of social and legal institutions, differences in competition law, the type of economy a country has, and legitimate doctrinal differences (such as the role of competition law in promoting a single market in Europe). The agreements can thus provide for clearer rights and obligations of both parties.

CONSISTENT REMEDIES

Beyond consultation regarding competition law enforcement which may affect another jurisdiction, consultative mechanisms in agreements commonly provide for dialogue to ensure that the remedies imposed in each country are consistent. Such provisions decrease the possibility that remedial actions, designed to limit the anti-competitive impact of the conduct under scrutiny, do not undermine each other. This can be particularly important in cross-border mergers and can avoid orders for different restructuring or divestment procedures.[13]

INTERNATIONAL OBLIGATIONS AS A MEANS OF ENSURING 'COMPETITION' ANALYSIS

International cooperation agreements may provide a mechanism to strengthen the likelihood that countries with such agreements undertake proper competition analysis. Given that competition laws operate under the power of constituency-serving governments, international commitment to a bilateral agreement is a public announcement of a commitment to cooperate in competition law matters. This may strengthen the hand of a competition agency in dealing with national groups and institutions who may attempt to influence the direction of competition-related policy or specific cases considered under domestic competition law (see World Bank, 1997, pp. 30—31). Such an observation may be particularly relevant to countries with relatively new competition law which may not have the political support to protect competition rather than domestic competitors.

Cooperation between authorities may also reduce the likelihood that particular disputes become politicized and so threaten the strict application of neutral legal and economic principles. As Klein (1997b) recently observed:

> If we antitrust enforcers fail to manage these differences through effective cooperation and coordination mechanisms, there will be a greatly increased risk that particular antitrust disputes will become politicized, with the obvious adverse effects on sound and predictable antitrust enforcement.

Concerns and Limitations

NON-BINDING, CASE-SPECIFIC COOPERATION

The cooperation agreements to date are simply enabling agreements. They only permit foreign competition authorities to cooperate when they want to. With nothing in the developing web of bilateral cooperation agreements that requires a nation to cooperate or enforce its own competition laws, the agreements represent incomplete solutions to the promotion of competition in globalizing markets. Neither party to an agreement is obligated to respond favourably to a request for assistance in providing information, even under a positive comity provision; nor were the agreements intended to create binding obligations on parties. Most agreements are expressly non-binding. Therefore, as their names suggest, they still require the voluntary *cooperation* of the other party.

Their voluntary nature allows for no certainty in the ironing out of jurisdiction in sensitive cases. An agency notified of possible anti-competitive activities within its borders must consider the foreign enforcement authority's request for assistance, but it retains complete discretion as to whether to initiate or expand enforcement activities. Even assuming cooperation is initiated, most agreements provide that one party may cancel, at any time, any coordinated efforts with notice and proceed to enforce its own laws independently.

Case-by-case cooperation also makes it easier to decline cooperation, in whole or in part, in particular cases. Given that most agreements provide for cooperation subject to a broad public interest evaluation by the requested party, cooperation is likely to be limited where it would be against a nation's interest (see Varney, 1995). Wide terms contained in the agreements such as 'significant interests', 'important interests' and 'within its reasonably available resources' allow for broad interpretation and provide a nationalistic prerequisite to cooperation. This diverts attention away from the effect on competition in a market to its effect on competition in a jurisdiction.

FAILURE TO REMOVE NARROW NATIONAL INTERESTS FROM COMPETITION LAW ENFORCEMENT

The ability of bilateral cooperation agreements to address international anti-competitive practices may be severely limited by nationalist interests. Under the agreements, nations will cooperate only if it serves their own immediate self-interests in specific cases. The bilateral approach fails to acknowledge the restrictions of a geographic jurisdiction in addressing international markets. No agreement requires domestic competition law enforcing bodies to look beyond national competition criteria in their own jurisdiction. However, it has been recognized that national competition criteria will not always be consistent with the interests of other countries (WTO, 1997, p. 58). Important competition effects outside a jurisdiction continue to go unrecognized, even with bilateral cooperation agreements. For example, Wood (1995), in explaining why the IAEAA was passed allowing the US to enter into competition MLATs, said:

> We did so because we believed that this was one of the best ways to promote effective enforcement of the antitrust laws in the interests of US markets and consumers. That, after all, is our job: through enforcement of the antitrust laws, to protect the competitive process in the United States from arrangements that threaten it.

Such a result is not the fault of competition agencies. National competition laws are national in focus and reflect, among other things, a country's policy objectives, political and legal systems, history and traditions. National competition laws reflect a domestic political response to perceived domestic realities and have never been expected to consider any efficiency/welfare effects outside of their jurisdiction. Even if criteria of allocative efficiency were solely applicable, the fact that such criteria are generally applied in respect of efficiency and welfare within the jurisdiction in question and may not take into account adverse effects on the welfare of producers and consumers abroad, means that national competition law enforcement will not give consideration to important effects in the international market.

The bilateral cooperation approach does not address the parochial flavour of competition laws and the need for their apolitical application (see Fox and Ordover, 1997). Instead, they reinforce the nationalistic focus of enforcement by specifically providing for requested agencies to decline cooperation when it may not be in the nation's interest to do so, irrespective of its global welfare effects or considerations. This is in contrast to the call for a global welfare standard.[14] Such a standard would enable national competition laws to take into account the effects on competition in a relevant international market as opposed to just a jurisdictional boundary.

With the national focus of competition law still intact, agency cooperation under bilateral agreements will be fruitful only when nations perceive their interests to be common and therefore choose to cooperate. Bilateral positive and negative comity will only work in situations where the perceived national interests of the countries concerned do not diverge. This provides a natural limit to the type of cooperation that can be extended under the agreements, for there are many instances where nations are likely to perceive their interests to be adversely affected: national industries policies; state sanctions of certain cartels; different conceptions regarding what is anti-competitive; different understanding of the underlying facts; other political pressures. Cooperation is also unlikely where allegedly anti-competitive private practices are encouraged or tolerated by national governments. Requests for cooperation in investigating such practices will almost certainly dictate a defensive attitude and so prevent cooperation and effective enforcement.

NO AGREEMENT ON ANY SUBSTANTIVE COMPETITION LAW
No bilateral cooperation agreements have attempted to harmonize any substantive competition law provisions. While there is an absence of agreement regarding substantive law and continuing important differences remain between jurisdictions, the scope for cooperation may be circumscribed in two ways.

First, domestic laws only provide the authority or legal power to authorities to investigate practices which contravene national law in a relevant national market. By extension, the business practice which is the subject of a request for assistance must be considered in breach of national law in the requested nation for that authority to have power to investigate it.

A competition authority does not have legal power to investigate practices which have no effect within its jurisdiction. This is because the powers of the authority must only be used to carry out the authority's function as defined by domestic legislation. As a result, serious limitations may confront actual cooperation efforts being undertaken. For example, most competition authorities will only have jurisdiction to use their investigatory powers where there is an infringement of their own competition laws. A requested authority may not necessarily have the authority to act where, despite the conduct having occurred within its jurisdiction, the effect of such conduct is not borne by the jurisdiction.[15] This is the result of domestic laws being framed in terms of an effect on 'a market' and there being either a provision or a presumption that such a market is within the confines of a jurisdiction. The focus simply on a national market can be explicitly displaced. See, for example, New Zealand and Australia's trans-Tasman competition provisions and the creation of a trans-Tasman market.[16]

If a competition authority were to exercise, for example, its search and seizure powers to obtain evidence for a requesting nation, solely on the basis of an effect in the requesting nation, the authority would probably be acting *ultra vires* (beyond its power). Therefore, any affected party would be entitled to seek an appropriate remedy from a court on the grounds that the authority had acted (or was about to act) beyond its powers.

For a bilateral agreement (including those in the form of a treaty) to deliver real cooperation, corresponding domestic legislation must be enacted by both parties to the agreement. Such legislation would need to enable a competition authority to exercise its powers when it received a request from the other party to the agreement. Without such legislation, the cooperative intention of an agreement cannot be realized unless an effect is also felt in a market in the requested country. The practice of some international treaties being subsequently enacted in the respective countries (by specific enactment, for example GATT, or automatically in the case of the US) may indicate the form that future bilateral cooperation agreements need to take. Without corresponding domestic legislation or automatic incorporation into domestic law, even treaties will have no binding effect on domestic law enforcement and therefore may also be limited.

Such limitations on the powers of competition authorities clearly illustrate the inadequacy of a consultative non-binding cooperation framework in attempting to accommodate the interests and concerns of trading partners, as opposed to rule-of-law systems for the domestic application of competition law. Even competition authorities party to a bilateral agreement cannot take into account considerations inconsistent with national law because the law's criteria are not being extended beyond a national jurisdiction. Moreover, where competition authorities are tempted to use any discretion available to them in a generous way, with a view to accommodating concerns expressed by another country under a cooperation agreement, there remains a risk that such decisions could be overturned by national courts.

The second problem arising from the failure of bilateral cooperation agreements to address differences in substantive competition law is the control of international practices on which competition authorities fail to agree. While cooperation success to date has largely occurred where two authorities approached alleged violations similarly,[17] there exist significantly different approaches to some competition issues. For example, different industry sectors have statutory exemptions and there is disagreement on the legal status of vertical restraints by a manufacturer on its distributors (Varney, 1995).

Given that cooperation is unlikely where a disagreement exists, the usefulness of bilateral cooperation agreements may be limited to those areas where there are shared values and norms about competition law. Rakovsky (1997) recognizes this:

> Of course, as we do not live in a perfect world, we should not expect that this cooperation framework would be sufficient to overcome all possible differences of approach which may stem from differences in substantive law or from the fact that the same behaviour by the same companies may have sometimes a very different effect on different markets.

Even assuming that nations share the goal of maximizing efficiency and national welfare, politics and national policy objectives may dictate important differences in the values and norms of competition authorities when they approach and enforce competition law. The perception (and problem) that some countries do not vigorously enforce their competition laws (if they have any) at a level that recognizes the importance of international competition is a vivid example of the problem. Authorities are unlikely always to agree upon what ought to be investigated and/or prosecuted (see Wood, 1992). Where there is no agreement, cooperation in the investigation or enforcement of competition law is highly unlikely and so leaves the bilateral agreements unable to address the problem.

A LIMITED NETWORK

Effective international competition is a global challenge and only a few industrialized countries have entered (or are ready to enter) bilateral agreements. Some major economies, such as Japan, are not party to any bilateral competition cooperation agreement.[18] Many countries therefore remain ill-equipped to address practices with a significant trans-border dimension. As a result, even those countries which have bilateral agreements may not be able to deal with conduct which falls outside existing bilateral agreements; nor would even a complex web of bilateral agreements seem able to capture broad international anti-competitive activity. With few bilateral agreements in place, a significant number of countries and their business practices are capable of distorting international competition.

Several factors may inhibit the future ability of countries to negotiate and be actively involved in cooperation agreements. The cooperation approach requires certain prerequisites of countries, not least of which is the requirement to have a competition regime and authority. However, many countries do not have competition laws. Of those who do, most have had only brief experience with their law, and are still developing both the expertise and political support necessary for the law's sound and effective enforcement.

The concern must be that the bilateral cooperation approach looks set to leave many countries (in particular developing countries) out in the cold or destined to be junior partners of major industrialized economies. Hence, major economies such as the US will still be able to exert unilateral pressures. Generally speaking, developing countries are likely to prefer multilateral rules and transparent implementation by an independent party (see World Bank, 1998, Chapter 5).

Without wide-scale cooperation agreements in place, there remains the ability for companies to exploit the division of the world into separate sovereign jurisdictions. Just as all the intellectual property protection across the western world is of little use if counterfeit factories flourish, international markets will continue to be distorted if developing countries are not parties to a 'solution'. For example, the bilateral cooperation approach does not address the situation where a cartel carefully does most of its business in a country which has weak or no competition law and which is not a party to any bilateral cooperation agreement.

Despite progress with the bilateral cooperation approach there will be room for 'competition havens'. Knowing they exist, some companies (or even countries) could exploit the gap and direct and attract investment to countries with no bilateral agreements or competition law (Wood, 1996).

SUPPLEMENT TO UNILATERALISM
No bilateral cooperation agreement prohibits a country from falling back to unilateral action if it so chooses. All agreements provide avenues for each jurisdiction to assert its own competition laws without the cooperation of the other. Therefore, whilst the trend has been away from extraterritorial application of national laws, the capability to do so sits unusually alongside the cooperation agreement to which the US is party. The US, in its recent guidelines,[19] confirms that extraterritorial application of its laws is, as Klein (1997a) expressed it, an essential 'component of a program for ensuring effective anti-trust enforcement in an age of global markets'.

Contrary to what US officials assert, there is an inconsistency in the commitment to cooperation on the one hand, and, on the other hand, the desire to retain the right to bring unilateral action in US courts via extraterritorial provisions when the necessary effects are occurring in the US (see Wood, 1995). Such an avenue allows the US to return to the more aggressive posture of the past if it believes cooperation is not delivering adequate results. It is difficult to accept that a mature system of cooperation, which includes provision for positive comity, should coexist with the possibility of unilateral action that would be carried out by country A against restrictive practices implemented in the territory of country B which have no effect on the market or consumers of A. Unilateral confrontational tools are regarded by many as second-best solutions that should only be used as a last resort in compelling cases.[20]

There would also be concern if countries could acquire information under cooperation agreements and then cancel such cooperation and enforce its competition laws unilaterally. The risk, which has been expressed in foreign government and business circles, is that cooperation agreements may assist countries in competition matters that look like trade 'market access' cases (see Klein, 1997b).

Requirements for a 'solution'

Present bilateral cooperation agreements have inherent limitations. If the bilateral cooperation approach is to have a realistic chance of providing a solution to current international competition concerns, present and future agreements have to be deepened. Among other things, agreements need to be more widespread, reflect more binding commitment (in particular to positive comity provisions) and more meaningful cooperation, and address the current void where countries' interests diverge and cooperation is not forthcoming.

Current bilateral agreements leave cooperation limited. In their present form bilateral agreements will not be able to address adequately international competition concerns and effective competition law enforcement in international markets. As voluntary consultative mechanisms, their capabilities extend to general exchanges of views on approaches to competition law matters and to preventing conflicts arising where both parties have an interest in a particular case. They do not attempt to reconcile different substantive approaches to competition law or provide mechanisms to settle differences between competition agencies where interests diverge.

If competition laws are to address the problem of private restraints affecting international competition, it is vitally important to ensure that such laws are designed to maximize consumer welfare and economic efficiency in those markets, not just within a jurisdiction. This would seem an inherent limitation of the bilateral cooperation agreement approach, for the agreements rely solely on national criteria and competition laws to protect competition in markets which increasingly exist beyond a nation's jurisdiction.

Bilateral agreements must be deepened if they are to provide any realistic means of ensuring effective competition in international markets. Such a suggestion is not new. In 1995 a European Commission Group of Experts proposed a deepening of the US—EC cooperation agreement as 'a priority' (European Commission, 1995). The 1994 passing of the IAEAA is an indication of US willingness to deepen cooperation in respect of the sharing of confidential information, even if it has had limited success to date.

However, the deepening of present and future bilateral agreements will not be easy. Any attempt to deepen cooperation must first gain national acceptance. The difficulty with this is that much of what is required to deepen cooperation raises serious sovereignty issues. For example, any suggestion that the statutory restrictions on disclosure of confidential information should be relaxed is bound to be controversial.[21] The EU is still assessing whether it has the political will among its members before seeking deeper cooperation or passing IAEAA-equivalent legislation (Schaub, 1996). This issue is politically sensitive and so domestic support for such initiatives cannot be taken for granted.

STRONGER POSITIVE COMITY COMMITMENT

Although the necessity for positive comity has been recognized in the 'second generation' agreements and the latest OECD Recommendations, much remains to be done to strengthen the comity provisions. Positive comity provisions remain voluntary and so continue to suffer from incentive problems on the part of the requested authority. As earlier noted, the requested country may in some instances also lack the authority to act. Countries are free to decline requests where these are contrary to sovereign interests and thus are unlikely to be accepted where countries have conflicting interests.

Enforcement agencies that are parties to bilateral cooperation agreements need to be more responsive to all complaints from foreign countries or persons. Aside from the 1998 Agreement between the US and the EU, few agreements contain presumptions and clarification of when positive comity is appropriate. Present positive comity provisions are also limited by an authority being unable to make a request of another country, unless the conduct in question violates the competition law of the requested country. The void remains of activity which may adversely affect competition in the requesting country yet would be permitted in the requested nation.

The recently signed Comity Antitrust Agreement between the US and the EU is an illustration of the direction required to ensure that positive comity provisions can and will be fully utilized. The agreement is a revised and reinforced version of the positive comity principle in the 1991 US—EC Agreement (see Cocuzza and Montini, 1998). The new agreement clarifies the situations that would presumptively call for referrals. It also creates a presumption that in certain circumstances a party will normally defer or suspend its own enforcement activities. However, the new positive comity provisions remain voluntary. While still implicit, such an agreement represents a greater commitment by both parties not to act unilaterally unless all means provided for by the comity provisions have been exhausted. Such provisions importantly allow for an improved balance in bilateral relations between countries where only one maintains its ability to exert jurisdiction extraterritorially.

Implementing widespread positive comity provisions may prove challenging. One wonders how two countries (such as Japan and the US), which could not even agree on the scope of comity in international law in the *Nippon* case, would be able to apply positive comity provisions. Some have suggested that for positive comity to work most effectively it requires some mutual recognition of outcome, both in abiding by the decision of the investigating authority and accepting the remedy imposed. This too would require a strong element of trust between the enforcing agencies, and at present seems highly unlikely.

MEANINGFUL EXCHANGES OF CONFIDENTIAL INFORMATION

The ban in most jurisdictions on the exchange of confidential information is a major obstacle to meaningful and effective cooperation even where a comprehensive bilateral agreement exists.[22] Access to confidential information collected by foreign enforcement agency would enhance efforts to combat international restrictive practices (see Rakovsky, 1997). Yet cartelists, operating in several countries, have some degree of comfort knowing that agencies investigating their activities cannot share with each other the findings of their separate investigations. Without the ability to share such information, in-depth case-specific cooperation is normally impossible and agencies are reliant upon the consent of the parties. Some recent investigations have shared confidential information but have done so due to the company consenting (for example, Microsoft). However, waivers by the parties being investigated is not the answer. Companies will only agree when it is clearly in their best interests and a request for waiver puts them on notice at a time when enforcement agencies would prefer it to be kept secret.

Confidentiality laws, which limit disclosure of information, exist for clearly legitimate reasons and serve an important policy.[23] Public dissemination of such information could be harmful to the firm that provided it, to the future information-gathering efforts of the agency and to consumer welfare. For example, unwarranted disclosure of confidential information which an authority has shared with another authority could undermine its own investigations and deter persons in the future from providing important information voluntarily. The principal challenge facing competition officials seeking means to enhance cooperation may be to find ways to permit the exchange of such information, in appropriate circumstances and subject to adequate procedural safeguards.

One means of authorizing information exchanges is suggested by the US in the passing of the IAEAA. However, this approach requires most nations to change laws that lift the limitations on information sharing. In some instances this would involve countries reversing blocking statutes recently put in place in an attempt to protect themselves from the extraterritorial reach of the US.[24] Such moves are likely to be controversial. Often such a suggestion draws attention from companies and lawyers, afraid that such provisions could be used to ship important information to another country (Ehlerman, 1994).

The competition community must explore means of protecting legitimate national interests, including safeguarding the confidentiality of business and official government information, even while they work more closely together to safeguard the interests of consumers in all countries. An essential step is that enforcement authorities recognize the legitimate concerns of businesses regarding the confidentiality of their information. However, the business and legal communities must also recognize the substantial social benefits that arise when enforcement agencies are given the proper tools to investigate mergers and restrictive trade practices with an international competition dimension.

Notes

1. In this chapter 'cooperation agreements' is used both in the collective sense of incorporating those in the form of a treaty, and also in the specific sense distinguishing agreements from treaties.
2. For a discussion on US agencies' attitude toward cooperation, see Varney (1995).
3. The Agreement was challenged before the European Court of Justice by France, supported by Spain and the Netherlands, for procedural reasons regarding the limits of the external powers of the EC Commission. According to Article 228 (1) of the EC Treaty, the European Commission has the power to negotiate but not conclude agreements with foreign countries; thus the European Commission was found to have acted in the absence of a delegation of powers by the Council. The Council of Ministers approved the Agreement and it entered into force on 10 April 1995. However, the effective date was applied retroactively to the original date of entry into force, 23 September 1991.
4. Agreement signed on 4 June 1998. For a brief summary of its content, see CCH Trade Regulation Reports no. 529, 10 June 1998.
5. Treaty between the Government of Canada and the Government of the United States of America on Mutual Legal Assistance in Criminal Matters. This came into force on 14 January 1990.
6. The agreement was considered crucial to the breaking up of two criminal price-fixing conspiracies in the *Fax Paper* and the *Plastic Dinnerware* cases.
7. Australia already had in place a statute under which confidential information could be shared with foreign competition authorities for use in civil cases — The Mutual Assistance in Business Regulation Act 1992.
8. Their communications have included formal notifications, regular consultations and informal contacts among heads and staff of agencies (see European Commission, 1997).
9. For more detailed analysis on the US—EU relationship, see Commission Report to the Council and the European Parliament on the Application of the Agreement between the European Communities and the Government of the United States of America Regarding the Application of Their Competition Laws. Com (96)479 Final.
10. It has been observed that the cooperation witnessed in the *Microsoft* or *Nielson* cases between the US and the EC would have been possible in the absence of

an agreement.
11. Ehlermann (1994) observes that negotiations began in early 1991 and were successfully concluded on 23 September 1991.
12. Court enters consent decree to resolve 1994 charges against Microsoft's practices, 69 Antitrust & Trade Reg. Rep. (BNA) 268 (24 August 1995). For further discussion, see Keegan (1996).
13. For example, *Shell/Montecatini* Commission Decision 94/811/EC of 8 June 1994 and *Montedison/Shell*, FTC Docket No. C-3580 (25 May 1995). Here both authorities consulted at length in order to obtain a settlement that would not only satisfy the FTC's competitive concerns but also that would not conflict with the provisions of the EC's decision.
14. Crampton and Witterick (1996) recognize the need for a total international welfare standard.
15. See Jardine (1996) for an interesting discussion on 'reverse positive comity'.
16. These are discussed in Chapter 5.
17. Even in the *Boeing* case, where the US and the EC reached famously different conclusions, officials believed that this did not show the ineffectiveness of the agreements as both authorities had used similar approaches (see Valentine, 1997).
18. Japan's bilateral economic relationship with the US is now largely governed by the June 1993 Framework for a New Economic Partnership, and the June 1997 Enhanced Initiative on Deregulation and Competition Policy announced by Clinton and Hashimoto.
19. The US DOJ and the FTC jointly issued the most recent iteration of the Antitrust Enforcment Guidelines for International Operations. Section 3.1 states: 'With respect to foreign commerce other than imports, the Foreign Trade Antitrust Improvements Act of 1982 applies to foreign conduct that has a direct, substantial, and reasonably forseeable effect on US commerce.'
20. See Crampton and Witterick (1996). For a contrary view see generally Meltz (1996).
21. For example, International Chamber of Commerce, 'Competition law: business concerns about confidentiality of corporate information' (press release, 26 September 1995).
22. Except for the US and Australia, countries generally do not have laws that permit them to offer investigatory assistance to foreign competition agencies.
23. For good discussions of reasons, see Rakovsky (1997) and World Bank (1997).
24. France and the United Kingdom adopted blocking statutes which prohibited their nations and companies from informing foreign public authorities, in any manner, about documents or information where this would impair the nation's sovereignty or essential interests.

PART THREE

The Approaches of Regional Trading Arrangements

4. The European Union

The European Union (EU) was the first regional trade agreement to adopt region-wide 'competition policy'. The EU is also the most important case among the regional trading agreements of policies to promote competition because of the deep integration in the area, which includes competition law and other policies which impact upon competition, and because of the large number of countries now involved in these policies. The 1957 Treaty of Rome contains several chapters relating to competition law. This gives competition law in the EU a constitutional basis which is unique among the regional trading agreements with elements of regional competition law.

This chapter provides a broad review of the policies of the EU which impact on competition, focusing on the international dimensions of competition law at the EU level.

Policies to Promote Competition at the EU-Level

The EU has developed a broad set of policies which promote competition in EU markets for all goods and services and factors. They encompass both public and private actions.

The foundation of these policies is the Common Market. Along with common policies in designated areas, the Common Market was the vehicle for the economic integration planned in the Treaty of Rome. The Treaty guaranteed freedom of movement within the area of goods, services, persons and capital, that is, the establishment of a Common Market. Border barriers to the movement of produced commodities and non-produced factors were removed by the end of the initial ten-year transition period. These measures were strengthened by the 1987 Single Act which established the concept of a Single Market. This was defined as 'an area without frontiers in which the free movement of goods, persons, services and capital is ensured'. It was accomplished by the removal of non-border and regulatory measures which restricted movements of commodities and factors by 1992. These measures were strengthened again by the Maastricht Treaty which laid down that 'the activities of the Member States and the Community shall [be] conducted in accordance with the principle of an open market economy with free competition'. This declared the basic importance of policies to promote competition in the EU. It represented the unequivocal triumph of free market ideas:

> The open economy/free-competition principle would seem to
> represent a definitive shift away from the last remnants of the
> highly interventionist economic policies of the 1950s (e.g. a high
> degree of state ownership of companies, far-reaching sectoral
> policies, a tendency to subsidise loss-making firms for purposes of
> employment, protection via trade policy or public procurement).
> The long-term significance of this principle could therefore be
> considerable.   (Pelkmans, 1997, p. 42)

Under the four freedoms, a number of steps were taken to liberalize the
markets for commodities and factors. For example, exchange controls,
which restricted the movements of both goods and capital, were declared
illegal for intra-area trade in goods by the European Court in 1974 and
finally removed for all trade by a Directive in 1988. As a part of the
creation of the European Monetary Union, restrictions on financial capital
flows between member states were prohibited outright by the Maastricht
Treaty. One peculiarity of the EU is the absence of a set of rules at the EU
level for foreign direct investment as such, either for EU or for non-EU
companies. However, a number of articles indirectly provide for freedom of
FDI within the EU. Intra-EU rights of establishment for enterprises,
service providers and self-employed individuals are guaranteed under Articles
52—66 and these rights have been clarified under various Directives
(Swann, 1988, pp. 164—68, and Moussis, 1997, Chapter 2). Freedom to
repatriate income and capital and other aspects of the freedom of movement
of capital relevant to foreign direct capital flows are guaranteed by other
articles of the Treaty.

Free movement of goods, services, labour and capital requires national
treatment as well as the removal of border restrictions. In principle, these
are guaranteed by the Treaty. Workers of a member state enjoy national
treatment in all member states, and corporations which invest and
incorporate in the EU enjoy national treatment and, therefore, EU treatment.
In practice a number of restrictions on the full recognition of national
treatment remain. The EU has pioneered a number of mechanisms to
ensure that full national treatment is enjoyed *de facto*; these include mutual
recognition of industrial standards and labour qualifications and the creation
of Community companies.

Competition across the national borders of the member states may also
be restricted by the existence of differences in national laws concerning
business law, taxes and regulations. As a part of the Common Market, the
Treaty of Rome established a general policy of 'approximating' economic
policies to reduce the impact of such differences. These became 'common
policies or activities' in the Maastricht Treaty.

Competition across national borders of course involves competition
from non-member states. Foreign direct investment from outside the EU
has been liberalized unilaterally by the individual members of the area, with
some sectoral exceptions. The same is not true of border restrictions on
trade in goods *vis-à-vis* non-member states. Trade policy is one area of

common policy and is, therefore, the exclusive responsibility of the EU. The EU has not unilaterally lowered border barriers and retains tariffs and non-tariff barriers, especially those peak levels which apply to problem areas such as textiles and clothing, automobiles and agriculture.

While the EU has no systematic policies for the deregulation of regulated industries, there has in recent years been substantial deregulation in many industries under a variety of EU provisions, including freedom of movement, Council Regulations, Directives and EU competition law (see Pelkmans, 1997, Chapters 7 and 8, and case studies in Buigues, Jacquemin and Sapir, 1995). Under Article 222 of the Treaty of Rome, the EU is neutral with respect to private or public ownership of enterprises. The strong shift towards greater market orientation in the individual member countries and European Commission surveillance of state-owned enterprises have led to the steady privatization of formerly state-owned enterprises in all current member countries, especially in the public utilities and transport sectors.

Industrial policy is another area where EU-level policies impact on competition. Article 92 of the Treaty of Rome forbids 'state aids' which distort trade between member states and Article 130 of the Maastricht Treaty states categorically that EU industrial policy 'does not provide a basis for the introduction by the Community of any measure which may distort competition'. (State aids are defined broadly to cover not only direct grants but also low-interest loans, tax relief and any gratuitous advantage in general.) Despite these policies, in practice there has been considerable conflict between competition and state aids which are intended to prop up ailing industries or promote industrial champions or high-technology industries, as revealed in a number of industry case studies in Buigues, Jacquemin and Sapir (1995). These authors find a lack of coordination between industrial policy, competition policies and trade policies (including anti-dumping). An important part of industrial policy is the granting of state aids. The general view among economists is that the EU controls on state aids have not been effective, though they have been tightened again in 1998.

Overall, these policies have resulted in major liberalization of all markets within the EU area and have, therefore, intensified competition. This intra-EU liberalization has not yet, however, achieved the degree of freedom of movement and the degree of competition found among the states of the US federation and other federations. With respect to competition from non-member state sources, border trade barriers and industrial policies restrict competition in some areas.

Competition Law at the EU-Level

'Competition policy' has been one of the cornerstones of the policies of the EC since its inception. A common competition policy was one of only four areas of common policies originally provided for in the Treaty of Rome; the others were a common trade policy, a common agricultural policy and a common transport policy. A common competition policy was envisaged as a complement to the Common Market which would prevent private restraints on trade from denying the full benefits of the removal of public restraints and would ensure competitive markets. This central role of competition policy has been strengthened in the revisions of the Treaty in the Single Act and the Maastricht Treaty.

Competition law (including state aids) is the vehicle of this common competition policy. Following the analytical framework laid down in Chapter 2, we now consider the coverage of the competition law and the objectives of this law. The coverage of the competition law can be considered in terms of the countries covered, the division between EU-level and national-level jurisdictions, the types of conduct covered and sectoral dimensions. The country coverage and the division between EU-level and national-level jurisdictions are of special interest in the case of the EU.

The country coverage of competition law extends beyond the 15 full members of the EU to the members of the European Economic Area (EEA) and the Associated States of the Central and East European countries (CEECs) and the Mediterranean. The EEA Agreement was signed in 1992. Under the Agreement, the members of the EEA were required to modify the competition law provisions of the European Free Trade Area (EFTA) of which they were members to conform to the *acquis communitaire* of the EU including its competition law (see Stragier, 1993, and Smith, 1998). This alignment was seen as a crucial step in the pre-accession preparation of the EEA states for full membership of the EU, at which time they would of course have to adopt the competition law of the EU in full. EFTA established an EFTA Surveillance Authority and an EFTA Court. These are supranational authorities which parallel the European Commission and the European Court in the EU and cooperate with the European Commission and the European Court on competition law matters. Until the time when the EEA countries become full members, they are not subject to Directorate-General IV (DG IV). One special feature of the EEA Agreement is that the EU countries exempted the EEA countries from all contingent protection actions, including anti-dumping actions. Indeed, this was another factor which led the EU to insist upon conformity between the competition law and procedures of the EFTA countries and those of the EU (cf. the experience of Australia and New Zealand in the CER, as discussed in Chapter 5). Since the EEA entered into force, Austria, Finland and Sweden have become full members of the EU. This leaves only Iceland, Norway and Liechtenstein in the EEA.

Similar arrangements apply under the European Agreements with the ten CEEC Associated States, which were signed between 1991 and 1996. Under the terms of their European Agreements, these countries are required to introduce and align their national competition laws (including those relating to state aids) to the principles of competition law in the Treaty of

Rome if they wish to be considered for full membership. The nature of these obligations is clarified in the White Paper of the Commission of the European Communities (CEC, 1995). These obligations on the CEECs are stricter than those which apply to full members of the EU. There has been a vigorous debate as to whether EU regional-level competition law is suitable to individual transition states (see Estrin and Holmes, 1998). Unlike the EEA states, exports from the CEECs to the EU are not exempt from possible anti-dumping actions and other contingent protection by the EU, although at a December 1994 meeting of the European Council, the European Commission notified the signatories of the European Agreements of requests for anti-dumping investigation and consulted with them in the investigations.

The Association Agreements between the EU and the five Mediterranean countries (Israel, Jordan, Morocco, Palestine Authority and Tunisia), signed between 1995 and 1997, contain provisions which require the principles of a market economy, including provisions relating to competition law, to be put into effect by these countries (European Commission Directorate-General IV, 1997, p. 88).

A decision of the EC—Turkey Association Council, which came into effect at the end of 1995, contains provisions requiring the application of the principles and criteria of EU competition policy and the approximation of competition law (European Commission Directorate-General for Economic and Financial Affairs, 1998, p. 195).

The second dimension of coverage is the division between EU level and national jurisdictions. This is determined by the principle of subsidiarity. This principle was first laid down explicitly in the Maastricht Treaty though it has evolved during the whole history of the EU. It divides between the national government level and the EU level functions which are not the exclusive competence of the Community. Article 3B of the Maastricht Treaty declares:

> In areas which do not fall within its exclusive competence, the Community shall take action, in accordance with the principle of subsidiarity, only if and in so far as the objectives of the proposed actions cannot be sufficiently achieved by the member States and can therefore, by reason of the scale or effect of the proposed action, be better achieved by the Community.
> Any action by the Community shall not go beyond what is necessary to achieve the objectives of the Treaty.

It is a complex doctrine (see CEPR, 1993, and Pelkmans, 1997, Chapters 4 and 12): 'Subsidiarity may be the most contentious abstract noun to have entered European politics since 1789. And it is certainly the most abstract' (CEPR, 1993, p. 1).

In the case of competition law, the exclusive assignment of laws to the EU level is restricted to competition issues which affect actual or potential intra-EU trade. It does not include merger controls. All competition issues which do not affect intra-EU trade are the responsibility of the national governments of the member states. This has meant that the EU level has taken responsibility for all the international dimensions of competition law, including those which affect trade and competition between the EU countries and third countries, while the national competition authorities deal with those which affect only the markets in these individual countries.

Subsidiarity is a most interesting doctrine in the context of the international dimensions of competition law. It derives from a view that there are certain functions of governments which require law at the EU level because there are cross-border spillover 'effects' of competition and national competition law which can only be overcome by an EU-level law. In the EU these are known as 'spillovers' or 'negative externality' effects. These are what were called in Chapter 2 Type 1 and Type 2 market failures. Thus the application of subsidiarity to competition law in the Treaty of Rome and the Maastricht Treaty is an explicit recognition of these effects as the basis of regional-level competition law, and the choice of a centralized supranational authority rather than a coordination of the actions of the competition authorities of the member states (see CEPR, 1993; and Pelkmans, 1997, Chapter 4).

The third dimension of coverage is that of the extent of conduct covered. This coverage is unusually wide, and includes all standard aspects of unilateral conduct, horizontal and vertical restraints and mergers, plus government conduct in the forms of state aids, state monopolies and regulatory structures. The core of competition law in the EU derives from the Treaty of Rome plus the Merger Regulations. Article 3 sets out 'the institution of a system ensuring that competition in the common market is not distorted' as one of the activities of the Community. Article 85 prohibits cartels and other restrictive agreements. This is the article under which most investigations and cases have taken place. Article 86 deals with abuse of dominant positions and Article 92 forbids state aids that distort trade between member states. A number of other articles deal with particular restrictions on competition such as state monopolies (Article 37) and public undertakings with special and exclusive rights (Article 90) or with particular sectors, such as transport and agriculture and energy, which may have competition dimensions. There are no explicit provisions relating to mergers in the Treaty of Rome. The Merger Regulations were added in 1990 as a result of dissatisfaction with the powers under Articles 85 and 86 relating to mergers and the increase in mergers during the 1980s, and amended in 1997 with effect from 1 March 1998.

Both Articles 85 and 86 give particular examples of practices which may restrict competition or abuse a dominant position and are, therefore, prohibited. Article 85 lists as prohibited agreements those which:

(a)   directly or indirectly fix purchases or selling prices or any other trading conditions;

(b) limit or control production, markets, technical development, or investment;
(c) share markets or sources of supply;
(d) apply dissimilar conditions to equivalent transactions with other trading parties, thereby placing them at a competitive disadvantage;
(e) make the conclusion of contracts subject to acceptance by the other parties of supplementary obligations which, by their nature or according to commercial usage, have no connections with the subject of such contracts.

Article 86 lists as prohibited practices which are an abuse of a dominant position those which consist in:

(a) directly or indirectly imposing unfair purchase or selling prices or other unfair trading conditions;
(b) limiting production, markets or technical development to the prejudice of consumers;
(c) applying dissimilar conditions for equivalent transactions with other trading parties, thereby placing them at a competitive disadvantage;
(d) making the conclusion of contracts subject to acceptance by the other parties of supplementary obligations which, by their nature or commercial usage, have no connection with the subject of such contracts.

Export cartels organized by EU producers and import cartels in other countries relating to imports from the EU are outside the scope of Article 85.1 and, therefore, permitted; but import cartels by undertakings in the EU and export cartels among non-EU producers relating to exports to the EU fall within the scope of Article 85.1.

In the present context, the Merger Regulations are the most explicit attempt to allocate power between the jurisdictions at the levels of the EU and the national governments under the principle of subsidiarity. The 1990 Merger Regulations stipulated that mergers, acquisitions and 'concentrative' joint ventures should be notified to the Commission when they are between parties whose combined world-wide annual turnover exceeds ECU 5 billion and the Community-wide turnover of each of at least two of the undertakings concerned is more than ECU 250 million and 'unless the parties conduct two-thirds or more of their business in one and the same member state'. All three conditions have to be met. The conditions mean that the merger powers do not go exclusively to the EU level, even when they involve cross-border aspects: '[The second condition] is a clear and precise attempt to base centralization upon the extent of the spillovers between member states' (CEPR, 1993, p. 135). The 1998 revised Merger Regulations maintained the thresholds. (The Commission had proposed that the thresholds be lowered but this was not approved by the Council.)

It also harmonized the treatment of mergers involving joint ventures and simplified the notification procedures.

The CEPR (1993, pp. 135—37) evaluates the net gains from centralizing merger controls at the EU-level compared to the net gains from coordination among the national-level competition authorities. It sees the net gains at each level as a trade-off between the loss from regulatory capture (see Neven, Nuttall and Seabright, 1993, on this aspect) and gains from the capture of cross-border spillovers. Its conclusion is that:

> merger control is an area in which cooperation to secure the benefits of policy coordination is a particularly unsatisfactory alternative to centralization, because of the highly discretionary nature of the policy to be implemented and the consequent difficulty for twelve member states in observing whether each is abiding by the terms of a collective agreement. Overall, merger policy is a good illustration of a case where the gains from centralization are high; but it is also a warning that the central institutions need to be designed in such a way as to ensure that these gains are not dissipated through an increase in rent-seeking and regulatory capture. (CEPR, 1993, pp. 136—37)

In practice, however, the merger thresholds, and especially the Community-wide turnover threshold, have meant that more than 90 per cent of proposed mergers in which one or more parties is located in the EU escape EU control (Sleuwaegen, 1998). The merger regulations have also been criticized for a lack of transparency and flexibility (Sleuwaegen, 1998).

The fourth dimension of coverage is that of the number of sectors exempted. There are general exemptions for coal, iron and steel products, but these are handled in a similar way under the European Coal and Steel Community (ECSC) Treaty which coexists with the Treaty of Rome. Labour and collective bargains are excluded and there are partial exclusions for agriculture and defence and special rules for transport and financial institutions (see OECD, 1996a, chapter on the EU). Undertakings by cartels relating to exports from the European Community are generally exempt.

The objectives of EU competition law are somewhat unclear. Article 3 makes it plain that competition law is an area of common policy to support the achievement of a Common Market. Article 85 prohibits:

> all agreements between undertakings, decisions by associations of undertakings and concerted practices which may affect trade between Member States and which have as their object or effect the prevention, restriction or distortion of competition within the common market . . .

However, Article 85.3 goes on to permit any agreement, decision and practice which contributes to improving the production or distribution of goods or to promoting technical or economic progress, while allowing consumers a fair share of the resulting benefits, and which does not

(a) impose on the undertakings concerned restrictions which are not indispensable to the attainment of these objectives;
(b) afford such undertakings the possibility of eliminating competition in respect of a substantial part of the products in question.

Article 86 more simply prohibits any abuse which is 'incompatible with the common market in so far as it may affect trade between Member States'.

Similarly, Article 92 declares any aid which

> distorts or threatens to distort competition by favouring certain undertakings or the production of certain goods shall, in so far as it affects trade between States, be incompatible with the common market.

Thus, there are multiple objectives: one is the prevention of conduct which distorts competition, and another is the prevention of distortion of trade between member states. Article 85 refers to both producer efficiency and consumer interests and it recognizes the benefits of technical and economic progress. In relation to the set of persons covered by these objectives, Article 3(F) of the Treaty of Rome and the explicit references to trade between member states in Articles 85 and 86 imply that the law is concerned only with the welfare of residents within the jurisdiction (Jacquemin, 1993, p. 96). The non-efficiency objectives could lead the Commission to decisions which conflict with those based on efficiency alone (Weatherill and Beaumont, 1993).

The administration of EU-level competition law has been granted to the EC by the Council. It is the responsibility of DG IV, which is headed by a Commissioner. DG IV is a supranational competition authority and the European Court of Justice is a supranational court with jurisdiction in the EU area.

The application and interpretation of these laws is complex and constantly evolving. It is beyond the scope of this book. In addition to the revision of the Merger Regulations, the EU in 1997 published a Green Paper on vertical restraints as a prelude to a revision of the administration of the law relating to these restraints, and the Commission has decided to undertake a similar exercise with respect to horizontal restraints. (For recent reviews of EU competition law, see McGowan, 1995; OECD, 1996a; Pelkmans, 1997, Chapter 12; Young and Metcalfe, 1997; European Commission Directorate-General IV, 1997.)

We can note some general features which are germane to the questions of how to coordinate or centralize competition law across national boundaries:

- The mention of both producer efficiency and consumer interests permits a rule of reason approach to balance costs and benefits, though there is a legal debate about the extent of the rule of reason in EU law (see Bourtese, 1994).
- Exemptions or exclusions are provided for under a number of provisions. Article 85.3 excludes agreements which have benefits that offset the restrictions on competition and trade. These exemptions can be granted by decision (individual exemptions) or by regulation (block exemptions). They may have conditions attached and are granted for a fixed period. Coal products and the labour markets are specifically excluded. There are partial exclusions which apply to particular sectors or small and medium enterprises in particular circumstances (see OECD, 1996a, chapter on European Union).
- Coordination procedures have been developed between the European Commission and the competition law authorities of the member states to avoid conduct being examined at two levels (European Commission, 1997). If conduct or a merger or acquisition falls within the scope of the Community law, it is reviewed only at the EU-level. The regulations and notices relating to both Articles 85 and 86 and to mergers were amended in 1997 to ensure a 'one-stop shop' (European Commission Directorate-General IV, 1997). This avoids more than one authority examining such conduct or proposed mergers or acquisitions. Similar procedures have been developed in the EEA to avoid conduct being examined, in this case, by both the Commission and the EFTA Surveillance Authority and in the courts to distinguish the roles of the courts at the EU level and the national level.
- Procedures were developed for the sharing of information between the European Commission and the national authorities. Article 20 of the EU Council Regulations 17/62 binds both the Commission and the national authorities to keep the information secret.

The Extra-EU Dimensions of Competition Law

The extraterritorial application of national competition laws is one means whereby a country may seek to prevent or remedy alleged anti-competitive conduct which is located in another jurisdiction and has a negative spillover on residents of the country. On the face of it, extraterritoriality appears to apply quite widely in the EU, as the Treaty of Rome states that conduct which affects trade within the Community is subject to the law, irrespective of where the conduct originates and of the nationality of the parties. The European Commission has made it clear that the law applies to agreements between the EU and outside parties which affect imports (but not exports) and to parties wholly outside the EU jurisdiction (Rose, 1994, Chapter 2).

This has been confirmed by the European Court. In the *Wood Pulp* case, the Court ruled that Article 85 (1) applied to foreign companies selling into the Community without any presence in its territory whatsoever. The Court has taken a narrower view than the Commission and required proof of the implementation of the conduct within the EU. This is known as the 'implementation' doctrine. It is a doctrine implied by other provisions of the Treaty: 'Thus jurisdiction is grounded on the territoriality principle while there is an extraterritorial dimension in terms of enforcement' (Jacquemin, 1993, p. 95). The doctrine is more limited than the US explicit 'effects' doctrine in that it does not apply to conduct wholly outside the EU and it does not apply to exports.

While the EU has been less aggressive in its application of extraterritoriality than the US, it has applied the doctrine from time to time. It has been applied to mergers as well as to horizontal and vertical restraints (see Sleuwaegen, 1998). The Merger Regulations apply explicitly to companies which have their headquarters outside the EU. The extraterritorial application of EU law by the Commission in the proposed Boeing/McDonnell Douglas merger led to intensive discussions between the European Commission and the US Federal Trade Commission under the terms of the bilateral agreement between the EU and the US. In this case, the two merging companies were located outside the EU jurisdiction but the only other competitor remaining, Airbus, was an EU company. The case was examined simultaneously by the US and EU authorities. (For the views of the European Commission, see European Commission Directorate-General IV, 1997, Chapter III, and for further discussion, see Chapter 3 above.)

A bilateral agreement between the Government of the United States and the Commission of the European Communities regarding the Application of their Competition Laws was concluded in 1991 and finally approved by the European Council in 1995. It provides for notification, exchange of information and negative and positive comity (details are provided in Chapter 3).

The European Commission considers that the bilateral agreement has not been altogether satisfactory (European Commission Directorate-General IV, 1997, and European Commission, 1998). In 1998 a new Agreement with the US was approved by the Council. This strengthens the provisions for positive comity. Under the new Agreement, one of the parties is to adjourn or stay its own activity in respect of an anti-competitive practice which primarily affects the territory of the other, provided the other is disposed to act. The Commission hopes that the application of the primary effect rule will reduce extraterritorial applications of competition rules and the frictions deriving from them (European Commission Directorate-General IV, 1997, p. 19). European Commission (1998) discusses the possibilities of developing 'second generation' agreements which go beyond the OECD Recommendations and existing bilateral agreements in making it possible to share confidential information and use compulsory process on behalf of the other party.

The EU has been the single most important force with respect to discussion of the possibilities of developing multilateral competition law. The discussion of these issues by Sir Leon Brittan, a former Competition Commissioner (in Brittan, 1992), was one of the first to examine the issues during the Uruguay Round. Before the WTO Ministerial Meeting in Singapore, the European Commission commissioned a group of experts to prepare a report (European Commission Directorate-General IV, 1996), commonly known as the Van Miert Report. This group recommended a gradual building-block approach, based on the development of national competition laws in all countries, a core of 'common principles', and cooperation under bilateral agreements. This report laid the foundations for EU views on the issues concerning problems of cross-border competition. At the Singapore Ministerial Conference, the EU in its so-called 'non-paper' proposed that the WTO explore the feasibility of an international framework for competition rules in the WTO (European Commission, 1997). This could include the development of effective domestic competition law in all countries and the identification of a core of 'common principles', the establishment of an instrument of cooperation between national competition authorities, and the use of the WTO dispute settlement procedures. One can note too that many of the individuals advocating some form of multilateral competition law are from EU countries (see, for example, the writings of Jacquemin, 1993; Nicolaides, 1996; and Petersmann, 1996 and 1998).

At the WTO Working Group, the EU continues to favour an evolutionary approach; with developments on several levels. Many developing countries do not have an understanding of the role of competition law and many do not have comprehensive competition laws. The views were spelt out in a communication to the European Council entitled *Towards an International Framework of Competition Rules*, submitted by Sir Leon Brittan and Karel Van Miert (European Commission, 1996) and in Brittan (1997). The communication notes that:

> [a] premise of this communication is that the creation of an International Competition Authority, with its own powers of investigation and enforcement, is not a feasible option for the medium term. Countries at this stage would be unwilling to accept the constraints on national sovereignty and policies that such a structure would impose. The proposals set out below . . . reflect a more modest approach.

They develop further the possibilities of competition policies based on the WTO. These include principles that each country would develop competition laws and methods of enforcing them through the judiciary and access for private parties to national authorities. They also include improved bilateral cooperation, possibly based on the positive comity procedures which have now been incorporated in the new US—EU bilateral cooperation agreement, and improved WTO dispute settlement procedures to ensure the enforcement multilaterally of national laws. Brittan (1997) recommends the adoption of a non-binding basis of standards such as those embodied in the OECD 'hard-core' cartel agreement.

The EU has also taken the view that dumping should not be discussed by the WTO Working Group. The EU views dumping as a trade matter. It does not advocate the replacement of trade remedies against dumping by competition law remedies at the multilateral level, as it has done at the EU regional level. It does believe, however, that stronger enforcement of competition laws may reduce the incidence of dumping, as some dumping is the result of anti-competitive cartels.

These views with respect to multilateral competition law reflect the general success of the development of EU-level competition law within the EU.

Anti-dumping and Countervailing Duty Action in the EU

Anti-dumping action in the EU comes under trade policy, not competition policy (under DG IV). It is, however, considered here because of the overlap between competition law and trade law in this area and the importance of anti-dumping action in current debates about the interaction between international trade and competition and the development of multi-national competition law.

Because trade policy has been one of the common areas of policy since the formation of the European Community, anti-dumping action comes under the Directorate-General I (DG I) of the EC. As a part of the Common Market, anti-dumping action was prohibited in relation to imports from other EU countries by the Treaty of Rome. (During the transition period Article 91 permitted members to petition the European Commission to authorize anti-dumping action.) The rationale appears to have been simply that anti-dumping actions as a form of border trade restriction have no place in a common market with freedom of trade (Hoekman, 1998).

This prohibition has been extended to the three EFTA members of the EEA. In the negotiations leading to the formation of the EEA and in the discussions with Associated States in East Europe and the Mediterranean, the EU has made it plain that the cessation of anti-dumping action can occur only when markets are fully integrated. Consequently, anti-dumping action applies to imports from outside the EU and the EEA.

When taking anti-dumping action against imports from outside the EU and the EAA, the EU is bound, as a member of the WTO, by the WTO rules. These require proof of dumping, of injury or threatened injury and cause of injury. An anti-dumping unit within the Commission investigates complaints. These investigations establish the dumping margin and the injury margin (the margin by which imports undercut the EU price and therefore cause injury). One feature of the EU trade law is a Community interest clause which allows the authorities, when investigating a complaint, to determine whether anti-dumping action would be 'in the interests of the Community'. However, this is not an overriding provision as it exists alongside a need to eliminate the trade-distorting effects of injurious dumping and does not appear to have had a substantial restraining effect on anti-dumping actions.

Another feature of· the EU practice of anti-dumping actions is the increasing frequency of use of cumulation across source countries to establish injury to EU producers. (Cumulation is discussed further in Chapter 6 with reference to the US, and in Chapter 11 with reference to the WTO rules.) This has made it easier for the Commission to prove injury and has thereby increased the frequency of anti-dumping actions. Tharakan, Greenaway and Tharakan (1998) find that 66.3 per cent of all injury determinations over the period 1980—97 were determined on the basis of the cumulation of imported market shares. Following the line of analysis of US anti-dumping actions by Hansen and Prusa (1996), they verify that cumulation has had an effect on the affirmative finding of injury which is 'super-additive', that is, greater than the effect predicted on the basis of the summation of the countries' import shares.

The WTO statistics show the EU to be the second most frequent actor against dumping, after the US, in terms of anti-dumping measures in force in 1996, the latest year for which statistics are available (WTO, 1997a, Table V.4). The EU accounted for 17 per cent of the global total. This is a high figure, especially given that most EU international trade is with other members of the EU or EEA, which are exempt from anti-dumping action. The EU, unlike the US, makes extensive use of price undertakings in place of anti-dumping duties.

The EU is one of the countries or blocs of countries with anti-dumping laws in which there is evidence that anti-dumping action has itself had anti-competitive effects in some instances by, for example, reinforcing the position of a domestic cartel (Montagnon, 1990, pp. 79-81; Messerlin and Reed, 1995; and Veugelers and Vandenbussche, 1998).

There is a clear inconsistency between the anti-dumping law and the competition law of the EU. EU competition law does not expressly prohibit selling below cost (though some EU countries such as France do have national laws which prohibit this practice). It is doubtful that even intra-EU predatory pricing falls within the scope of the EU competition law, unless it results from the concerted action of a group of exporters. One consequence of the coexistence of competition law and international trade law in this area is that conduct which is not actionable for a European seller in the home market of the seller or elsewhere in the EU is actionable when the seller is outside the EU. This is discriminatory.

Countervailing (or anti-subsidy) duties pose some of the same issues as anti-dumping action. They are permissible under Article VI of the GATT, subject to proof of subsidization, injury and cause of injury. As noted above, the EU is exceptional in that subsidies (state aids) are within the scope of competition law at the EU level. As with anti-dumping action, there is an overlap and a conflict between EU international trade law and competition law in this area. Countervailing action can be taken against subsidies which are actionable under WTO rules but are not actionable or are not acted upon under EU competition law. But the conflict is much less important because the EU takes much less action against subsidized trade than against dumped trade, having only two measures in force in 1996 (WTO, 1997a, Table V.2).

Convergence of Competition Laws among the EU Countries

Of the six original member states of the EEC in 1957 only (West) Germany had comprehensive national competition laws. While the Treaty of Rome and subsequent treaties do not have an explicit requirement that all member states have competition law, it would be difficult for the member states to operate in the EU without such laws. All of the original six and now all of the current 15 member states have comprehensive competition laws. This spread of national competition laws among the member states is due in large measure to the EU-level competition law in the treaties.

Convergence of competition law means more than the introduction of national competition laws. It also comprises all aspects of these laws across countries — such as their scope, methods of analysis and enforcement. That raises the question: can national-level laws and EU-level laws coexist when the national laws have provisions that are different from the comparable provisions of the EU-level laws?

If conduct is clearly examinable under national laws because it does not affect EU trade and/or competition, there is no conflict. But if it does affect both national trade and EU trade and/or competition, a conflict may arise. In a key 1969 decision the European Court of Justice ruled that national authorities could proceed in parallel against practices in question but, if a conflict arose, the Community law would prevail. Most EU member states have amended their national legislation to bring it into greater conformity with EU law, largely on the basis of Articles 85 and 86 of the Treaty or Rome (see Young and Metcalfe, 1997). This is true of the major countries such as Germany and France, and the UK is currently revising its competition laws. Pelkmans (1997, p. 185, n. 4) notes that 'today all EU Member States have well-developed competition policies, having gradually been attuned closely to the main rules of the EC-wide regime. So it would seem that the common policy, in conjunction with deepened market integration, has induced approximation of the (residual) national regimes.'

He adds: 'One wonders whether this outcome would have been accomplished merely via coordination.'

However, numerous differences persist between the laws of national authorities and these laws and the EU-level law. There are substantial differences in the scope of the laws because the coverage of some practices or conduct such as resale price maintenance and mergers differ and because of differences in sectoral exemptions and exclusions (see OECD, 1996a). In relation to objectives, which are central to the outcome of investigations, the national laws of some countries have supplementary objectives such as competitiveness in foreign markets (the UK) or national development. The competition laws of some member states (the UK and Germany) have a 'national interest' provision which allows a balance of consumer and producer interests whereas others do not, and the EU does not have an explicit Community interest provision in its competition laws. Some of the national governments have a more tolerant view of competition problems than the EU. McGowan (1995, p. 188) concludes: 'There remains a tension in the Community between the traditional outlook in many countries and the Commission's approach, and that tension is exacerbated when the latter seeks to extend the scope of the policy or otherwise limit the conduct of national governments.'

These persisting differences themselves create a pressure for greater convergence. The European Commission DG IV (1997, p. 15) has noted that the division of responsibilities between the EU level and the national level will only work well if the national authorities are prepared to apply Community level law at the national level. Otherwise, 'this would bring with it the danger of forum shopping, with firms seeking out the jurisdiction of the authority they feel will be most favourable to their interests'. In its 1997 notice on cooperation between the national competition authorities and the Commission, the Commission called on member states which have not already done so to adopt legislation enabling their competition authority to implement Articles 85 (1) and 86 of the Treaty of Rome effectively (European Commission, 1997). The same pressure for greater convergence has been observed in other policy areas in the EU, such as VAT tax rates. In all cases it is due to the incentives which exist under divergent laws for agents to take evasive action and circumvent EU laws or regulations.

The competition provisions of the European Agreements are profoundly affecting the evolution of competition law in the CEECs. Before the Agreements were signed, Romania had no comprehensive national competition law and the others had gaps in the coverage of their laws, especially with respect to vertical restraints and mergers, and weak enforcement (EBRD, 1995). Since the Agreements were concluded, they have all developed comprehensive national laws and stronger enforcement. They have all aligned their national laws with the EU law. Consequently, the competition laws of the ten countries have converged both within the group and to those of the EU. (One can note that unwillingness to align its relatively lax competition laws with those of the EU was one of the reasons why Switzerland was not willing to participate in the EEA.)

Thus the EU has brought about a substantial convergence of national competition laws among 25 countries as well as the superimposition of common EU-level competition laws on its member states. It remains to be seen how effective this convergence will be in practice, especially for the transition economies.

Observations on the Extra-EU Dimensions of Competition Law

The complex relations between competition law at the EU level and the national level and the deep integration of the EU which includes the development of common policies in the areas of trade and industrial policy make the international dimensions of EU competition law a particularly interesting case.

The EU has brought about the introduction of national competition laws in its full and associated members and there has been substantial convergence of these laws and their enforcement. At the EU level, the competition law has been steadily strengthened and it has devised procedures with the national-level competition authorities in order to avoid duplication and for the exchange of information.

This chapter reveals a number of aspects which may provide lessons for the evolution of multi-national competition law. It has shown the possibilities of developing near-uniform (or 'approximate' laws, in the terminology of the EU) among the members of a regional trading arrangement. This has involved the establishment of a number of precedents at this level; these include the basic doctrine of subsidiarity, the establishment of a supranational authority and rules of cooperation between the regional-level authorities and the national authorities. Countries wishing to accede to the EU are willing to adopt the *acquis communitaire* because they will gain preferential access to the large EU markets. This helps to explain the EU's ability to achieve such rapid policy convergence. A further feature of the EU model is that if and when countries become full members, they will be subject to the considerable powers of a common supranational authority.

In reviewing the case studies in Buigues et al. (1995, p. vii), Karl Van Miert, the present Competition Commissioner, concluded: 'One particular issue in which the Communities' experience may have an important lesson to offer is with regard to the relationship between competition law and industrial policy. I believe that Community experience has proven that modern industrial policy and competition policy are complementary, mutually dependent policies.' This experience of the EU shows the importance of coordination among other policies that promote competition. The coordination of 'competition policy' on the one hand and international trade and industrial policies on the other has been less than perfect. They have been in conflict in some industries.

5. Closer Economic Relations Agreement[1]

In 1983 Australia and New Zealand formed a free trade area under an agreement known as the Australia New Zealand Closer Economic Relations Agreement (ANZCERTA or CER for short). Free trade in goods (but not all services) was achieved between Australia and New Zealand in 1990. This ended a seven-year adjustment period in line with the Agreement and the 1988 Review of this Agreement. CER has treated goods and services differentially. From the point of view of promoting competition, some of the measures which have been adopted by the two countries with the effect of making goods and services markets more competitive have been adopted unilaterally and some in the context of the CER Agreement.

Policies to Promote Competition in the CER Countries

In both countries the scope of policy directed at competition has been broad even if not always explicit. Competition law is but one of several instruments that has aimed to promote competition; others include industry deregulation, privatization and the reduction of restrictions on foreign capital flows. An important connection was made at a policy level between reducing artificial market entry barriers and enhancing the competitive process. In combination the progressive reduction in border barriers to trade, the lessening of restrictions on the inflow of foreign capital and the microeconomic reforms have had the effect of opening up Australian and New Zealand markets — notably to foreign investors and foreign traders, and to competition for goods and services including non-tradables.

New Zealand policymakers drew on the economic arguments of contestability and transaction cost analysis and forged a strong link between competition and efficiency — efficiency being regarded as the essential foundation for international competitiveness and competition being the preferred, but not the sole, means of achieving this. Indeed, it is the competition—efficiency—economic welfare paradigm that has governed the New Zealand government's approach (and increasingly the Australian government's approach) to domestic policy reforms and to deregulation in particular.

For both market opening and the efficient functioning of markets, the coordinated and broadly consistent application of various policy instruments relating to trade and competition has been important. There has clearly been a major alignment between the objectives and instruments of competition-driven policy, the aims of market contestability and the removal of artificial barriers to competitive market entry. The freer flow of capital is especially important for facilitating competition in service industries where a commercial presence is required; and deregulation in industries such as telecommunications is clearly a necessary supplement to the freer flow of capital which enables increased investment in those industries.

Undoubtedly, the overall impact of these policy changes has been an increase in the level and modes of competition in Australia and New Zealand. As a consequence there has been a much sharper focus by business on efficient allocation and use of resources.

Intra-area competition in markets is a wider issue than foreign access via removal of border barriers. A freeing of trade between Australia and New Zealand, by itself, would not have resulted in the level of competition and the focus on efficiency now observed. Very evident in retrospect is a strong interconnectedness among the different policy elements of the trans-Tasman experience, including between free trade and the interest in business law harmonization and between the prior convergence of (and general familiarity with) each country's competition law and the political feasibility of repealing the trans-Tasman anti-dumping remedy.

In CER the objective of competition and of 'equal opportunity and equal treatment for both countries and both industries' (Burdon, 1996) has been the explicit driving force behind what has been achieved to date and behind residual policy issues which include the services protocol, rules of origin, intermediate goods (industry assistance), foreign direct investment and taxation. Market integration under CER has involved cooperation and coordination in respect of both border and non-border policies.

Part of the broader CER picture are: the 1996 Agreement on Joint Food Standards; the 1996 Agreements on Trans-Tasman Mutual Recognition and on the Single Aviation Market; the 1997 Arrangement on Food Inspection Measures; the revised Government Procurement Agreement; and the freedom of trans-Tasman labour movement (although this measure is not part of the CER Agreement). These measures have been introduced without any trans-national institutions.[2] The CER experience has demonstrated that formal trans-national institutional arrangements are not necessary to the progress of economic integration.

In 1998 the CER Protocol on Trade in Services was used to remove one remaining measure which restricted trade and competition: the content standard for television of the Australian Broadcasting Authority (ABA). It took court action by a group of New Zealand television production companies, which concluded with a successful appeal to the High Court of Australia (*Project Blue Sky* v. *Australian Broadcasting Authority* [1998]) before the path was clear for New Zealand television programmes to be treated as local content in the ABA's quota system. The High Court ruled that excluding New Zealand programmes from 'Australian programmes' was in breach of Australia's CER obligations and the obligations relating to comparable access and treatment as unequivocally expressed in the Protocol for Trade in Services.[3] The impugned standard of the ABA provided that (unsubsidized) Australian programmes be at least 55 per cent, from the beginning of 1998, of all programmes broadcast between 6 a.m. and midnight, and consequently New Zealand programmes had to compete with all other programmes (both Australian and third country) for the remaining 45 per cent of the time slots available. Since New Zealand programmes could not meet the Australian provenance requirement such access rights were less favourable and therefore, the High Court found, in breach of the CER Services Protocol. The ABA is undertaking a review of the standard. The matter is not concluded.

Total freedom of movement in respect of direct foreign investment has not, however, been accomplished under CER.[4] The respective Ministers of Finance have confirmed that trans-Tasman direct investment should be subject to minimum constraint and they have made explicit their aim to avoid further restrictions on investors to the fullest possible extent. But there remains a political risk of the present liberal practice being reversed at some time in the future.

Australia and New Zealand have each exhibited strong unilateralism in moving towards freeing trade *vis-à-vis* third countries and strong deregulation in many industries. Both are clearly well on track towards the APEC goal announced at the Bogor Meeting of APEC Leaders in 1994 of zero tariffs for developed economies by 2010; their tariff reduction commitments, made in their Individual Action Plans for APEC, are faster and deeper than their Uruguay Round commitments (PECC, 1996).

Competition Law in the CER Countries

Despite the trade and investment liberalization and internal deregulation that has occurred within Australia and New Zealand, competition law remains an important complementary policy instrument in the promotion of competition. Competition law is clearly seen as a continuing insurance against those commercial actions which could undermine the governments' achievements in opening markets and removing regulatory barriers to competition.

In New Zealand, the Commerce Act 1986 was a major step in competition law reform. Its objective was to promote competition in markets within New Zealand. While efficiency was not adopted as an explicit objective there was a general understanding that competition was being promoted as the preferred means for achieving efficient economic outcomes and that efficiency would become the primary determinant of successful business operation in more open and competitive markets.

At the time New Zealand's Commerce Act 1986 was introduced, the official view was that a strengthened and comprehensive competition law was needed to allow deregulation of industry to work. In other words, the stronger competitive pressures on firms as a result of deregulation and loss of government protections should not be diminished by the substitution of commercial restrictions on competition, either by way of business acquisitions or through collusive or unilateral conduct. The new competition rules were to be the vehicle for addressing constraints imposed by private regulators on the ability of others to operate their businesses independently (Vautier, 1987). Their main use now is likely to be in respect of those industries characterized by natural monopoly and access issues, major technology changes and significant restructuring or decline.

The enforcement resolve has been intensifying in both countries. In Australia's case there have been competition law extensions (1995) in the form of access and industry-specific requirements; and in New Zealand's case there is a government review of Commerce Act penalties and remedies (New Zealand Ministry of Commerce, 1998a) including discussion of optimal pecuniary penalties and the role of criminal sanctions. In addition, the New Zealand Government has passed industry-specific legislation centred on electricity distribution reform through compulsory ownership separation of electricity lines from electricity generation and retail activities (New Zealand Government, 1998). The Parliamentary Committee considering the draft legislation cited officials' advice that corporate (as distinct from ownership) separation, as well as information disclosure and Commerce Act powers, were 'second best solutions to the problems' (New Zealand Government Commerce Committee, 1998). The structural solution of mandatory ownership separation — without compensation — was judged to be the preferred way of delivering 'the best outcomes to [electricity] consumers'.

Clearly, the Commerce Act has been judged inadequate to deal with the following risks which the new electricity reform law is designed to address:

* anti-competitive restrictions on access to electricity distribution lines for competing retailers;
* cross-subsidization of electricity generation activities from electricity distribution lines; and
* cross-subsidization of electricity retail activities from electricity distribution lines.

While the Commerce Act has been described as 'the cornerstone of [New Zealand's] "light-handed" regulation policy' (New Zealand Commerce Commission, 1998a) the government has to some extent undermined confidence in its own competition law regime.

Convergence of competition laws between the CER countries

The 1983 CER Agreement envisaged, albeit in a limited way, that Australia and New Zealand would work towards business law harmonization (in the sense of general conformity not uniformity) as part of the joint agenda. The national competition laws were seen as the most amenable candidate, despite their inherently complex nature, and broad similarity has been achieved.

However, the policy rationale for such convergence was never rigorously presented (Farmer, 1990, pp. 45—49). There was an underlying policy assumption that statutory convergence would be good for business in the context of a free trade area and an integrating 'single market'. In turn this was taken to mean that the cost of transacting business in the two economies would be lowered. But harmonization has been made conditional upon finding that differences in laws and regulatory practices actually increase the transaction and compliance costs of businesses operating in both Australia and New Zealand (Burdon and McMullan, 1995). This is a more discerning approach and, justifiably, more cautious than the initial official view that harmonization would remove impediments to trade.

For its statutory framework New Zealand's Commerce Act drew heavily on Australia's Trade Practices Act 1974. With the shared tradition of the Westminster judicial system, this enabled New Zealand to draw on Australia's institutional design and legal precedent. But also, since the 1983 CER Agreement, business generally accepted (indeed sometimes promoted) that competition law harmonization was properly on the CER agenda.

In terms of statutory language, scope and procedure, the two national laws were very similar by the time free trade across the Tasman (in goods but not all services) was achieved in 1990. Business practices such as exclusive dealing, tie-in sales, price fixing and market sharing could fall within their general prohibitions. Both statutes treat export exemptions the same in that the restrictive trade practice proscriptions do not apply to contractual provisions that relate exclusively to the export of goods or services, if particulars are given to the relevant authority. A greater degree of harmonization was achieved when Australia later extended coverage of its Act to the trading activities of states, when it made provision for resale price maintenance to be an authorized practice (that is, subject to a public benefit test), and when it removed a specific prohibition on price discrimination that was likely to have the effect of substantially lessening competition.

Australia's repeal of its separate price discrimination provision warrants some comment. The Hilmer Committee (1993), to which this change is attributed, considered that price discrimination generally enhanced economic efficiency — except in the cases of anti-competitive agreements or misuse of market power which could be dealt with elsewhere under the Trade Practices Act. Debate as to whether or not a specific prohibition on price discrimination encouraged or restricted competition seems to have been resolved by the repeal in favour of the latter. However, the primary reason given for the repeal was that only one successful case had ever been taken under the provision and, on its strict terms, the provision was unlikely to be a relevant part of Australian competition law in the future. This argument was supported by the fact that other provisions in the law were equipped to deal with price discrimination that warranted intervention.

In 1986 the New Zealand legislature did not feel compelled to adopt the Australian provision but it took Australia over ten years to repeal its separate price discrimination provision, despite several repeal recommendations in the past. If an anti-dumping remedy were not appropriate in a free trade area, then the continued presence of a separate price discrimination provision in the Australian statute (in relation to domestic commerce) would be an anomaly.

As a result of each country retaining legislative discretion, some noticeable areas of difference between Australia's and New Zealand's competition laws remain. These are specified in Vautier and Lloyd (1997, p. 50). They include competition thresholds, the criteria for public benefit assessments, and the form and extent of intervention in respect of natural monopolies and access issues.

In 1995 Australia went beyond its existing misuse of market power provisions to insert into its Trade Practices Act a major section on access to services (Part IIIA) which provides for the designation of essential services and for arbitration on access to those services. Miller (1998, p. 115) quotes the Australian Competition Tribunal[5] on the objectives:

> Part IIIA is based on the notion that competition, efficiency and public interest are increased by overriding the exclusive rights of the owners of 'monopoly' facilities to determine the terms and conditions on which they will focus their services.

The focus is on service of facilities of national significance where duplication or replication would be uneconomic and where access to them would promote competition in another market.

Also inserted was a special regime for regulating conduct in the telecommunications industry (Part XIB). This goes beyond the s.46 prohibition on misuse of market power for an anti-competitive purpose. If a carrier or carriage service provider has a substantial degree of power in a telecommunications market it also engages in anti-competitive conduct if the effect or likely effect of taking advantage of that power is a substantial lessening of competition in that or any other telecommunications market.

Despite these substantial areas of difference, Australia and New Zealand are the only two economies within APEC whose competition laws can really be said to be harmonized. This is verified by the indices of competition law similarity for country pairs developed by Bollard and Vautier (1998) for eleven APEC economies. (The indices are reproduced in Table 9.1, p. 144.)

But, even if it is accepted that bilateral convergence of competition law under CER was carried out in highly favourable circumstances, it has been a slow and somewhat erratic process. There has been unilateral harmonization: through one country (New Zealand in this case) broadly adopting another country's law and enforcement structure (Australia's in this case). There has also been some harmonization at a bilateral level, notably in respect of the trans-Tasman competition provisions (discussed later in this chapter). In respect of other areas of the law such as domestic price discrimination, harmonization might well have been a consequence but not an objective of a particular change in national policy.

There has been debate from time to time regarding the remaining differences between Australia's Trade Practices Act and New Zealand's Commerce Act, but this has tended to be in terms of fairness rather than of transaction costs. There seems to be broad acceptance that Australia and New Zealand should each retain an element of regulatory independence which emphasizes 'best' law rather than simply harmonized law. The perceived advantage of this element of regulatory competition seems to outweigh any perceived transaction costs that may be associated with divergence. Further, there has not been a strong call by business for a common judicial system or for a trans-national appeal authority.

Of course, even with harmonization of statutory language and general policy approach between two national laws there is room for differences in their interpretation and application. This is because there are two separate and independent judicial systems and no supranational judicial authority or appeal procedure (although mutual recognition of the professions may stimulate greater cross-fertilization). There is New Zealand Court precedent which favours recourse (but not exclusively) to Australian judicial authority (although the reverse has not tended to apply), with both the High Court and Court of Appeal viewing CER as a basis for fostering consistency in the application of both competition and fair trading legislation (Vautier, 1990).

In short, despite a considerable degree of statutory convergence, business is not assured of certainty in respect of decision outcomes in the other country; nor could one realistically assume that it would be — even in its own country. This is especially true under the (mainly) rule of reason approach to competition law in Australia and New Zealand which relies on case-by-case application of generally applicable competition standards, rather than *per se* prohibitions of specific forms of conduct.

Anti-Dumping Action[6] and Industry Assistance in the CER Countries

CER's free trade achievement was accompanied by the removal of the trans-Tasman anti-dumping remedy in conjunction with the introduction of specific trans-Tasman competition law provisions. This made it the second regional trading arrangement (after the EU) to eliminate anti-dumping action within the region. In 1988 Australia and New Zealand agreed to cease payment of bounties and other production subsidies affecting their international trade; and, since 1990, the two CER member countries have vigorously reduced overall subsidies and other financial forms of assistance to producers. In view of the special structure of trans-Tasman trade, which is dominated by manufactured/higher processed goods, it is manufacturing subsidies that are of particular relevance in the CER context. This elimination of subsidies affecting trans-Tasman trade and competition was a remarkable achievement as no other regional trading agreement has succeeded in eliminating production subsidies which distort production and trade within the region. It goes considerably further than attempts to regulate subsidies (or state aids as they are known) in the EU. None the less, the trans-Tasman countervailing duty remedy was retained.

As a part of the 1988 CER Review Australia and New Zealand concluded an Agreed Minute on Industry Assistance which committed them to eliminating subsidies which distort trans-Tasman trade. These include bounties and other subsidies based on national production as well as export subsidies. This action was based on the principle that 'bounties and subsidies aimed at stimulating production and providing protection of Australian (and New Zealand) industries from trans-Tasman competition can no longer be regarded as viable instruments of industry policy'. From 1 July 1990 both governments ceased export incentives and subsidies on goods exported to the other CER country. Furthermore, under the Agreed Minute they committed themselves from 1 January 1989 to trying to avoid the adoption of industry-specific measures which would have adverse effects on competition between industries in the free trade area.

The 1983 CER Agreement itself does not proscribe national subsidies or other forms of assistance to industries and it permits the use of countervailing measures. As the Australian and New Zealand markets became integrated there was a sense that countervailing duties and anti-dumping would disappear or, at least, play a minor role. Reference is made in official CER documents to 'closely aligning' the countries' systems for the benefit of third-country actions but no rationale for or against the removal of trans-Tasman procedures appears in this context. A likely explanation of why countervailing duties were not reformed was that the problem they are supposed to address had not (and still has not) disappeared.

The policy shift away from anti-dumping remedies for trans-Tasman trade was formally instituted by the Protocol to ANZCERTA on Acceleration of Free Trade in Goods, signed on 18 August 1988. Article 4(1) provided that:

> The Member States agree that anti-dumping measures in respect of goods originating in the territory of the other Member State are not appropriate from the time of achievement of both free trade in goods between the Member States on 1 July 1990 and the

application of their competition laws to relevant anti-competitive conduct affecting trans-Tasman trade in goods.

This passage suggests two pre-conditions to the conclusion that anti-dumping remedies were no longer appropriate: first, the achievement of full free trade across the Tasman in goods; secondly, certain trans-Tasman competition law provisions had to be in place. Each country had to take steps to make sure its competition laws applied to the relevant area of anti-competitive conduct affecting trans-Tasman trade in goods (Articles 4(2)(a)—(e) and 4(4)). There was a fallback clause in case either country had to delay the introduction of the new statutory remedies (Article 4(5)) but this was not used and the complete policy reforms went into effect on 1 July 1990. Each country had obligations not to initiate any new anti-dumping action against goods originating in the territory of the other country from 1 July 1990 and not to continue any investigations or impose any new duties. Existing levies were to be revoked, price undertakings released and other measures removed.

Two steps were to be taken by each country: New Zealand had to amend the Dumping and Countervailing Duties Act 1988 to remove Australia from the scope of anti-dumping duties; and, secondly, it had to amend the Commerce Act 1986 to insert a new provision covering anti-competitive use of market power in trans-Tasman markets. Similarly, Australia had to limit the reach of its Customs Tariff (Anti-Dumping) Act 1975 so that anti-dumping duties could not be applied to New Zealand goods; and, secondly, it had to insert a new provision into its Trade Practices Act 1974.

The original CER Treaty of 1983 did not really limit use of the trans-Tasman anti-dumping remedy. Article 15 covered anti-dumping action by declaring that dumping of goods was inconsistent with the objectives of CER. There were then detailed requirements to consult with, and to disclose all relevant information to, the other Member State when a complaint of dumping was received and when provisional measures were imposed. Apart from these requirements, Article 15(2) expressly preserved the discretion of each country to decide to levy anti-dumping duties conditional upon the relevant statutory tests being met.

By the time removal of the trans-Tasman anti-dumping remedy came into effect on 1 July 1990, anti-dumping duties, undertakings or other remedies applied to only two New Zealand products and one Australian product. In 1989 and early 1990 no new investigations were pursued against the other CER country. The Uruguay Round, concluded in December 1993, led to a major overhaul of New Zealand's and Australia's trade remedies regimes to conform with the international rules on how and when anti-dumping duties may be imposed on foreign traded goods. Anti-dumping procedures in Australia and New Zealand are concerned solely with the effects of alleged dumping on producers in the target industry and, at the time of writing, there was no national interest clause which would allow the anti-dumping authorities to take into account possible off-setting benefits in terms of relatively low-priced imports to final consumers. The procedures also ignore the interests of those producers who buy the dumped goods and who are faced with higher prices in the event that an anti-dumping duty or price undertaking is imposed.

Economists emphasize that anti-dumping actions are a form of contingent protection against low-priced imports rather than a safeguard against predatory pricing or unfair competition. Lloyd (1977) found evidence that in a substantial proportion of cases in Australia anti-dumping action was taken when there was a decline in the competitiveness of domestic production, especially in periods of downturn in the macroeconomy. At such times complainants frequently seek other forms of protection. Later evidence (Vautier and Lloyd, 1997, App. I) strongly supports the contention that such action in Australia has provided contingent protection.

From 1990 an anti-dumping remedy was not available under CER. Any nationalistic idea that local industries should be protected from competing trans-Tasman imports at 'unfairly low prices' was abandoned. The removal of the trans-Tasman remedy ensured that trans-Tasman anti-dumping activity which was not harmful to the importing countries was eliminated.[7] The residual risk that economically harmful predatory dumping might occur was answered by the trans-Tasman competition provisions — the subject of the next section in this chapter.

With the removal of the trans-Tasman anti-dumping remedy the spotlight turned to anti-dumping actions against imports from third countries. WTO statistics reveal that Australia and New Zealand are two of the most frequent appliers of anti-dumping duties, especially in relation to their share of world trade. WTO (1997a, Table V.4) shows that Australia and New Zealand accounted for 5.2 per cent and 3.0 per cent respectively of all anti-dumping measures in force on 31 December 1996, whereas they accounted for only 1.2 per cent and 0.3 per cent respectively of the total value of all merchandise trade (WTO, 1997a, Table 1.5). An obvious question arises: under what circumstances might Australia and New Zealand consider removing all remaining anti-dumping remedies? This question lies outside the scope of this study and, indeed, outside the present policy intentions of both countries. A recent New Zealand review of trade remedies stated explicitly that it did not seek to address the question of replacing anti-dumping laws (by competition law) (New Zealand Ministry of Commerce, 1998b, p. 28).

The 1990 Trans-Tasman Competition Provisions

Coincident with removing the trans-Tasman anti-dumping remedy in 1990 the 'trans-Tasman competition provisions'[8] were enacted by each CER partner. These provide the only legal remedy for firms in Australia and New

Zealand concerned about trans-Tasman business conduct. Vautier and Lloyd (1997, pp. 64—102) provide a thorough examination of the trans-Tasman competition provisions and compare them with the superseded anti-dumping remedy. They review the 1990 policy shift in terms of its rationale, its significance and reactions to it, and document research on the overall impact of the 1990 amendments, including the results of a 1996 Business Survey in Australia and New Zealand.

The trans-Tasman competition provisions were simply an extraterritorial extension of their pre-existing parent provisions[9] which prohibit the use of a dominant market position (or, in Australia, the use of a substantial degree of market power) for the purpose of restricting/preventing entry or competitive conduct. The result is that the ability to take an action for abuse of market power in New Zealand for example, under its Commerce Act, no longer depends on:

(a)   the defendant being a New Zealand domiciled entity, i.e. 'any person resident or carrying on business in New Zealand'; and/or
(b)   the source of the defendant's market power being a New Zealand market.

In addition to these substantive provisions the 1990 competition law amendments introduced important ancillary enforcement measures. The rules of evidence were altered to allow the gathering of evidence by a court in one CER country from the other CER country. A court of one country can issue subpoenas to be served on persons in the other country. If appropriate, a court can conduct its proceedings in the other country. These powers go well beyond those incorporated in the bilateral cooperation agreements discussed in Chapter 3. Certain cooperative evidence-gathering, information-sharing and preliminary investigation powers were also introduced to facilitate the work of the two enforcement agencies, the Commerce Commission and the (now) Australian Competition and Consumer Commission (Baxt, 1990).

Thus the provisions were a useful extension of each country's competition law, by means of market definition and jurisdiction; and the concept of a trans-Tasman market (i.e. inclusive of a market in Australia *and* New Zealand) was formally incorporated in the Australian statute. None the less, the extension was limited in that it did not add substantively to the competition law remedies already available.

Another limitation was that the new provisions excluded (impact) markets exclusively for services. This is a peculiarity in the trans-Tasman competition provisions, especially in view of the absence of any such limitation in the parent provisions. It is evident that this outcome was influenced by the scope of the superseded trans-Tasman anti-dumping law which pertained only to goods in the importing country, that is the country in which the impact of dumping occurred. To the extent that business was seeking assurances that a substitute and like remedy would be available, the close linkage between the scope of the new competition provisions and the former anti-dumping rules is perhaps explicable. Despite a recommendation from the CER Steering Committee of Officials (1990) to remove the anomaly there has been no legislative response. The issue is not unimportant, both as a matter of principle and given that CER covers services which in both Australia and New Zealand account for a relatively high proportion of total trade (PECC, 1996).

Although the trans-Tasman competition provisions adopted by each country reflect a formally agreed common objective and fit well with the generally harmonized national competition laws, there are important differences between the provisions in the two countries. The main difference lies in the market power threshold (adopted from each parent provision) which activates the trans-Tasman provisions: 'a dominant position in a market' (New Zealand) versus 'a substantial degree of market power' (Australia). Debate over the threshold differences was vociferous at the time of the 1990 amendments. New Zealand business believed that the Australian threshold would be easier to breach than the supposedly higher dominance threshold. This would mean that New Zealand firms exporting into Australia would be more vulnerable to a claim under s.46A of Australia's Trade Practices Act than Australian firms exporting to New Zealand under s.36A of the Commerce Act. The CER governments remain of the view that the two threshold tests are not so dissimilar as to cause undue prejudice or practical difficulty in the operation of the provisions and that identical language is not required for the statutory provisions to work effectively and fairly.

Comparing the anti-dumping and competition law remedies

The 1990 amendments represented a policy shift that was not a straightforward swap of one regulatory tool for another. Rather, it was tantamount to a redirection of trans-Tasman trade policy through greater emphasis on the competitive process and the interests of buyers, rather than on 'fairness' and the interests of domestic producers alone. The policy shift was intended to direct attention to those actions of powerful firms likely to harm the competitive process itself. Thus the trans-Tasman competition provisions focus on the competition implications of conduct with far greater precision than the former anti-dumping measures (New Zealand Ministry of Commerce, 1989). Aimed at preventing abuse of market power, they were not a direct substitute for the traditional anti-dumping trade remedy which exposed a wider range of price discrimination. Anti-dumping duties and competition law remedies are each aimed at a different market problem; they have different objectives, they target a different range of business conduct, and they employ different analytical tests, tools and procedures to achieve a determination.

In approving the policy shift in favour of trans-Tasman competition law (albeit limited to the unilateral conduct of powerful firms) it seems that the

CER governments judged trans-Tasman anti-dumping law to be over-inclusive, with the risk that legitimate price competition could be caught. They narrowed the extent of protection available to domestic manufacturers from trans-Tasman pricing behaviour. They also changed the form of protection in that they opened new avenues of complaint, notwithstanding the exclusion of conduct impacting upon services markets. In addition, firms with a trans-Tasman predation complaint were accorded the right to take private enforcement action through the courts.

The notion of a single market has been emphasized as an influence behind the policy shift. For example, the Australian Department of Foreign Affairs and Trade (1995) said that, at the time, 'dumping remedies were seen as being less relevant to trans-Tasman trade than they had been in the past as the scope for price discrimination between domestic and export markets was reduced by a single market'. Now that neither Australia's nor New Zealand's competition law contains a prohibition on price discrimination in domestic markets, the logic for removing the trans-Tasman anti-dumping remedy for trans-national price discrimination in a free trade area is even clearer.

What was missing from the explicit policy rationale was the desirability of removing the risk that trans-Tasman anti-dumping activity would be used by industry as a protective device in response to the falling levels of industry protection. In hindsight, at least, the trans-Tasman reforms agreed in 1988 were part of the CER governments' strategy to eliminate protection for domestic manufacturers from non-dumped goods imported from the other country. The removal of that risk in the context of CER has to be one of the main achievements of the policy shift.

The trans-Tasman competition provisions were clearly driven more by the residual price discrimination concern than by any broader policy objective to apply a competition standard to all forms of conduct affecting all trans-Tasman trade. Given their limited scope, it seems clear that the new provisions were promulgated more with a view to assuaging the fears of domestic manufacturers over the loss of the trans-Tasman anti-dumping remedy than with a view to having a comprehensive trans-Tasman competition law.

A broad-based trans-Tasman competition law was neither the main achievement nor the main objective of the 1990 amendments. Such a shift in policy would have required a much more comprehensive approach to the application of competition law to trans-Tasman trade. It would have required extension of the trans-Tasman provisions to collusive price-fixing and other contracts and arrangements (such as trans-Tasman market sharing) which have the purpose or effect of substantially lessen competition in an impact market and to cover vertical practices and mergers. For example, any collusion between actual or potential competitors across the Tasman should be treated as seriously as collusive conduct prohibited within each of the national jurisdictions. It appears, however, that these issues are not presently a high priority for either policymakers or the enforcement agencies.

Non-use of the trans-Tasman competition provisions

Despite the notion of a single market, opportunities for both price and non-price predation were expected to remain. But, to date, neither the Commerce Commission nor the (now) Australian Competition and Consumer Commission has taken a prosecution action under the trans-Tasman competition provisions. At the time these were introduced, some commentators expected that firms would be eager to use them against trans-Tasman rivals (Baxt, 1990, p. 119). Court action is the only legal avenue for dealing with the trans-Tasman and parent provisions. However, no private litigation has yet been mounted in New Zealand, and since an early unsuccessful interlocutory claim by an Australian distributor under s.46A (*Berlaz Pty Limited & Ors* v. *Fine Leather Care Products Limited,* 1991) there has been no further private litigation.

One possible deterrent to the use of competition legislation is the cost, delay and uncertainty of pursuing private litigation. However, on the basis of market evidence obtained by Vautier and Lloyd (1997), it would not be possible to mount a convincing case that these factors have played a significant part in limiting the number of disputes coming to light under the trans-Tasman provisions, nor is it apparent that there is a problem of under-enforcement by the relevant Commissions. No procedural, technical or jurisdictional factors emerged that might tend to inhibit firms from making use of the trans-Tasman competition remedy should an appropriate circumstance arise.

The fact that (apart from the *Berlaz* decision) there are no decided court cases is only partly instructive about the role of the trans-Tasman competition provisions. Complaints may be made to the competition authorities and dealt with by informal investigation without ever getting to the stage of requiring judicial determination. There may be various reasons why complaints are not taken further: the alleged conduct or market characteristics do not fit the statutory parameters; a case does not fit the Commission's enforcement priorities even though there may be a *prima facie* breach; or the Commission effects a settlement. It is generally true that the vast majority of private actions settle out of court before a full hearing takes place.

The Extra-CER Dimensions of Competition Law

As in other regional trading arrangements, CER countries have adopted provisions in relation to competition issues arising out of trade and commerce with third countries.

The first of these provisions is the possible extraterritorial application by Australia and New Zealand of their competition laws with respect to third countries. Both the Australian and New Zealand competition statutes give similar expression to the general extraterritorial provision which covers conduct engaged in outside Australia and New Zealand respectively by any person resident or carrying on business in one of those countries to the extent that such conduct affects a market in that country. These provisions follow the US 'effects doctrine'. To our knowledge, in practice these provisions have really only applied to mergers or takeovers, and more particularly in Australia where detailed procedures are set out in their legislation. Even then there are practical difficulties which may in part explain the unusual settlement reached between New Zealand's Commerce Commission and firms in Australia's and New Zealand's sugar industry. This followed an investigation into complex transactions involving parent companies in Australia which would have 'the effect of combining New Zealand's only sugar refinery, owned by New Zealand Sugar, and Mackay's sugar importing and distribution businesses'. As part of the settlement, the Commerce Commission undertook not to take court action and, as one of three undertakings, the companies would 'not seek to renew the anti-dumping duties on imported refined sugar from Malaysia, which are due to expire in November [1998]' (New Zealand Commerce Commission, 1998b).

The second provision relates to bilateral competition agreements. In Chapter 3 we noted that Australia has bilateral agreements with the US and Chinese Taipei, and New Zealand has a bilateral agreement with Chinese Taipei. A Joint Statement between the Commerce Commission and the Trade Practices Commission was made pursuant to the 1990 trans-Tasman competition provisions and should therefore be regarded as a part of the CER regional trading arrangement rather than a bilateral agreement. The two countries also have a bilateral agreement, the 1994 Cooperation and Coordination Agreement between the Australian Trade Practices Commission and the New Zealand Commerce Commission, relating to cooperation in respect of all other competition provisions in their statutes. This is outside the CER Agreement and is referred to in Chapter 3.

In their independent Communications to the WTO Working Group on the Interaction between International Trade and Competition, Australia and New Zealand go beyond competition law to take a broad approach to 'competition policy', each referring to deregulation in particular. New Zealand has emphasized competition and regulatory principles to guide policymakers towards a coherent approach to all aspects of economic policy. A single primary objective of efficient production and consumption in the economy is stressed.

Applying a Competition Framework

An important theme of this book is that an integrated policy approach is required to address properly competition and efficiency in markets. This section provides some Australian and New Zealand examples of how this can be done. The examples relating to parallel importing and producer boards have recently emerged in the context of globalizing markets and illustrate the benefits of viewing them within an integrated policy framework. The New Zealand Government is presently reviewing how traditional trade remedies might have regard to competition and national interest considerations. This section concludes with a business perspective which reinforces the broad approach to policy relating to competition in trans-Tasman and other markets.

Parallel importing

In recent years the issue of parallel importing has received much more attention in Australia, New Zealand and several other countries. The prohibition of parallel importing comes about because the importing country's own intellectual property legislation restricts imports to the holders of copyright or their authorized distributors.

The New Zealand Copyright (Removal of Prohibition on Parallel Importing) Amendment Act 1998 removed the parallel importing prohibition contained in the Copyright Act 1994.[10] At the same time the penalties for piracy or counterfeit of copyrighted goods were trebled. Trademark law was unchanged. New Zealand's copyright regime, by comparison with other countries, was quite pervasive in that no new or used goods were exempt from the prohibition on parallel importing (New Zealand Institute of Economic Research, 1998).

At the time of writing, in Australia the Copyright Amendment Bill had just been passed by both Houses of Parliament. This Bill removes the current prohibition on parallel importing of sound recordings and exclusive brand name goods. Penalties were also increased and measures introduced to raise the probability of detecting piracy or counterfeit goods.

The CER partners are seeking to open further their markets to foreign trade and price competition. This does not, in their view, undermine copyright protection for foreign suppliers or inhibit private contractual arrangements that copyright holders may wish to enter into with their distributors.

Whatever the ultimate (and uncertain) impact in Australia and New Zealand of removing exclusive distributor rights covering a range of branded/copyright products, the basis for the governments' policy change is clear. The potential for customer benefit from permitting intra-brand competition on price, service and quality through freer trade is considered at least to outweigh the potential detriments. These potential detriments are said to relate to free-riding (by purchasers of parallel imports) on the information/service provided by the copyright owner or exclusive licensee, the likely redistribution of commercial opportunities, and a disincentive to innovate and/or invest in Australia and New Zealand. The changes are based on the assumption that final consumers as well as customers in the productive sector are discerning enough to be able to compare quality-adjusted prices for final goods or intermediate componentry/machine parts and assess the likelihood of guaranteed service back-up being available.

Strong statutory protection against parallel importing — reminiscent of protection via the former import licensing regimes for goods — was questionable for trans-Tasman trade in the context of CER's free trade area. It would have been in the EU too, had parallel importing not been considered central to the notion of a common market. But the Australian and New Zealand governments have gone further than repealing the prohibition on intra-regional trade. They have confronted the wider international issue in repealing prohibitions on imports from all sources, thereby removing a legislatively condoned restriction upon competition.

Of course, the actual opportunities available to any parallel importer depend heavily on the extent to which particular product markets are already open and efficiently functioning as a result of competition. Effective inter-brand competition is especially important in this context and may well provide a commercial deterrent to some parallel imports. Innovators, licensed manufacturers and distributors may still enter into and enforce private contracts to the extent that they seek to compete with parallel importing and preserve opportunities for profitable cross-border price discrimination; and to the extent that an 'economically rational rate of return on investment' is seen to be threatened by the legislative changes in Australia and New Zealand.

These changes to parallel importing in both Australia and New Zealand have faced strong US opposition and direct expressions of concern by the USTR. USTR's Ambassador Barshefsky termed New Zealand's decision 'unfortunate' and threatened that it 'will undermine US domestic support for efforts to enhance and expand [the US/New Zealand] bilateral trade and investment relationship' (USTR, 1998b). The US is particularly concerned about the 'precedent-setting action by an OECD nation [which places New Zealand outside of common international practice] that could have an adverse impact on *overall world trade*' (USIS, 1998; emphasis added).

The US intercessions have placed both Australia and New Zealand on USTR's special 301 watch list: a means 'of monitoring progress in implementing commitments [by US trading partners] with regard to the protection of intellectual property rights and for *providing comparable market access* for US intellectual property products' (emphasis added). This is notwithstanding US acceptance that the new regime does not contravene either WTO rules, including the TRIPS agreement, or any international treaty obligations (*New Zealand Herald,* 1998). Furthermore, it is understood that the World Intellectual Property Organization (WIPO) does not regard parallel importing as threatening copyright interests and considers that its abolition would not breach the Berne Convention.

The position of the US Administration, that intellectual property should be protected by prohibitions on parallel importing, appears to drive off concerns of US owners of copyright material that they would not now enjoy protection comparable to that which would be available to Australian and New Zealand owners of copyright through protections available in the US against unauthorized parallel importing. This position rests on a notion of negative reciprocity and cuts across the positive role of unilateral initiatives in the context of globalizing markets. The US argues that New Zealand's 'removal of the ban on parallel imports primarily impacts intellectual property protection for innovators [and] is not simply an "open trade" or "competitiveness" issue' (and yet section 301 is a retaliatory trade instrument). Exclusive control of distribution into *countries* is regarded as an economic right of copyright owners which allows them to optimize their *country* income and share by *tailoring* to that country, for example in terms of timing. In other words, *US trade* interests are at stake. The effect of parallel importing restrictions is to increase US export prices and export income for the particular products.

Certainly, firms will seek to take advantage of market segmentation caused by country differences in the balance of supply and demand. (This is termed multi-market or third-degree price discrimination, the overall welfare effects of which are ambiguous. See Tirole, 1990, section 3.2.) Globalization itself will not remove such tailoring opportunities, but pro-competitive domestic policies (and deregulation in particular) will tend to reduce them. Country boundaries are becoming less relevant to the conduct of both consumers and producers in globalizing markets. Whether there will on balance be positive or negative trade effects is uncertain.

If Australia and New Zealand were to maintain the trade prohibitions in question, one consequence would be the granting to US (and other) companies of an extraterritorial right to control distribution of particular products in these foreign countries, thereby protecting US (and other) trade interests. It is argued that such distribution monopolies are 'not an essential tool to protect copyright' (Oxley, 1997, p. 4). Parallel imports including brands are legally manufactured/genuine products (although not necessarily identical, depending on the extent of country tailoring). Their copyright protection is not at issue (unless undetected piracy increases). A genuine import, even if unauthorized by the copyright holder or exclusive licensee, is still protected by copyright.

In effect, the CER partners are now taking the view that it is not their role to enforce authorization to distribute these genuine products even though industry concerns have been voiced in both Australia and New Zealand, particularly in respect of local book publishing and sound recording productions. To the extent that this opposition to parallel importing reflects concern that the prices of books and CDs will fall, we infer that the opponents' justification for retaining the prohibition is the protection afforded to producers, by umbrella pricing for consumers, that will support higher-cost local productions.

The debate over parallel importing — with its trade, intellectual property and competition dimensions — provides an excellent example of how a generic competition framework based on generally applicable competition principles would provide an invaluable reference point for addressing such cross-border trade frictions. It is also an excellent example of a truly trade-related competition issue; and one that from the perspective of the CER governments and no doubt of consumers should be steered by competition and welfare criteria.

The CER governments believe that prohibitions on parallel importing constrain trade *and* price competition from all foreign sources. While actual impacts on price competition and service and other terms of provision are uncertain (as are the net trade and investment implications), and while these will vary between different product categories, it can be inferred from the policy changes that, at worst, national economic welfare impacts are expected to be neutral. This assumes that there will be no market closures as a result of the policy changes.

The US position causes some consternation in Australia and New Zealand, given their shared commitments with the United States to trade liberalization both in APEC and the WTO. The issue is not simply a bilateral one. To quote New Zealand's Commerce Minister (*The Independent*, 1 July 1998): 'Our approach is that this is competition policy.'

It is worth quoting here from the United States Communication to the WTO Working Group on the Interaction between Trade and Competition Policy (1997b):

> [The WTO] Working Group will have accomplished much if we succeed merely in establishing a shared understanding of the basic precepts of competition policy and the substance and emphasis these precepts are given under various national and regional systems. The importance of building this educational foundation should not be underestimated, as the meaning and impact of competition policy can manifest itself quite differently when one considers that common economic and legal concepts can sometimes take on divergent meanings as they evolve through different cultures of policy, administration and jurisprudence.
>
> Once this knowledge and understanding are firmly established, the United States believes that much might also be gained from learning and exploring the manner in which the development and application of competition law and policy can contribute to the fuller realization of the objectives of trade liberalization and the multilateral trading system . . . This exploration could include consideration of means of *promoting the adoption of sound competition principles* as well as ways to improve and strengthen international cooperation in the application and enforcement of competition laws. Through these efforts, we can profitably fulfil

the [WTO] Ministerial mandate to examine the interaction between competition policy and trade with a view towards furthering greater *market access,* economic growth and sustainable development. (Emphases added)

A finding of whether or not a business (or government) action is anti-competitive is not simply dependent on a measure of that action's impact on the exporting country's trade. The relevant concern is competition and efficiency in the global markets.

Producer boards

Australia and New Zealand each have several statutory marketing boards which are a form of state trading enterprise. There is some concern in both countries about the operations of these boards. This concern is partly about WTO consistency; a separate WTO working party is looking at state trading enterprises. It is also partly about the restrictions on the opportunities for overseas trading by domestic producers, particularly the development of new products and new markets. New Zealand is taking a leading role in reviewing these enterprises in an international context.

The New Zealand Government intends (over, say, 3—5 years) to dismantle special statutory backing for all producer boards. This reflects, in part, a continuing reduction in government intervention in primary industries; but, mainly, the rationale is that this is a trade-related issue and one where international pressure will increasingly be brought to bear. New Zealand's Trade Minister has stressed (Smith, 1997) that:

> State trading will inevitably be addressed in the next round of [WTO] negotiations. And it directly affects New Zealand [and Australia] because our marketing boards fall under the WTO definition of state trading enterprises. The pressure is coming from the US. State trading is the agriculture issue for them . . . The US argue that [legislated] export monopoly powers enable . . . 'unfair competition' — price pooling, price discrimination, predatory pricing.

Undoubtedly, the proposed reform is seen by the New Zealand Government as further demonstration of New Zealand's contribution to broad goals through unilateral leadership. It is ironical that one of the complex issues raised by the reform is the need 'to ensure that New Zealand [continues] to be able to administer [tariff] *quota markets,* and meet . . . obligations with respect to those quotas to the satisfaction of our trading partners' (Smith, 1998; emphasis added).

Once again, a competition framework would assist in distilling and reconciling the various (but related) perspectives on an important multi-national issue in the interests of a more coherent approach.

The current New Zealand review of anti-dumping action

A recent New Zealand government discussion paper reviewing trade remedies (New Zealand Ministry of Commerce, 1998b) was 'based on the premise that trade remedy action against imported goods should take account of national interest criteria'. The continuing rationale for trade remedies, in the context of government policy for more open markets and effective competition within them, was clearly a major consideration in the review. The review recognized that redressing injury to domestic producers via anti-dumping (and other trade remedies) may not increase national welfare. Submissions were invited on the following issues, *inter alia*:

- how the application of trade remedies could take account of the interests of consumers or other producer considerations (net national benefit);
- whether a common framework and administrative structure could be developed to cover all forms of trade remedy action;
- the extent to which competition policy considerations should be incorporated into trade remedy analysis.

In a subsequent document which discusses the issues arising from submissions, the New Zealand Ministry of Commerce (1998c) cited the concern that a national benefit test

> would not accord with New Zealand's international commitment to the condemnation of dumping which causes or threatens material injury, and . . . it would not be appropriate for New Zealand unilaterally to adopt any additional threshold in anti-dumping cases when the level of anti-dumping actions is increasing in Asia.

In response the Ministry rightly commented that the WTO permits actions against dumping but places no obligation on its members to take such actions. Further, inconsistencies in the policies of other countries is not a good reason to avoid unilateral policy improvement where there is a national benefit.

The Ministry equated a competition policy approach with a competition law approach. It seems that the officials' main purpose was to emphasize the economic efficiency objective of competition law (which is not restricted to protecting producers' interests). Clearly, officials were also aware of the net national benefit approach used to describe the authorization process (contained in the competition laws of both New Zealand and Australia) whereby a business acquisition or restrictive business practice[11] can be authorized on grounds that public benefit outweighs any detriment to competition. For New Zealand competition law cases, the link between net national benefit and national economic welfare is strong, given the requirement (under direction of the Commerce Act) to accommodate efficiency considerations in public benefit assessments.

Amongst the main conclusions of the officials' trade remedies review were that analysing dumping in a competition framework would accommodate economic benefits to the importing country; dumping would probably apply to less trade; and an economic rationale for any intervention would receive greater emphasis. The Ministry was realistic in suggesting that national border remedies for dumping would be likely to continue in the foreseeable future. However, this does not preclude unilateral initiatives to bring a competition perspective to bear on the analysis of dumping claims, for example by adding a mandatory price predation test for all dumping complaints. There is no economic justification for leaving anti-dumping remedies outside a competition framework, either in a national economy committed to effective competition and overall welfare enhancement or in a grouping of economies committed to trade liberalization and economic integration. Only where cross-border price discrimination contains elements which allegedly contravene agreed competition standards should intervention (judicial not governmental) be countenanced. At least as far as CER and the EU are concerned, the view that price discrimination is no longer a trade issue but rather a competition issue underpins their policy approach.

Some business perspectives

Respondents to a 1996 business survey of 108 firms based in Australia/New Zealand (Vautier and Lloyd, 1997, pp. 97—101 and App. III) made very little reference to business conduct in the form of restrictive practices — either in trans-Tasman markets (where there is a relatively high degree of economic integration) or in respect of third countries (where there is a growing level of trade and economic interaction). There were residual trans-Tasman 'dumping' concerns.

The most noticeable feature of the responses relating to third countries was the extent to which they reflected problems for business (and particularly for competitiveness), not from private actions but from government actions or inaction (covering tariffs, non-tariff barriers and industry assistance). Various government interventions were clearly seen as inimical to competition. Perceived competition problems were thus broadly scoped; they were not confined to those problems which are usually covered by competition law. Clearly, there was a concern about the ability of third-country suppliers to export from monopoly or protected positions — although typically competition law, even in developed economies, does not preclude the retention of monopoly positions.

Overall, an important feature of the business perspectives revealed by the survey was their reinforcement of a broad approach to policy relating to competition in trans-Tasman and other markets.

Notes

1. The relevant trans-Tasman experience is fully documented in Vautier and Lloyd (1997). This chapter draws heavily on that study.
2. Pursuant to a 1991 treaty, a CER institution JAS—ANZ (Joint Accreditation System — Australia and New Zealand) was established, with the limited role of providing accreditation for (standards) conformity assessment bodies. The Australia New Zealand Food Authority, established in 1996 and charged with establishing common food standards pursuant to the Agreement on Joint Food Standards, was the second formal institution created under CER; but even this is the former and renamed (Australian) National Food Authority with New Zealand admitted to full membership.
3. Articles 4 and 5(1) of the Protocol require, respectively, that:

   > Each Member State shall grant to persons of the other Member State and services provided by them access rights in its market no less favourable than those allowed to its own persons and services provided by them [and that]
   > Each Member State shall accord to persons of the other Member State and services provided by them treatment no less favourable than that accorded in like circumstances to its persons and services provided by them.

4. Any formal investment agreement would need to be consistent with international obligations relating to investment flows (Finance Ministers of Australia and New Zealand Correspondence, 1996).
5. The Tribunal can, upon application, review ACCC determinations by way of a re-hearing.
6. For a brief history of trade remedies in Australia and New Zealand and a case-study of anti-dumping and countervailing action in Australia, see Vautier and Lloyd (1997, pp. 53—64 and App. I).
7. The CER Agreement makes provision for anti-dumping action on behalf of a third country.
8. S.36A of New Zealand's Commerce Act and s.46A of Australia's Trade Practices Act.
9. S.36 of New Zealand's Commerce Act and s.46 of Australia's Trade Practices Act.
10. Because of the Medicines Act, parallel importing of pharmaceuticals is unlikely, although Crown entities are not prohibited from doing so.
11. That is, other than the trans-Tasman competition provisions (ss.36A, 46A) or their parent provisions (ss.36, 46).

6. The Americas

Multiple Initiatives

There are a number of trade liberalization initiatives in the Americas or the so-called Western Hemisphere (see PECC, 1997c, for an excellent review). They include: NAFTA; the Canada—Chile Free Trade Agreement; the 1990 Enterprise for the Americas Initiative, in the first year of which the United States signed a trade and investment framework agreement with nearly every eligible Latin American country; the Southern Common Market (MERCOSUR), the largest of the South American regional groupings, covering Argentina, Brazil, Paraguay and Uruguay, with Chile and Bolivia as associate members and not part of the common external tariff agreement; the Andean Community, comprising Bolivia, Colombia, Ecuador, Peru and Venezuela; and the Group of Three, comprising Colombia, Mexico and Venezuela. All these, except the Enterprise for the Americas Initiative, contain chapters or protocols relating to competition policy or law. We shall consider these agreements. Each of the Latin American groupings has an interest in trade and investment liberalization and economic integration.

Of most potential significance is the proposed Free Trade Area of the Americas (FTAA).[1] This would result in the world's largest regional trading arrangement, involving over 30 countries and over 700 million people. In their third joint Declaration (1997), Ministers Responsible for Trade agreed that countries may negotiate and join the FTAA individually or as members of a sub-regional integration group negotiating as a unit. We also look at the 'competition policy' aspects of this initiative.

The structure of this chapter is as follows: first, we examine each of the three arrangements involving one or more of the NAFTA partners — NAFTA itself, the Canada—Chile Free Trade Agreement and the Group of Three; secondly, MERCOSUR and the Andean Community; and thirdly, the FTAA.

NAFTA

The experience in NAFTA is another important example of the possibilities and difficulties of developing a regional approach to cross-border competition. NAFTA is the second largest regional trading arrangement but the provisions in the agreement relating to 'competition policy' are rudimentary compared to those of the EU and CER. This is despite the fact that many anti-trust concepts were first developed in the US and anti-trust law is pursued more aggressively in the US than in any other country. For the last 50 years or more the US has been the global centre of economic analysis, including industrial organization and other areas of economics which are used in the analysis of competition problems. Canada and the US were the first countries to develop comprehensive competition laws, in 1888 and 1890 respectively.[2] The US has pioneered the development of bilateral cooperation agreements and was the leading force behind many of the developments of international trade law and policy at the multilateral level in the Uruguay Round and since the Round was concluded in 1993. The chapter in NAFTA dealing with 'competition policy' was largely shaped by the US. For these reasons more attention is paid in this chapter to the views of one country, the US, than in other chapters dealing with regional trading agreements.

Policies to promote competition and competition law in the NAFTA countries

The US in particular, Canada and, more recently, Mexico have developed polices to promote competition but they are exclusively national policies. The US has been for more than 100 years the bastion of free enterprise. Whereas almost all other countries favoured state provision of public utilities and many infrastructure services, in the US, apart from postal services, these were provided by (regulated) private companies. There have been few restrictions on inflows and outflows of FDI for decades. The US has a generally low level of border restrictions on trade in goods with some notable exceptions such as agricultural quotas and the Jones Act restricting coastal navigation. Services are traded freely with few exceptions.

Canada is today one of the more liberal states in terms of restrictions on trade in goods, services and FDI and in terms of the level of regulation of most industries. But it has not always been so liberal. It has a long history of restrictions on border trade and is still significantly less open than the US to trade in both goods and services. It also has a long history of restrictions on inflows of FDI. In the 1970s it introduced a Foreign Investment Review Agency to screen foreign investment proposals and a National Energy Program which severely restricted FDI in the Canadian oil and gas industry. These restrictions have been substantially relaxed subsequently, but in NAFTA negotiations Canada insisted on a 'cultural industry' exclusion for FDI flows in NAFTA.

Mexico began an aggressive programme to liberalize the economy in the 1990s. This included privatization, deregulation, price liberalization and international trade liberalization. These policies involved a major shift towards increased competition among private producers. The replacement of a limited and ineffective set of laws against monopolies by a comprehensive national competition law was seen as essential to ensure competition in markets. This law applied to the newly privatized markets and the public sector except for those strategic areas expressly reserved to the state by the Mexican Constitution.

NAFTA's Chapter 15, dealing with competition policy, is essentially competition law. The chapter has only five pages (out of the 2,000 pages in total) and there are only four substantive articles. Article 1501 (Competition Law) imposes on the member countries a general obligation to maintain and enforce a competition law and to cooperate with each other in the enforcement of these national laws. Cooperation comprises mutual legal assistance, notification, consultation and exchange of information. No party may have recourse to dispute settlement under the Agreement for any matter arising under this Article. Articles 1502 and 1503 provide rules for monopolies (sole providers or purchasers of a good or service) and state enterprises. These provisions do not do proscribe monopolies or state enterprises but do proscribe acts which are inconsistent with obligations of members under the Agreement or which nullify or impair benefits of the Agreement. Article 1504 establishes a Working Group on Trade and Competition to examine the issues concerning the relationship between competition laws and policies and trade in the NAFTA area. (Johnson, 1994, provides a comprehensive review of the Agreement.)

Thus, the obligations of the member countries are limited to maintaining and enforcing a competition law and to cooperating with each other in the enforcement of these national laws. There are no common rules in the sense of the EU-level competition law and no supranational authority. The chapter takes a behavioural and not a structural approach, in that neither monopolies nor state enterprises are prohibited. Nor are particular practices, such as differential pricing or cross-subsidization, prohibited unless they are used as instruments of anti-competitive behaviour. But the parties are to ensure that any designated privately owned or government monopoly, *inter alia,*

> provides non-discriminatory treatment to investments of investors, to goods and service providers of the other Party in its purchase or sale of the monopoly good or service in the relevant market. [Non-discriminatory treatment is defined as the better of national treatment and most-favoured-nation treatment.]

It is clear that the provisions contained in this chapter are sensitive not only to the ability to 'enhance the fulfilment of the objectives of [the] Agreement' (in the case of competition law), but also to the mutual desire to avoid nullification or impairment of the benefits expected to flow from the Agreement (in the case of monopolies and state enterprises).

Because there is no dispute settlement procedure relating to competition law matters, any dispute between members has to be resolved under bilateral competition cooperation agreements, in the case of Canada and the US, or are probably left unresolved. The cooperation provisions are much less extensive than those in the bilateral 1995 US—Canada Agreement (and in the 1991 and 1998 US—EU Agreements). The American Bar Association (1994) recommended that the members consider a formal cooperation agreement as a part of NAFTA which would include comity.

This limited approach to competition law within NAFTA reflects the views of the member countries that a national competition law is an essential component of efficient market behaviour and that bilateral cooperation is the best means to deal with cross-border issues. The obligation to have national competition laws was put there primarily to ensure that Mexico, which did not have a competition law before the Agreement, would introduce a national law and to foster cooperation among the three national authorities. The substantive provisions cover only monopolies and state enterprises. The chapter essentially lays down general provisions for national governments to follow but it does not establish any competition standards. There are no specific provisions relating to abuse of dominance, collusion, vertical restraints or mergers.

This NAFTA approach reflects the approach of the members to the regional agreement as a whole. Unlike the EU, and to a considerable extent the CER and MERCOSUR Agreements also, the NAFTA members are not pursuing a common or single market with a high degree of integration of the markets of the member countries. NAFTA is primarily a free trade agreement. In respect of 'competition policy', NAFTA has, under the leadership of the US, concentrated on competition law alone. This is a narrow view of competition and competition-related policies. The concentration on monopolies and state trading enterprises reflects the view of the US that monopoly structures are particularly conducive to anti-competitive conduct and its suspicion of state trading.

The Working Group on Trade and Competition has submitted an Interim Report (NAFTA Working Group on Trade and Competition, 1997). This report was confined to comparing national competition laws and studying specific issues relating to trade and competition.

US national competition law is laid down in several Federal statutes, of which the most important are the Sherman Act (which deals with monopolies and unilateral conduct, and anti-competitive agreements), the Clayton Act (which deals with mergers) and the Robinson—Patman Act (which deals with price discrimination). The Webb—Pomerene Act exempts export cartels from anti-trust prosecution, provided they do not restrain the export trade of any domestic competitor or enhance or depress prices within the US. There are two competition authorities: the Antitrust Division of the Department of Justice and the Federal Trade Commission. The Federal legislation applies, under the US Constitution, to all business and transactions involved in interstate commerce or, if the activities are local, affecting interstate commerce. The states also have comparable competition laws relating to anti-competitive conduct within each state.

For the purpose of comparison with other countries and questions such
as convergence, we can note that the US anti-trust law has a number of
broad distinguishing features:

- US laws now have a stronger consumer welfare orientation, but
sometimes this is interpreted in terms of consumer surplus only and
sometimes in terms of consumer and producer surplus (total welfare).
- There is a *per se* prohibition of hard-core cartel behaviour, including
price fixing, bid rigging, group boycotts and market sharing
agreements, but other behaviour is subject to the rule of reason
approach.
- There are few exclusions in the US compared to other countries.
There are no general exclusions but some industries are partially
excluded in various circumstances under a number of Acts (see
OECD, 1996a, pp. 165—87).
- Private individuals may sue for damages which result from breaches
of competition laws. Individuals as well as corporations are subject
to prosecution.
- Remedies are varied and punishment may be heavy. Violations
under the Sherman Act have from the beginning been punishable as
crimes as well as civil violations; criminal prosecutions are generally
limited to cases of *per se* horizontal price fixing, bid rigging, market
division and customer allocation. Punishments for criminal
violations are subject to fines of up to US$10 million for corporate
defendants and jail sentences of up to three years and/or fines of up
to US$350,000 for individual defendants. In civil cases, the
Antitrust Division and private parties may sue for treble damages.

Canadian competition law follows broadly that of the US but there are
some significant differences in coverage, remedies, analysis and other
features. (Goldman, Bodrug, and Warner, 1997, review Canadian
competition law, and American Bar Association, 1994, makes a comparison
between Canadian and US competition laws.) There is a single Federal Act,
the 1986 Competition Act. The objectives of Canadian competition law are
less clearly oriented to the enhancement of consumer welfare than those of
the US laws. The 1986 Canadian Competition Act specifies four policy
objectives:

(i)   to promote the efficiency and adaptability of the . . . economy;
(ii) to expand opportunities for Canadian participation in world
markets, while at the same time recognizing the role of foreign
competition in Canada; (iii)   to ensure that small and medium-sized
businesses have an equitable opportunity to participate in the
Canadian economy; (iv)   to provide consumers with competitive
prices and product choices.

There may be conflict between these multiple objectives.

The coverage of conduct and sectors is broad, like that of the US. There are differences in the treatment and analysis of particular practices compared to the US; for example, under the Competition Act, an anti-competitive merger is one which is likely to prevent or lessen competition, but Canada has formally adopted an efficiency defence in its law. Again like the EU and some other countries but not the US, Canada has an explicit concern for the abuse of power on excluded competitors. Labour activities are generally excluded. There are no total sectoral exclusions but some sectors are partially excluded or excluded in certain circumstance (see OECD, 1996a, pp. 19—68). In particular, export cartels are exempt under conditions similar to those in the US; export-related agreements are permitted, provided they do not reduce the real value of exports or restrict any person from exporting or lessen competition in the supply of services facilitating exports from Canada. Like the EU, it treats small and medium-sized enterprises less strictly.

Remedies are similar to those of the US. Canadian competition law was exclusively criminal legislation before 1986, but legislation that year made abuse of dominance and various other horizontal and vertical restraints and mergers no longer criminal offences but retained criminal law and remedies for the most egregious conduct such as conspiracy, bid rigging and predatory pricing. Prison sentences are used much less frequently than in the US. Private persons may initiate acts when a criminal provision of the Act or an order of the Tribunal or courts has been violated but private actions are much less common than in the US. Single damages and costs may be recovered.

In 1992 the Congress of the United Mexican States passed a new Federal law which became effective in June 1993. There is a single Act, the Federal Law on Economic Competition, and a single competition authority, the Federal Competition Commission. The law covers horizontal and vertical restraints and mergers. There is an exemption for export cartels under specified conditions. (For a description of the Mexican laws, see American Bar Association, 1994, ch. 2, and OECD, 1996a, pp. 127—36.) The only general exclusion is strategic areas and other areas designated in the Constitution and there are no partial exclusions. The principal objective of the new law is to protect competition in Mexican markets and enhance economic efficiency. A limited form of private action is provided in the law for persons who have demonstrated that they have sustained damages as a result of a monopolistic practice or illegal concentration. Single damages may be awarded. (President Salinas's proposal for double damages was not adopted by the Congress.) The law does not refer to its effect outside Mexico.

The international dimensions of US competition law

The US government has been the most active in the application of national competition laws extraterritorially and in the development of bilateral cooperation agreements.

The reach of US anti-trust law is not limited to conduct located within the US. Under the Sherman Act, conduct relating to US imports that harms consumers in the US may be subject to the jurisdiction of US antitrust laws irrespective of where such conduct occurs or the nationality of the parties involved. Conduct relating to non-import foreign commerce is subject to US law only if it has a 'direct, substantial or reasonably foreseeable' effect on non-import trade or commerce. Under the Clayton Act, mergers and acquisitions involving parties outside the US are similarly subject to the jurisdiction of US law. Foreign sovereigns and their instrumentalities are generally immune from suit in US courts. This application of extraterritoriality is known as the 'effects doctrine', a reference to the effects of conduct outside the US on US persons.

The US enforcement procedures are set out in the Antitrust Enforcement Guidelines for International Operations, last amended in 1995, and issued then for the first time jointly by the DOJ and the FTC. The Guidelines set out a number of factors which are to be taken into account. The first of these is 'the relative significance to the alleged violation of conduct within the United States, as compared to the conduct abroad'. They also include the presence or absence of a purpose to affect US consumers, markets or exports, the degree of conflict with foreign national law, and the effectiveness of foreign enforcement as compared with US enforcement. The last has caused concern in some foreign countries.

The DOJ has considerable discretion in enforcing the laws extraterritorially. In 1992, it announced an expansion of enforcement policy to cover conduct occurring overseas which violates US anti-trust laws and where US courts have jurisdiction, if it is clear that the conduct has a direct, substantial and reasonably foreseeable effect on *exports* of goods and services from the US. This represented a change from the earlier guidelines which required harm to US consumers before action could be taken. It effectively brought conduct in other countries which allegedly affects US exports within the scope of the extraterritorial application of its competition laws. In enforcing the law relating to mergers and acquisitions, the DOJ generally applies the 'direct, substantial or reasonably foreseeable' standard to mergers and acquisitions.

In enforcing the anti-trust laws extraterritorially, the DOJ recognizes the considerations of comity among nations and has committed itself to consider the legitimate interests of other nations in accordance with the OECD Recommendations relating to bilateral cooperation agreements and with bilateral agreements between the US and foreign governments or bodies, where applicable. It carries out a comity analysis before taking action. It considers whether the significant interest of any foreign government or body would be affected. This includes circumstances in which the conduct is prohibited under the laws of the nation or nations in which it occurs or if the conduct is not prohibited but not encouraged under the laws or policies of the nation or nations concerned.

The US has applied its anti-trust laws extraterritorially on numerous occasions (as it has applied extraterritorially US laws concerning export controls, FDI and securities), chiefly to foreign conduct affecting US imports and only in a few cases to conduct affecting exports. The extraterritorial application of US anti-trust laws, and in particular attempts to order production or disclosure of documents outside the US, have been vigorously opposed by the governments of some of the nations involved, including the UK, France and the EU, and its NAFTA partner, Canada. These countries see the interests of their persons or trade as being adversely affected. In such cases, they are reacting to what the WTO calls 'negative spillovers' from the actions of national competition authorities. In effect, they interpret their interests as being affected more broadly than the US does under its comity analyses. They are also objecting to what they see as an infringement of national sovereignty. Some governments have responded by passing legislation to forbid compliance with US authorities seeking to enforce these laws extraterritorially or to block the effects of the US actions.

A number of US academic lawyers have defended the extraterritorial application of US antitrust laws in the context of a lack of alternative options to counter adverse effects on the US from conduct originating in other countries (that is, Type 1 policy failures, in the terminology of Chapter 2) which affect the US. Baker et al. (1997, p. 442) conclude:

> Thus, absent a seamless international antitrust code, global allocative efficiency is better served by overlapping jurisdiction (e.g. based on an 'effects test') than by gaps in jurisdiction which would allow anti-competitive conduct to fall between the cracks of domestic competition law regimes.

In effect, it is justified as a last-resort policy to correct negative spillovers from private conduct.[3]   On the other hand, Baker et al. (1997) advocate bilateral cooperation in place of the conflict-generating unilateral application of laws. There is, in addition, the question of whether this extraterritorial application of laws aimed at protecting the interests of the nation will also protect the interest of the world as whole, as noted in Chapter 2.

Some sections of the Canadian Competition Act apply only to conduct in Canada, but other sections do not expressly limit the application in this regard (Goldman, Bodrug and Warner, 1997, and the American Bar Association, 1994, pp. 25—26).

Canada has been affected by a number of cases in which the US anti-trust authorities have acted against companies in Canada. In some of these cases, the US action may have been in the interests of Canada and, in the words of one commentator, Canadians 'don't so much complain about the injury as the insult' (Goldman, Bodrug and Warner, 1997, p. 65).

In relation to bilateral cooperation agreements in the area of competition law, the US has been the leading force (see Table 3.1, p. 34). The Agreement signed with the Federal Republic of Germany in 1976 was the first such agreement and subsequently the US has signed agreements with Australia (1982), the EU (1991, supplemented by a new agreement in 1998) and Canada (1984, superseded by a new agreement in 1995), but, one may note, not to date with Mexico.

In relation to the discussions concerning the possible development of a multilateral approach to anti-trust at the OECD and in the WTO Working Group, the US has advocated a minimalist role for international competition law. In particular, the US is strongly opposed to multilateral competition law being developed in the WTO or elsewhere. It favours the development of competition laws in all countries and an expansion of the existing network of bilateral competition law agreements to obtain evidence. This is the same approach as that embedded in Chapter 15 of NAFTA.

Anti-dumping and countervailing duty action in the NAFTA countries

In contrast to the EU, CER and the Canada—Chile Agreement, the NAFTA countries have not waived the application of anti-dumping actions against other members of the agreement, nor have they eliminated subsidies affecting the trade and production of the countries. In the NAFTA negotiations, Canada sought to have Canadian exports to the US made exempt from anti-dumping and countervailing duties but the US strongly opposed this.

However, the Canada—US Free Trade Agreement, which preceded NAFTA, established special dispute settlement procedures for both anti-dumping and countervailing duties, and similar procedures now apply under the dispute settlement procedures laid down in Chapter 19 of NAFTA. Binational panels are provided to hear appeals concerning decisions of the administering authorities in the three countries. These panels review the decisions but cannot substitute a different finding or determination. They seem to have had little effect on the anti-dumping actions. NAFTA also created a NAFTA Trade Remedies Working Group to consider the application of trade remedies within the NAFTA area. This Working Group reported in 1997 but did not make any recommendations for fundamental reform of the trade remedies legislation in member countries. However, the American Bar Association (1994, ch. 6) and a number of individuals in both the US and Canada (see Goldman, Bodrug and Warner, 1997, and references therein) have called for a replacement of trade remedies by competition law remedies or an alignment of competition and trade laws.

Anti-dumping action in the NAFTA countries is exclusively the responsibility of the individual countries. As all three current members of NAFTA are members of the WTO, they are bound by the WTO rules relating to anti-dumping actions.

The US is the most frequent and the most aggressive applier of anti-dumping action among WTO members. WTO statistics show that in 1996 the US had more than twice as many anti-dumping actions in force than the EU, which is the second most frequent applier of these measures (WTO, 1997a, Table V.4). The US accounted for 34.5 per cent of the world total whereas it accounted for 15.1 per cent of total world imports of goods in the same year (WTO, 1997a, Table II.7). In the same year, Canada and Mexico ranked third and fourth in the number of measures in force, with 10.6 and 10.1 per cent of the world total respectively. Mexico is by far the most important applier of these measures among developing countries. Together, the three countries accounted for 55.3 per cent of the world total. Moreover, the number of petitions and applications is increasing in all three countries.

In the US, as in some other countries, the determination of dumping and of injury are handled by two different agencies, the Department of Commerce (DOC) and the International Trade Commission (ITC) respectively. One feature of the US practice is that it uses price undertakings much less than the EU and some other countries. In the US, anti-dumping duties are levied to the full amount of the dumping margin which has been proven.

The high and rising level of anti-dumping actions in the US can be explained by a number of changes to US legislation, in association with reductions in tariff barriers which have exposed some uncompetitive producers. Since the 1970s a sequence of amendments have made it easier to take anti-dumping actions (see Prusa, 1998, Table 3). One important change was the expanded definition of 'less than fair value' sales to include sales below cost of production in the 1974 Trade Act. Thus, dumping was extended beyond price discrimination and a finding of dumping was made easier. Since the mid-1970s the rejection rate for the determination of dumping in dumping petitions has plummeted. In the period from 1989 to 1994, the rejection rate by the DOC has been zero per cent! It has rejected only two out of 100 cases in the last decade (Prusa, 1998).

Another change in US practice which explains the increase in the number of petitions and the success of findings of injury in these petitions is cumulation of imports across countries for the purpose of assessing injury. In 1984 the US Congress enacted a provision that requires the ITC to cumulate imports across exporting countries. This has greatly lowered the injury standard. Prusa (1998) argues that cumulation has significantly increased the number of petitions filed in the US and has led to smaller importers being named. It has also changed the finding of injury from negative to affirmative 'in dozens, perhaps hundreds, of cases'.

There is general agreement among commentators in the US that the US application of anti-dumping duties is essentially protectionist. This has been acknowledged by the US Council of Economic Advisers (1994).

Canada's anti-dumping laws and procedures broadly follow those of the US. Like the US, Canadian laws include below-average cost pricing as a form of dumping; Canada seldom uses negotiated price undertakings, and anti-dumping duties are levied to the full amount of the proven dumping margin. Canadian anti-dumping law has a public interest provision which allows consumer interests to be included.

There is one feature of the Canadian law which is unique and especially interesting in the present context. It allows considerations relating to competition to be taken into account. The Competition Bureau may, on the initiative of the Director or at the request of the Canadian International Trade Tribunal (CITT), which investigates complaints of dumping, advise the CITT on either the margin of dumping or the competition effects of anti-dumping action as part of the determination of injury. Thus, the CITT can take into consideration pro-competitive effects of dumping or anti-competitive effects of anti-dumping action. Goldman, Bodrug and Warner (1997, p. 75) assess the outcome of these possibilities:

> Canada has evolved procedural and substantive innovations that may allow for competition policy concerns to enter into the analysis to some extent. However, the CITT has recognised that there is a fundamental policy conflict between the two statutory regimes and has generally been reluctant to embrace competition policy concepts.

In relation to countervailing duty actions, the picture is similar, though the number of actions is much smaller. The US is by far the most important applier of countervailing duties. In 1996, it had 60.4 per cent of the total measures in force in the world economy (67 out of 111); Canada and Mexico had five and two respectively (WTO, 1997a, Table V.2). Together the three NAFTA countries accounted for 66.6 per cent of the world total.

Convergence of competition laws among the NAFTA countries

The national laws of the three countries have been converging over the last decade or so and are now broadly similar. Those of the US and Mexico countries prohibit *per se* price fixing and cartels and the law of Canada prohibits conspiracies or agreements to restrain or injure competition unduly. All three contain provisions for the notification of mergers and pre-merger reviews. All three countries are federations with competition laws at the federal and the state/province level.

Convergence extends beyond coverage of conduct. We emphasize in this book the importance of the objectives of the law and the quality of competition analysis in determining whether or not the rulings of competition authorities lead to greater efficiency in the economy. There is

little sign of convergence of objectives among the NAFTA countries.
The Canadian laws are closer to the laws of the US than those of any other country. This similarity extends to all aspects of the law: coverage in relation to conduct and sectors, remedies and private actions, but less so to the objectives. Canadian enforcement authorities and courts have been considerably influenced by US jurisprudence and often look to US precedents for guidance.

Mexico made a big step forward in its laws and a major step towards convergence with its NAFTA partners when it adopted a comprehensive competition law in 1992. This was a part of the economic reforms necessary to prepare Mexico for entry into NAFTA. In March 1998, the Federal Competition Commission created a series of regulations, including guidelines for mergers and acquisitions that are similar to those of Canada and the US in all relevant aspects.

The final report of the NAFTA Chapter 15 Working Group on Trade and Competition, which is due at the end of 1998, may recommend further developments at the NAFTA level in relation to competition laws and policies. We have noted above that there are no bilateral cooperation agreements between the US and Canada on the one hand and Mexico on the other, no prohibition on anti-dumping actions within the region and no recourse to the NAFTA dispute settlement procedures for competition law matters covered by Chapter 15.

Canada—Chile Free Trade Agreement

The Canada—Chile Free Trade Agreement (1996), supported by July 1997 implementation legislation, contains a chapter headed 'Competition Policy, Monopolies and State Enterprises'. The provisions contained therein are identical to those in NAFTA except that there is no provision for a Working Group on Competition as in NAFTA Article 1504. Consequently, the comments made above in respect of Chapter 15 of NAFTA apply equally here.

Also of relevance to their competition framework, Canada and Chile negotiated a mutual exemption — with a maximum six-year phase-in period — from the application of anti-dumping duties in the free trade area.

Group of Three (G-3)

The Group of Three is an agreement establishing a customs union between Colombia, Mexico and Venezuela. The chapter dealing with competition, Chapter XVI of the G-3 Treaty,[4] is restricted to the conduct of state enterprises and government monopolies in Colombia, Mexico and Venezuela. State enterprises in one of the member countries must accord non-discriminatory treatment to persons in the other member countries with respect to 'similar commercial transactions' (goods and services). As in the provisions of NAFTA and the Canada—Chile Free Trade Agreement, non-discriminatory treatment is defined to mean the better of national treatment and most-favoured-nation treatment.

With the exception of procurement for governmental purposes, government monopolies and state enterprises are to apply only commercial criteria in relation to the purchase or sale of a monopoly good or service in the relevant market of a party's territory; and a monopoly position may not be used anti-competitively in a non-monopolized market with adverse cross-border effects. The G-3 Agreement provided for a Committee on Competition to be established to prepare reports and make recommendations 'on further work on relevant issues concerning the relationship between competition laws and policies and trade in the free-trade area'.

MERCOSUR

The 1996 competition protocol

The 1996 Protocol of the Defense of Competition in MERCOSUR was, at July 1998, pending Congressional approval by three of MERCOSUR's four member countries for enforceability as national law. (Only Paraguay had ratified the protocol.)

The preamble of the protocol focuses on the link between the free movement of goods and services amongst MERCOSUR members and equal conditions of free competition. The protocol rules are designed to apply to all persons and entities (including state monopolies) 'whose purpose is to influence or to bring influence to bear upon competition in the framework of the MERCOSUR and consequently to influence trade between the [member states]'. These rules are clearly aimed at spillover effects with adverse impacts on competition and trade. Where the influence on competition is limited to a member's respective territory, the conduct in question falls within the exclusive competence of that member state.

Targeted conduct is clearly that which has the purpose or final effect of restricting, limiting, falsifying or distorting competition or access to the market, or which constitutes an abuse of the dominant position and the relevant goods and services market in the MERCOSUR framework *and* which affects inter-member trade. The protocol alerts market players that a wide range of conduct might be caught. Indeed, 17 different practices are listed, including price fixing, artificial market division, tying, preventing competitor access to raw materials, investment goods or technologies or distribution channels. Importantly, market success through efficiency is itself protected.

The protocol is applied by the Trade Commission of the MERCOSUR and by the Committee for the Defense of Competition (an inter-government body comprising those in each state responsible for the application of the protocol). The Committee can apply preventative measures, including the cessation of a practice subject to inquiry. Where differences regarding the application of procedures arise, an opinion can be requested from the MERCOSUR Trade Commission (comprising one member from each of the four states). If the MERCOSUR Trade Commission cannot reach a consensus the Common Market Group makes a ruling. Failing consensus in that Group, a member state could resort directly to MERCOSUR's Dispute Settlement Protocol.

Part of the protocol deals with cooperation and technical consultation between the national enforcement agencies — but it is noted that, at the time of writing, neither Paraguay nor Uruguay had competition-specific legislation or institutions, nor was there work-in-progress to this end.

Importantly, the protocol envisages an autonomous competition agency in each member country and the application of the law to all public and private enterprises.

The MERCOSUR Trade Commission, while taking into account the ruling or conclusions of the inter-government Committee, shall — in the absence of Committee consensus — make its own ruling and specify the sanctions to be applied by the relevant national enforcement authority.

Assuming adequate technical and other resources, the MERCOSUR protocol has the potential to pursue investigations of public or private practices with extra-territorial effects on competition and trade. Arguably, a MERCOSUR-wide view, particularly if it permeates national approaches to competition issues, would help avoid the spillover conduct within the region which is the target of the protocol.

The protocol itself is intended to be a force for a comprehensive convergence of approach to competition. Article 7 requires the member states to adopt, by the end of 1998:

> [c]ommon rules for the control of acts and contracts, of any kind, which may limit or in any way cause prejudice to free trade, or result in the domination of the relevant regional market of goods and services, including which result in economic concentration, with a view to preventing their possible anti-competitive effects in the framework of the MERCOSUR.

And Article 32 requires the states within two years of the protocol coming into force

> to draft joint standards and mechanisms which shall govern State aid which is susceptible to limit, restrict, falsify or distort competition and to affect [MERCOSUR] trade . . . To this end, progress made on the subject of public policies which distort competitiveness and the relevant standards of the WTO shall be taken into consideration . . .

Brazil's influence

It seems that the ultimate direction of MERCOSUR's approach to competition will depend largely on Brazil's influence. In 1994, that country expressly emphasized the protection of competition (as distinct from anti-trust) as an objective. This helps to explain why the competition theme seems to be developing well in the Latin American countries.

The key Brazilian agency, CADE (the Administrative Economic Protection Council), is described as both an advocate for competition and a consumer advocate (OAS, 1998b). However, 'the absence of a culture of competition' and 'the lack of coordination with other public policies' are recognized as important matters still to be dealt with. It is encouraging that CADE has been charged with finding ways to coordinate its activities with the rest of government. Obstacles to be overcome explicitly include the lack of coordination between CADE and government policies on industry, foreign trade and privatization; the tension between industry restructuring and concentration; the relevance of tariff and non-tariff barriers to any assessment of damage from concentration or alleged anti-competitive conduct; and the need for CADE to be a more active participant in the process of privatization where infrastructure and strategic inputs can raise competition problems.

Thus it appears that Brazil has the potential to exercise leadership both within MERCOSUR and in any other trading arrangements to which it becomes a party, in respect of a coherent approach to the promotion of competition.

It is noteworthy that Brazil's report on competition policy and laws in 1994—96 (OAS, 1998b) highlights the following: '[N]o international agreement has focused on harmonizing or developing *principles* related to the defense of competition' (emphasis added). The report goes on to say: 'At any rate, it is becoming necessary to replace anti-dumping provisions with harmonized competition laws.'

Andean Community

Reflecting a growing market orientation, the five Presidents of the Andean Community promulgated the Commission of the Cartagena Agreement (Decision 285) in 1991.[5] This created common rules 'for the prevention or correction of distortions in competition caused by practices that restrict the competition'. According to the OAS, this Decision was the first attempt in Latin America to address competition issues at a regional level[6] even though at the time Colombia was the only member with a national competition law.

Several features are worthy of comment:

(a)　　The emphasis is expressly on distortions/restrictions to competition but only in so far as these would undermine the integration process in the Andean Community. However, the Decision is littered with the language of 'damage or imminent damage to production or exports' and the 'cause and effects between the practices and the damage or imminent damage'. So, in fact, the analytical framework seems more akin to anti-dumping actions and to the issue of nullification and impairment than to competition in a relevant market.

(b)　　The relevant Board has supranational authority in respect of regional practices, that is practices of companies that engage in economic activity in one or more of the member countries.

(c)　　However, the relevant authority cannot initiate its own investigations; these have to be requested by either member countries or companies which have a 'legitimate interest'.

(d)　　A remedy to apply preferential tariffs to affected imported products targets the injury rather than the practice(s) that caused it.

While it seems doubtful that this initiative of the Andean Community has promoted competition in the region it may well have stimulated members, notably Peru and Venezuela, to adopt a national approach to the promotion of 'free competition': 'enabling private initiative to develop in ways that yield the greatest benefits for users and consumers' (OAS, 1998a). Peru's Commission on Free Competition is also specifically charged with monitoring the taxation practices of municipalities to ensure that they do not create public restrictions to trade in goods and services as, for example, in the case of licensing fees for announcements and advertisements. The Commission has also been closely involved with the privatization process.

The Commission is described as a 'technically administratively independent agency' of Peru's INDECOPI, the National Institute for the Protection of Free Competition and Intellectual Property, whose responsibilities include anti-dumping and countervailing duties, technical barriers, intellectual property rights and economic deregulation. This structure seems to provide an excellent basis for developing a coherent approach to the promotion of competition.

FTAA

Declarations and principles

The First Summit of the Americas in 1994 culminated in the signing by the leaders of 34 countries of the Miami Declaration of Principles and Plan of Action. This is seen as a broad social and economic agenda aimed at raising living standards, improving working conditions and better protecting the environment. Differences in the size and level of development of participating economies would be taken into account. The Second Summit in April 1998 formally launched negotiations for a free trade agreement by 2005 with concrete progress by 2000.

The Leaders' Declaration at the Second Summit of the Americas (1998b) noted 'real economic benefits in the Americas resulting from more open trade, transparency in economic regulations, sound, market-based economic policies, as well as efforts by the private sector to increase its competitiveness'.

The ultimate aim of the proposed Free Trade Area of the Americas and its broad work agenda are set against what has occurred over the past decade in terms of macroeconomic reforms, more open trade policies and the creation of market conditions more attractive to private investment. Statements emphasize cooperative efforts to promote prosperity through increased economic integration and more open economies.

Trade ministers at their first Western Hemisphere Trade Ministerial Meeting in mid-1995 agreed that the FTAA will be a 'single undertaking' comprising mutual rights and obligations; ultimately all countries will assume all of the obligations of the FTAA, with no 'free-riders'.

It was also agreed that the FTAA would be comprehensive and WTO-consistent, meaning that WTO obligations would become the baseline for future negotiations. However, one of the general principles for guiding the FTAA negotiations is to improve, wherever possible and appropriate, on WTO rules and disciplines. The US, at least, holds the view that negotiations should aim to go beyond WTO obligations.

Because FTAA is envisaged as a free trade area, the framework is to be governed by the language of agreements, rules and obligations. Common rules are seen as a way of harmonizing and locking in market-opening measures, especially given the agreed guiding principle that all member countries 'shall ensure that their laws, regulations and administrative procedures conform to their obligations under the FTAA agreement'.

It appears that, like APEC, proponents of the FTAA see leadership at a regional level as a way of influencing multilateral agreements. But there is an important underlying assumption: that it would be appropriate for the WTO to have comprehensive and agreed rules in all the new areas.

FTAA working groups

Ministers responsible for trade, meeting between 1995 and 1997, established 12 FTAA working groups:

- Market Access;
- Investment;
- Services;
- Government Procurement;
- Dispute Settlement;

- Intellectual Property Rights;
- Subsidies, Anti-dumping and Countervailing Duties;
- Competition Policy;
- Standards and Technical Barriers to Trade;
- Customs Procedures and Rules of Origin;
- Smaller Economies;
- Sanitary and Phytosanitary Measures.

Under the auspices of a vice-ministerial trade negotiations committee (TNC), the first eight of these groups plus Agriculture (to which the objectives of the Market Access group also apply) became negotiating groups[7] at the San Jose Trade Ministerial Meeting in March 1998. Their work is to commence no later than September 1998.

One thing is apparent from the list of FTAA working and negotiating groups: they are broad in scope and are centred around policy areas of significance for competition in markets, even if not explicitly so. Thus it seems likely that the explicit 'Competition Policy' label assigned to one of the groups will be narrowly defined to cover anti-competitive commercial conduct.

Competition policy

The 18 countries attending the second meeting of that working group charged the chair with the preparation of a preliminary discussion draft on convergence and divergence in respect of internal laws and regulations relating to business practices. Clearly, the group also saw the need to be informed about the latest developments in competition policy in international bodies, such as the WTO and OECD.

Objectives of the Competition Policy negotiations are:

a. General objectives:
  - to guarantee that the benefits of the FTAA liberalization process not be undermined by anti-competitive business practices.
b. Specific objectives:
  - to advance towards the establishment of juridical and institutional coverage at the national, sub-regional or regional level, that proscribes the carrying out of anti-competitive business practices;
  - to develop mechanisms that facilitate and promote the development of competition policy and guarantee the enforcement of regulations on free competition among and within countries of the Hemisphere. (Ministerial Declaration of San Jose Summit of the Americas, 1998, p. 9)

The general objective is very much in line with the general rationale adopted internationally for prohibiting anti-competitive business practices in globalizing markets. Use of the word 'guarantee' could reflect a special determination to ensure effective enforcement. The enforcement point is picked up in the second of the specific objectives, both in respect of intra-national and inter-national competition. The first objective is interesting in that it contemplates the possibility that the focus might be at the national, sub-regional or regional level:

> A crucial issue [for smaller economies] would be the implementation of technical assistance and cooperation programs. These could be designed to support national efforts in the sphere of competition policy, including the design of national legislation and the establishment of adequate enforcement agencies. (OAS, 1997)

What is important is the apparent link between the liberalization process (the means) and 'free competition' (the desired outcome but itself a means to achieving the broader social and economic agenda). The liberalization process is to be stimulated by a number of government initiated measures, including:

- the progressive elimination of tariffs and non-tariff barriers as well as other measures with equivalent effects which restrict trade between participating countries (Market Access);
- the establishment of a 'fair and transparent legal framework' with emphasis on a stable and predictable investment environment; protection of investors and investments; avoidance of creating obstacles to investments from outside the FTAA (Investment);
- the examination of ways to deepen, if appropriate, existing WTO disciplines on subsidies and countervailing measures; and the improvement, where possible, of the rules and procedures regarding the operation and application of trade remedy laws in order to avoid creating unjustified barriers to trade in the hemisphere (Subsidies, Anti-dumping and Countervailing Duties);
- the achievement of a normative framework that ensures openness and transparency of government procurement processes (Government Procurement);
- the promotion of adequate and effective protection of intellectual property rights, taking changes in technology into account (Intellectual Property Rights);
- the establishment of disciplines to progressively liberalize services trade (Services).

The way in which these government measures are expressed has helped to shape a comprehensive competition framework for guiding the various negotiating processes. Both facilitation and liberalization are envisaged. There is alertness to the risk that a free trade area could itself raise barriers to others, for example through rules of origin and investment rules. A guiding set of competition principles would not only give added support to this developing competition framework but also increase the coherence of the negotiating processes as they develop through the various negotiating groups.

While the emphasis of the Competition Policy group is on anti-competitive business practices, the group's terms of reference do not prejudge the best means for addressing these. In other words, it seems to leave open the possibility that either or both general competition laws and industry-specific regulations may be appropriate.

On the issue of policy coherence it is noteworthy that the ministers responsible for trade — both in the main text of their March 1998 Ministerial Declaration and in Annexe II, 'Objective by Issue Area', attached to it — said the following:

> Work in different groups may be interrelated, such as agriculture and market access; services[8] and investment; competition policy and subsidies, antidumping and countervailing duties; among others. The [Trade Negotiations Committee] shall identify linkages and outline appropriate procedures to ensure timely and effective coordination. We agree to give the mandate to the relevant negotiating groups to study issues relating to: the interaction between trade and competition policy, including antidumping measures; market access and agriculture; in order to identify any areas that may merit further consideration by us.

The 1998 statement went on to say: 'The groups involved will report their results to the [Trade Negotiations Committee] no later than December 2000. This is without prejudice to decisions made by the TNC to dissolve, establish or merge groups. Likewise, the negotiating groups may establish ad-hoc working groups.'

Thus, it seems that the decision to establish the TNC at vice-ministerial level, with the ministers responsible for trade exercising ultimate oversight and management of the negotiations, could be instrumental in building a coherent competition framework. Certainly, the list of illustrative linkages — which, to the ministers' credit, did not avoid mention of anti-dumping — is welcome. But it also highlights the need for competition principles to guide what undoubtedly will be some contentious coordination issues. In the absence of some linking principles it will be even more difficult to forge the linkages that ministers have had the foresight to highlight, even if only in a preliminary way.

The FTAA principle of a 'single undertaking' with negotiations leading to a single comprehensive agreement to which each country will be committed, as distinct from separate sectoral agreements, is of particular significance here. Comprehensiveness itself will help to promote a coherent approach.

Observations on the Americas

Responses from the various regional groupings in the Americas to the competition dimension of policy have been diverse. Tavares and Tineo (forthcoming) pose the question of how 'conditions of competition' in the hemisphere can be harmonized while preserving the variety of policy approaches. There appear to be two main groups in terms of their approaches, as stated in the articles dealing with 'competition policy'. One group involves the NAFTA countries, that is the countries in NAFTA itself and those in the Canada—Chile Free Trade Agreement and G-3. The other group involves the MERCOSUR and ANDEAN Community countries.

The first group is most remarkable for its narrow conception of 'competition policy' as contained in their agreements. NAFTA and the Canada—Chile Agreement require a competition law in each member country. The specific provisions of these agreeements refer only to monopolies and state trading enterprises. None of these three agreements has created a supranational authority. The focus instead is on national responsibilities. The NAFTA and Canada—Chile agreements expressly rule out recourse to their dispute settlement procedures in respect of matters covered by the competition law section of the relevant chapters. It should be noted, however, that there is a provision in the Canada—Chile Agreement which abolishes anti-dumping actions on trade between the two countries.

The competition provisions of the MERCOSUR and Andean agreements are more explicit in terms of their coverage of conduct. This may be due to the fact that they are developing countries which do not have a long tradition of competition law and its enforcement. They could well prove useful for guiding competition approaches in developing economies. It is pleasing to see explicit recognition in MERCOSUR's Protocol of the role that efficiency can play in 'market conquest' (Article 5). This reduces the risk that increasing trade becomes a superior objective to efficiently functioning markets, whereas the link between competition and trade is thematic throughout the OAS work for the FTAA Working Group on Competition Policy. Both the Andean Decision and the MERCOSUR Protocol appear to contain supranational elements. However, the powers are unclear and untested.

It is perhaps surprising that the formal brief of the FTAA's working group on Competition Policy seems so narrow. In part, this possibly reflects the US position but also the hemisphere's relative inexperience outside Canada and the US of competition-driven policy instruments. Indeed, over half of the FTAA's potential members have no competition law or institution.

In reviewing the extensive work of the FTAA's working group on Competition Policy, it is a very healthy sign that the emphasis is on the promotion of competition generally rather than on anti-trust with its emphasis on private conduct and structures. The seeds have been sown for a coherent approach to competition in markets that are being deregulated, opened to international competition and privatized. While a culture of competition is some distance away, the competition frameworks that are evolving spark confidence that comprehensiveness and coherence are important beginnings. We believe that competition principles would further facilitate this directional shift and guide the resolution of policy conflicts that will inevitably be encountered on the way. The 1998 Ministerial Declaration features prominently the possible importance of linkages between different elements of the FTAA's work programme. In the short term it is not so much a matter of operationalizing these linkages but, rather, of identifying them; assessing the possible implications of pursuing them; and adopting competition principles for addressing them.

Tavares (1995) argues that both the FTAA and the multilateral trade agenda generate strong pressures for the convergence of public policies in Latin America. Tavares and Tineo (1998) suggest that the main problem for competition agencies in Latin America is coping with inconsistent government actions.

Notes

1. According to the US Department of Commerce, Bureau of the Census, South-Central America traded $63,034 million of exports and $53,666 million of imports in 1997; and North America $221,503 million of exports and $253,880 million of imports in the same period.
2. This disrègards the Magna Carta and early English Common Law, which some legal historians regard as the first competition law.
3. In the EU, Jacquemin (1993, p. 95) adopts a similar view.
4. Treaty on Free Trade of the Group of Three between the Republic of Colombia, the United Mexican States and the Republic of Venezuela (G-3) (1994); Chapter XVI: Policy regarding State Enterprises.
5. Decision 285: Norms for the Prevention or Correction of Distortions in Competition caused by Practices that Restrict Free Competition (1991).
6. The term 'regional' is used throughout this book in the WTO sense, that is, a free trade area or customs union among a group of countries. The OAS regards the whole of Latin America as a region and calls trading arrangements within this area 'sub-regional arrangements'.
7. The chairman and vice-chairman of each group will reflect geographic balance and the desirability of rotation each 18 months. Peru, which chaired the Competition Policy working group, is to be the first chair of the Competition Policy negotiating group, with Trinidad and Tobago as vice-chair.
8. At an early stage, the working group on Trade and Services undertook to keep its relationship with other working groups, including Investment, to the fore.

PART FOUR

Plurilateral Approaches

7. ITO, the GATT 1960 Decision and the United Nations

Independently of the OECD, plurilateral attempts to deal with international competition problems have been developed in three international organizations: GATT, the United Nations Economic and Social Council (ECOSOC) and the United Nations Conference on Trade and Development (UNCTAD).

ITO and the GATT 1960 Decision

The GATT Decision has a curious history. The GATT came into existence because of the failure of the International Trade Organization to be ratified by some of the participants in the negotiations in Havana in 1946 and 1947, chiefly the US. The GATT was based on the Chapter on Commercial Policy of the Havana Charter, and throughout its life it only applied provisionally. The ITO Charter contained another chapter: Chapter V on Restrictive Business Practices. If it had been ratified, the Charter would have regulated international trade and restrictive business practices under one agreement and administered the regulation through one organization, which would have changed the evolution of laws relating to international trade and competition. Despite its non-ratification, these provisions of the ITO have influenced the approach of the GATT (and other international organizations) to issues relating to international trade and competition.

Chapter V contained nine articles setting out the obligations of member governments to address restrictive business practices. The purpose of these provisions was defined as:

> to prevent, on the part of private or commercial public enterprises business practices affecting international trade which restrain competition, limit access to markets, or foster monopolistic control, whenever such practices have harmful effects on the expansion of production or trade and interfere with the achievement of any of the objectives [of the Charter].

The Chapter specified six practices that were considered to have harmful effects on production and trade when applied by an enterprise with effective control of trade and made provision for other practices to be added by agreement. These were:

(a) fixing prices, terms or conditions to be observed in dealing with others in the purchase or lease of any product;

(b) excluding enterprises from, or allocating or dividing, any territorial market or field of business activity, or allocating customers, or fixing quotas or purchase quotas;

(c) discriminating against particular enterprises;

(d) limiting production or fixing production quotas;

(e) preventing by agreement the development or application of technology or invention whether patented or unpatented; and

(f) extending the use of rights under patents, trade marks or copyrights granted by a member to matters which, according to its laws and regulations, are not within the scope of such grants, or to products or conditions of production, use or sale of which are likewise not the subject of such grants.

All of the listed practices related to horizontal restraints, including price fixing and market allocation, and two related to intellectual property rights restrictions. Although the main concern was with the effects of these practices on international trade, not with competition, and although the list did not include vertical restraints or mergers, the draft agreement was very far-reaching.

As a remnant of the Havana negotiations, the GATT did contain Article XXIX, 'Relation of this Agreement to the Havana Charter'. In the expectation that the Havana Charter would be ratified in the future, this Article states that 'contracting parties undertake to observe to the fullest extent of their executive authority the general principles of Chapters I to VI inclusive and of Chapter IX of the Havana Charter pending their acceptance of it in accordance with their constitutional procedures'. When it became clear that the Charter would not be ratified, a proposal to delete Article XXIX was adopted unanimously by the GATT. However, the failure of one contracting party to ratify the change to the General Agreement led to the continued inclusion of the Article in the text of the GATT, and it is still there today.

The Contracting Parties established a Group of Experts in 1958 to study whether and to what extent the GATT should deal with restrictive business practices. In their 1960 Report (GATT, 1961, pp. 170—79), the group was unable to reach a consensus. A majority considered that it would be unrealistic to recommend a multilateral agreement to control international restrictive business practices. However, they recognized that these practices could have a harmful effect on international trade and suggested that the best course was to encourage bilateral consultations between interested parties on specific practices upon request. The suggested procedure was to keep this outside the dispute settlement procedures laid down in Article XXIII. A minority proposed a multilateralized procedure to address restrictive business practice issues. A group of experts would deal with those issues that could not be settled bilaterally and would submit a report to the GATT Secretariat which would report annually to the Contracting Parties. This division is a forerunner of the division between those who have subsequently advocated a multilateral competition law in the GATT or WTO and those who prefer bilateral or plurilateral cooperation and discussion.

After considering the report of the Group of Experts, the Contracting Parties reached a decision in 1960. This is known as the Decision on Arrangements for Consultations on Restrictive Business Practices (GATT, 1961, pp. 28—29). This Decision recognized that business practices which restrict competition may restrict international trade in goods and thereby deny the benefits of tariff reductions and the removal of non-tariff barriers or frustrate other objectives of the General Agreement. It also recognized that international cooperation is needed to resolve complaints relating to such practices.

To deal with these problems, the Decision recommends that, at the request of any Contracting Party, a Contracting Party should enter into consultations on restrictive practices which harm international trade on a bilateral or many-country basis as appropriate. The party addressed should accord sympathetic consideration to the request with a view to reaching mutually satisfactory conclusions and, if it agrees, should take such measures as it deems appropriate to eliminate the harmful effects. The GATT Secretariat was to be advised of the outcome of the consultations by the Contracting Parties.

In terms of the analytical framework put forward in Chapter 2, it should be noted that these provisions relate to the business practices themselves. The source of the complaint does not have to be attributed to a government measure, as in the case of non-violation complaints coming before the Dispute Settlement Procedures of the WTO. As with other GATT rules and activities, these provisions are concerned with the effects of these practices on international trade rather than with competition and efficiency.

These consultation provisions have been invoked only three times, all relating to alleged restrictions on trade with Japan in photographic film and paper (see Chapter 12). Ironically, these cases were part of the grounds for complaints under the Dispute Settlement Procedures of the WTO.

ECOSOC and UNCTAD

After the failed attempt in the ITO, the first attempt to develop a plurilateral agreement relating to what is now called competition law was that of the United Nations ECOSOC. During the 1950s, there were efforts to deal with restrictive business practices at the Council. ECOSOC's Ad Hoc Committee on Restrictive Business Practices proposed an international code largely based on Chapter V of the Havana Charter. The proposal did not obtain sufficient support from member countries to enter into force. The UNCTAD attempt was partly a rival of the OECD Guidelines as it was designed to protect the interests of the developing countries.

In 1980, after almost ten years of negotiations, agreement was reached in UNCTAD on a plurilateral code of conduct relating to competition and international trade. This is known as the Set of Multilaterally Agreed Equitable Principles and Rules for the Control of Restrictive Business Practices (hereafter referred to as the UN Set); it is published in United Nations (1981). The United Nations General Assembly passed Resolution 35/63 in December 1980 which incorporated the UN Set.

In terms of our classification, the UN Set is a plurilateral agreement, as it is not binding on members of the UN. In terms of its coverage, it is an agreement which seeks to regulate private conduct and to provide a consultation mechanism; but UNCTAD has also sought to harmonize national legislation by developing a model law.

The UN Set follows the GATT in its objectives. The first objective is to ensure that restrictive business practices do not impede or negate the realization of benefits that should arise from the liberalization of tariffs and non-tariff barriers affecting world trade. It is primarily concerned with practices which affect the international trade and development of developing countries. It also seeks to achieve greater efficiency in international trade and development through the promotion of competition in markets, the control of concentration of economic power and the development of innovation, and to protect the interests of consumers.

The UN Set defines restrictive business practices to include acts or behaviour of enterprises which, through an abuse of dominant position, limit access to markets or otherwise unduly restrain competition. It lists some practices which enterprises should refrain from if they restrain competition:

(a) agreements fixing prices, including as to exports and imports;
(a) collusive tendering;
(c) market or customer allocation arrangements;
(d) allocation by quota as to sales and production;
(e) collective action to enforce arrangements, e.g. by concerted refusals to deal;
(f) concerted refusal of supplies to potential importers;
(g) collective denial of access to an arrangement, or association, which is crucial to competition.

In addition, the UN Set provides that enterprises should refrain from abusing a dominant position or otherwise unduly restraining competition by certain acts. These include:

(a) predatory behaviour towards competitors, such as using below-cost pricing to eliminate competitors;
(b) discriminatory (i.e. unjustifiably differentiated) pricing or terms or conditions in the supply or purchase of goods and services, including by means of the use of pricing policies in transactions between affiliated

enterprises which overcharge or undercharge for goods or services purchased or supplied as compared with prices for similar or comparable transactions outside the affiliated enteprises;

(c) mergers, takeovers, joint enterprises or other acquisitions of control, whether of a horizontal, vertical or conglomerate nature;

(d) fixing the prices at which goods exported can be resold in importing countries;

(e) restrictions on the importation of goods which have been legitimately marked abroad with a trademark identical with or similar to the trademark protected as to identical or similar goods in the importing country where the trademarks in question are of the same origin;

(f) when not for ensuring the achievement of legitimate business purposes, such as quality, safety, adequate distribution or service: (i) partial or complete refusal to deal on the enterprise's customary commercial terms; (ii) making the supply of particular goods or services dependent upon the acceptance of restrictions on the distribution or manufacture of competing or other goods; (iii) imposing retrictions concerning where, or to whom, or in what form or quantities, goods supplied or other goods may be sold or exported; (iv) making the supply of particular goods or services dependent upon the purchase of other goods or services from the supplier or his designee. (UN, 1981)

Vertical and horizontal restraints as well as mergers are part of this list which is the most detailed and comprehensive list of restrictive practices or conduct in plurilateral and multilateral agreements (cf. the lists for OECD the ITO and the GATT/WTO).

Section D, addressed to enterprises, calls for them to conform to the laws relating to restrictive business practices of the countries in which they operate and to refrain from the restrictive business practices which are listed in the Set.

Section E, addressed to the governments of the states, calls for the adoption and effective enforcement of appropriate national competition legislation and the implementing of judicial and administrative procedures. Section E also calls for exchange of information and cooperation in proceedings, subject to confidentiality safeguards. Section F provides for consultation procedures and technical cooperation for developing countries.

In terms of the policy framework put forward in Chapter 2 to evaluate each policy option, the UN Set follows the GATT Decision in being concerned with private conduct in all markets, and it follows the GATT and the GATT 1960 Decision in its trade objective. The UN Set tends to be more negative in its view of corporate behaviour, reflecting the ethos in UNCTAD at a time in which the multinational corporation in particular was viewed as an agent of production which was often in a dominant position and able to use its multinationality to reduce the benefits of foreign investment to recipient countries, especially developing countries.

The UN Set has had little influence on the conduct of enterprises or the evolution of international competition law. Its main contribution has been as a form of competition advocacy among the developing countries which has encouraged them to develop their own national competition legislation.

There is a sequel to the UNCTAD story. The former United Nations Commission on Transnational Corporations (UNCTC) (which is now a part of UNCTAD) attempted in the late 1980s to develop a United Nations Code on Transnational Corporations which would have reinforced the UN Set. The members could not agree on a final document. A report by the UNCTC noted that 'many of the concluded provisions of the proposed Code are markedly relevant to trade issues, especially in the area of trade in services' and that 'many of the issues involved in the Uruguay Round have been for years under negotiation in the Code exercise, and that some degree of consensus has been reached on them' (UNCTC, 1990, pp. 46—49).

8. OECD

The OECD has been the most active of all the international organizations in the field of international dimensions of competition policy. Its activities have ranged widely from the advocacy of a national competition policy in member countries (and non-member countries under technical assistance programmes) and the promotion of convergence among these national policies to recommendations relating to bilateral cooperation and to the development of plurilateral guidelines. This chapter reviews these activities. (A review of many of them by the OECD itself is provided in its Communication to the WTO Working Group (WTO, 1998f) and in the OECD Competition/Antitrust Policy Home Page at www.oecd.org/daf/ccp.)

Competition Policy in the OECD

Since its establishment the OECD has played a central role in encouraging governments to liberalize flows of FDI. The 1961 Code of Liberalization of Capital Movements and the Code of Liberalization of Current Invisible Operations were the first international (plurilateral) code for regulation of direct capital movements by governments. It has also promoted regulatory reform for the past 20 years and now has an organization-wide programme on deregulation.

From its inception, the OECD Committee of Experts on Restrictive Business Practices (renamed in 1987 the Committee on Competition Law and Policy, or CLP Committee for short) has provided a forum for the exchange of experiences of OECD member countries and insights from the member countries which are most experienced in competition law. The CLP Committee has worked on a broad range of issues concerning competition in member countries. These include examination of various business practices or business conduct. The Trade Committee has considered a number of features at the interface between international trade and competition.

The emphasis in recent years in the CLP Committee has been on the promotion of competition, including deregulation and liberalization of trade and foreign investment, as well as competition law. It has a Working Party on Regulatory Reform.

In the area of competition law, its work covers mergers and restraints which give rise to reduced competition as well as market abuses through monopolization and cartel action, such as market sharing and price fixing. The OECD favours 'adequate' or 'sound' competition rules rather than rigid minimum standards of behaviour. As it is frequently unclear how individual business conduct affects market competition, the OECD favours examination on a case-by-case basis, especially in relation to vertical restraints. It was for these reasons that the Committee abandoned the term 'restrictive trade practices' in its title. As an example, the CLP Committee focuses on the concept of predatory pricing and its harmful effects on the degree of competition, rather than on the trade law concept of dumping with its emphasis on injury to other competitors, and it has found that claims of predatory pricing are often unfounded (WTO, 1998f, II (c)). The OECD has been pressing members to reduce the number of exemptions in their national laws and it emphasizes the necessity of strong enforcement of these laws.

The work of the CLP Committeee has led to OECD Council Recommendations concerning cooperation between national law enforcement authorities and the avoidance of potential conflict between international trade and competition policies and other aspects of the international dimension of competition policy. The work of the CLP Committee and the Trade Committee has examined issues at the interface between international trade and competition policies. These areas are reviewed in the next two sections.

The OECD Recommendations for Bilateral Cooperation

The first efforts of the OECD in the area of international dimensions of competition policy were recommendations for bilateral cooperation in competition law enforcement. A series of OECD Council Recommendations concerning bilateral cooperation on anti-competitive practices affecting international trade were adopted in 1967, 1973, 1979, 1986 and 1995 (hereafter referred to as the OECD Recommendations). The revised 1995 Recommendations are reproduced in WTO (1998f, Annex IV).

These recommendations specify notification and consultation and cooperation procedures. Provisions referring to consultation and cooperation concern consultation and cooperation both between governments and between a government and enterprises. Recommendations are adopted by the OECD Council. While they are not legally binding, there is an expectation that member countries will move towards their implementation.

The instrument adopted in 1995 covers:

- notification of investigations to member countries whose interests may be affected;
- coordination of actions when two or more member countries proceed against the same anti-competitive practice, in so far as appropriate and practicable;

- cooperation in developing or applying mutually satisfactory and beneficial measures for dealing with anti-competitive practices in international trade and, to that effect, supplying each other with relevant information;
- consultations when a country considers that an investigation by another country may affect its important interests, or when enterprises situated in another member country have engaged in anti-competitive practices that substantially affect its interests; and
- commitment by the member country addressed to whatever remedial action it considers appropriate.

The Recommendations also set out detailed guiding principles for the implementation of notifications, exchanges of information, cooperation in investigations, proceedings and consultations. They recommend that these principles be taken into account in bilateral agreements for cooperation in the enforcement of national competition laws.

The Recommendations enjoin a member country addressed by another member country to give 'full and sympathetic consideration' to such views and factual materials as may be provided by the requesting country. But the Recommendations also recognize that there are restrictions on the information which the member country addressed may be able to disclose under its domestic laws, that the member countries will have to consider their own national interests, and that the coordination of action and consultation is on a voluntary basis.

These Recommendations have played an important part in the development of bilateral agreements on competition law and law enforcement. The 1967 Recommendation appears to be the origin of the principle of positive comity.

The International Dimensions of the OECD Competition Policy

As early as May 1982, OECD Ministers called for work to examine possible longer-term approaches for developing an international framework to deal with problems arising from the interface of competition and trade policies. The CLP Committee has a Working Party on International Competition Policy and there is a Joint Group on Trade and Competition which combines representatives of the CLP Committee and the OECD Trade Committee.

The Committee on Restrictive Business Practices and the CLP Committee have produced a series of monographs (for example, OECD, 1984a and b, 1996a and b) and round-table papers on issues at the interface between international trade and competition policies. These develop a comprehensive, if sometimes bland, view of the international dimensions of competition policy. Apart from the abortive attempts to incorporate discipline on restrictive business practices in the ITO in 1947, in the United Nations Economic and Social Council during the 1950s and in the 1960 report of the Group of Experts appointed by the GATT (see Chapter 7), this was the earliest work at the interface between competition and international trade policies.

The CLP Committee has surveyed trade policies which restrict competition and the operation of competition laws in international markets. The Committee has seen the interaction between trade and competition policies as one in which the liberalizing effects of lowering trade barriers and promoting competition reinforce each other. In recent years it has worked towards achieving greater coherence between trade and competition policies. It has reviewed international mergers and predatory pricing in international markets and has strongly condemned international cartels. Anti-competitive conduct should be evaluated on an economy-wide basis and the evaluation should consider the effects on both consumers and producers.

One part of this work was a convergence project whose aim was to promote the convergence of national competition laws among the members of the organization. The OECD prefers the term 'convergence' rather than harmonization. The convergence project produced an interim report in 1994 (OECD, 1994). The report found that there had been a substantial degree of convergence in member countries' competition laws in areas such as the objectives of the laws, analytical tools, enforcement practices and some areas of substantive law such as horizontal agreements and resale price maintenance; however, significant differences remained among the national laws with respect to the coverage of competition laws, the treatment of non-price vertical restraints, the abuse of dominance and monopolization, and merger review.

The convergence project has ceased but the general goal of convergence remains. Recently, in the CLP Committee and in the Joint Group on Trade and Competition, work has been devoted to developing a common cross-country approach to 'hard-core' cartels and to dominance and vertical restraints.

As a result of work done in the CLP Committee, the OECD Council has adopted a number of recommendations relating to the international dimensions of competition policy generally and competition law. In particular, in 1986 the OECD Council also adopted Recommendations for Cooperation between Member Countries in Areas of Potential Conflict between Trade and Competition Policies (reproduced in WTO, 1998f, Annex IV). These cover both trade policy measures which may adversely affect competition and competition laws which may adversely affect international trade. They advocate consultation and cooperation and transparency of laws. They also contain some specific recommendations, notably that governments should exercise care that proceedings under national laws dealing with anti-dumping action and countervailing duties are not misused for anti-competitive purposes, and that governments should not encourage the exercise of market power in foreign markets through the use of export cartels. These recommendations, like those relating to cooperation in competition law enforcement, are voluntary.

In 1978 the Council adopted Recommendations concerning Action against Restrictive Business Practices Affecting International Trade including those Involving Multinational Enterprises. Although restrictive business practices of multinational enterprises do not differ in form from those of purely national enterprises, they were considered important because of greater market power wielded by multinational enterprises. The aim is to prohibit or control restrictive business practices of multinational enterprises. They refer particularly to:

(a) actions adversely affecting competition in the relevant market by abusing a dominant position of market power by means of, for example:
   - anti-competitive acquisitions;
   - predatory behaviour towards competitors;
   - unreasonable refusal to deal;
   - anti-competitive abuse of industrial property rights;
   - discriminatory (i.e. unreasonably differentiated) pricing and using such pricing transactions between affiliated enterprises as a means of affecting adversely competition outside these enterprises;
(b) cartels or other restrictive agreements which without justification adversely affect or eliminate competition.

There are other Recommendations that relate to international dimensions of competition law or competition policy, at least in part. These include Recommendations concerning the Application of Competition Laws and Policy to Patent and Know-how Licensing Agreements, and those concerning Action against Restrictive Business Practices relating to the Use of Trademarks and Trademark Licences.

The latest Recommendations, adopted in March 1998, are the Recommendations Concerning Effective Action against Hard Core Cartels. These cartels are regarded as the single most harmful form of anti-competitive conduct. The Recommendations cover both domestic and international cartels. The term 'hard core' is applicable only to agreements among competitors or potential competitors and only to four specific categories of agreement. A hard-core cartel is defined as:

> An anticompetitive agreement, anticompetitive concerted practice, or anticompetitive arrangement by competitors to fix prices, make rigged bids (collusive tenders), establish output restrictions or quotas, or share or divide market by allocating customers, suppliers, territories, or lines of commerce.

The text encourages member countries to ensure that their competition laws effectively prevent hard-core cartels and it promotes international cooperation by positive comity in enforcing national laws prohibiting them. It asserts that most countries have a common interest in cooperating, but that they encourage cooperation only to the extent that such cooperation is consistent with a country's important interests, and the draft affirms a member country's right to decline to cooperate.

These OECD Recommendations are the first to define a particular type of anti-competitive conduct and recommend actions against it. No substantial progress has been made on developing a common approach to abuse of dominance or to vertical restraints. It is questionable whether a common approach can be developed in respect of particular forms of conduct because the boundary between pro-competitive and anti-competitive behaviour is typically unclear. The difficulties in dealing with them have been aggravated by major differences among the member countries in their approaches to competition laws in these areas. For example, the EU is disposed to seek a common approach in the OECD (and in the WTO) to abuse of dominance and vertical restraints whereas the US is not. There are also important differences in EU and US law in relation to particular items of business conduct such as boycotts. The rule of reason approach is being used more widely in place of *per se* prohibitions. This reflects the uncertainty as to how different forms of conduct affect competition and efficiency in markets.

Some members favour a more limited approach through the development of principles rather than the development of minimum standards relating to cartels, vertical restraints and mergers. This approach would be confined to general principles of transparency, non-discrimination and national treatment in competition law.

The Trade Committee has focused on new dimensions of market access, including the concept of international market contestability and regulatory reform issues from a trade perspective. As a background for possible future policy- and rules-making initiatives, the Committee has identified categories of private behaviour most likely to exert significant effects of market access and market presence:

> Exclusionary practices, predation and foreclosure effects stood out as issues deserving particular attention. Various types of vertical behaviour, particularly when engaged in firms with market power, were viewed as potentially restraining international competition and distort trade and investment flows. Such conduct includes, inter alia exclusive dealing arrangements, restrictions on pricing through resale pricing maintenance schemes, exclusive territory and tying arrangements. (WTO, 1998f, II (a))

This perspective presents these forms of conduct as trade-related issues. Implicitly, this uses trade maximization rather than welfare maximization as the objective function of policies.

Other Committees of the OECD have examined competition in international markets for maritime transport, international air transport and agro-food industries. These are sectors with a very high degree of domestic regulation and of barriers to free international trade. This sector-specific work has promoted international competition in these sectors and may assist multilateral agreements in these sectors which free international trade and domestic competition.

The current activities of the OECD Committees are substantially oriented towards the work programme of the WTO Working Group on the Interaction betwen International Trade and Competition.

The OECD Guidelines for Multinational Enterprises

The OECD has also developed Guidelines for Multinational Enterprises (hereafter referred to as OECD Guidelines) as an annex to the Declaration on International Investment and Multinational Enterprises (OECD, 1976). These Guidelines cover many aspects of multinational enterprises, including guidelines intended to avoid anti-competitive behaviour by these enterprises rather than by governments.

The OECD Guidelines list the conduct which is considered to restrict competition. Enterprises are enjoined to:

1. refrain from actions which would adversely affect competition in the relevant market by abusing a dominant position and market power, by means of, for example: (a) anticompetitive acquisitions: (b) predatory behaviour towards competition; (c) unreasonable refusal to deal; (d) anticompetitive abuse of industrial property rights; (e) discriminatory (i.e. unreasonably differentiated) pricing and using such pricing transactions between affiliated enterprises as a means of affecting adversely competition outside these enterprises;
2. allow purchasers, distributors and licensees freedom to resell, export, purchase and develop their operations consistent with law, trade conditions, the need for specialisation and sound commercial practice;
3. refrain from participating in or otherwise purposely strengthening the restrictive effects of international or domestic cartels or restrictive agreements which adversely affect or eliminate competition and which are not generally or specifically accepted under applicable national or international legislation . . . (OECD, 1976)

This list is illustrative but quite comprehensive. The emphasis is on preventing behaviour which would adversely affect competition rather than proscribing particular practices. The fourth paragraph, not quoted here, enjoins enterprises to consult and cooperate with competent authorities of countries whose interests are affected.

The Guidelines state explicitly that 'Observance of the guidelines is voluntary and not legally enforceable'. It appears that they have had little effect on enterprise behaviour.

In terms of the analytical framework adopted in Chapter 2, these Guidelines are framed with a desire to improve the efficiency in the global economy by reducing anti-competitive behaviour and they cover all markets but they are restricted to multi-national enterprises.

In summary, the work of the OECD in the area of 'competition policy' has had a major impact on both national competition law and multi-national mechanisms to deal with cross-border aspects of competition law. Its competition policy advocacy has encouraged the development of comprehensive national laws among members and non-members and it has sought to encourage convergence in their coverage and analysis. Member countries have a much better understanding of the positions of other nations. Since the Uruguay Round, the Trade Committee has been in the vanguard of the discussions on international contestability of markets (see OECD, 1995 and 1996b). On the other hand, much of the recent work of the OECD's CLP Committee and Trade Committee has focused on the 'new dimensions of market access'. This perspective tends to present competition issues as being trade-related and does not provide a sufficiently broad framework for the analysis of competition in globalizing markets.

9. APEC

The Institution

APEC was established in 1989 and now comprises 21 economies in the Asia-Pacific region. It is an inter-government forum fostering 'open regionalism' through consensus-driven economic cooperation. The Bogor Declaration, signed by APEC's Economic Leaders in 1994, gave formal expression to a goal of 'free and open trade and investment' by 2010 and 2020 for developed and developing economies respectively.

Economic cooperation within APEC is voluntary; therefore, progress towards agreed goals relies on the peer pressure of governments and on the habit of extensive consultation, information exchange and consensus-building. Much will also depend on the extent to which producers and consumers support and actively encourage the process.

The essence and distinguishing feature of APEC is found in its concept of concerted unilateralism which embodies the collective commitment to trade and investment liberalization within specified time-frames, while allowing for flexibility of response by member economies depending on their stage of development and national priorities. Concerted unilateralism provides opportunities for leadership; and it is a powerful point that unilateral market-opening actions by governments give less scope for others to run protectionist arguments.

Whatever APEC achieves in the long term, it will not be as a result of binding rules and negotiated concessions; nor is APEC dependent on the US President securing fast-track negotiating authority from Congress. Rather, APEC's achievements will depend upon a perceived mutuality of interest in cooperating towards transparent, comprehensive and non-discriminatory strategies for enlarging markets in a contestable way. Such mutuality of interest implies that national welfare considerations might sometimes have to give way to global welfare considerations.

Action Plans

Policy coherence

At their Osaka Meeting in December 1995, APEC's Economic Leaders adopted an Action Plan. This included action in 15 specific areas, of which competition policy was one. As an on-going exercise, APEC members are developing both a Collective Action Plan (CAP) and Individual Action

Plans (IAPs) covering these areas. If momentum can be maintained, this exercise will contribute to transparency of policy and purpose and also form a basis for monitoring progress towards agreed goals.

There is a risk, however, of too much policy fragmentation and, as a consequence, the obscuring of important policy linkages: for example, between services and investment; anti-dumping and competition; government procurement and competition; intellectual property and competition. Policy coherence will be an essential ingredient for real progress in APEC's liberalization agenda. This is in line with widespread calls, prompted by the financial crisis in Asia, for greater coherence between financial, trade and investment policies.

APEC's Committee on Trade and Investment (CTI) in February 1996 noted the central role of 'competition policy' in enhancing economic efficiency and that the globalization of business was creating new challenges for this policy area. At the same time, it agreed to merge the work areas of competition policy and law and deregulation in view of the linkages between them. While the Action Plans for the two areas remain separate, this was a very positive move by the CTI towards greater policy coherence — given the role that deregulation can play in reducing government barriers to competition as markets enlarge.

APEC will need to focus on how various policy areas can be better linked with the objective of promoting more open and efficient markets; for example, investment (with its current emphasis on implementing further liberalization of investment regimes of member economies); government procurement (transparency and non-binding principles); services (national treatment); standards and conformance (mutual recognition and transparency).

Greater policy coherence is likely to be required for any substantive progress towards realizing APEC's ambitious goals. A set of agreed competition principles would be invaluable as a unifying influence on policy development via the Action Plans. The process of concerted unilateralism lends itself to the adoption of non-binding competition, regulatory (and other) principles — collectively endorsed by the Leaders as a stimulus to progress and operationalized by individual member economies in the spirit of economic cooperation.

The competition policy area

APEC's initial interest in competition policy was stimulated by the view that this was one of the new trade-related issues. An effective competition policy (not defined) was perceived to be a support mechanism for trade liberalization and for the opening of markets in the Asia-Pacific region. There has also been interest in some APEC economies: in the elimination of anti-dumping remedies or in the application of a competition standard to anti-dumping rules; in the possibility of minimum competition standards, for example, the prohibition of 'hard-core' cartels; inter-agency cooperation on technical training and information exchange; and also cross-border convergence of both substantial and procedural provisions of national competition laws (covering business acquisitions as well as restrictive business practices).

The competition policy area of APEC's CAP encourages cooperation among the competition authorities (where they exist) with regard to notification, information exchange and consultation. It also encourages examination of the interrelationships between competition policies and laws and other policies related to trade and investment. The interrelationship between competition policy and/or laws and other policies related to trade and investment was on the Competition Workshop agenda of the Committee on Trade and Investment (CTI) in 1997. Competition and deregulation were centre stage in the following year: and it is hoped that CTI's proposed Trade Policy Dialogue on anti-dumping will serve to highlight the linkages between this trade policy instrument and competition objectives. The Trade Policy Dialogue allows an informal exchange of views 'as a useful means of broadening perspectives and sharing approaches on issues' (APEC, 1997b, p. 20). Indeed, a 'better appreciation by APEC officials of the broader policy context of competition law' is one of the expected benefits from pursuing the short-term deliverable outcome of competition policy seminars for APEC officials. Perhaps of most importance in the long run, the CAP asks members to consider developing non-binding principles on competition policy and laws in APEC.

Each Individual Action Plan originally revealed in Manila features a section on Competition Policy, with the following preamble:

Objective
APEC economies will enhance the competitive environment in the Asia-Pacific region by introducing or maintaining effective and adequate competition policy and/or laws and associated enforcement policies, ensuring the transparency of the above and promoting cooperation among APEC economies, thereby maximizing, *inter alia*, the efficient operation of markets, competition among producers and traders, and consumer benefits.

Guidelines
Each APEC economy will:
a. review its respective competition policy and/or laws and the enforcement thereof in terms of transparency;
b. implement as appropriate technical assistance in regard to policy development, legislative drafting, and the constitution, powers and functions of appropriate enforcement agencies; and
c. establish appropriate cooperation arrangements among APEC economies.

While the flavour of this preamble is predominantly legalistic, the ultimate objective of 'maximizing, *inter alia*, the efficient operation of markets, competition among producers and traders, and consumer benefits' is clearly not one that can be delivered by the enforcement of one policy instrument, namely competition law. This observation lends weight to the important reference in the Collective Action Plan to policy interrelationships.

The IAP's Competition Policy objective is also important for another reason: it is strongly oriented towards competition, efficiency and consumer welfare in globalizing markets. It is not simply trade-related.

The deregulation policy area

Each Individual Action Plan also features a separate section on deregulation, with the following preamble:

> Objective
> APEC economies will:
> a. promote the transparency of their respective regulatory regimes; and
> b. eliminate trade and investment distortion arising from domestic regulations which not only impede free and open trade and investment in the Asia-Pacific region but also are more trade and/or investment restricting than necessary to fulfil a legitimate objective.

This objective has more of a trade-related than a competition flavour. While APEC's CTI has recognized the interrelationship between the competition and deregulation policy areas in particular, this is not yet reflected in their respective objectives. The reason why deregulation is so important in the context of a trade and investment liberalization/facilitation agenda is because of its reinforcing role in promoting competition and efficiency in globalizing markets, not because of its role in maximizing trade and investment flows.

Key features of competition policy and deregulation areas of Individual Action Plans

The key features of the competition policy and deregulation areas of the APEC member economies' IAPs, contained in Manila's Action Plan for APEC (MAPA), are highlighted in Vautier and Lloyd (1997, App. IV). They reveal a range of views on what is encompassed by competition policy. New Zealand and the Philippines envisage the broadest scope, inclusive of competition law, in contrast to the United States IAP, which focuses on anti-trust laws alone.

While there are several references in the IAPs to the goal of more efficient markets, there is more frequent reference to free and fair competition and trade as well as to the problems of unethical trade and market concentration. The competition and efficiency welfare paradigm is not embedded, even in the competition policy area. So long as fairness and protection for producers remains a rationale for anti-dumping action and other policy actions that impact upon competition in markets, it will be harder to bring transnational competition issues within a competition—efficiency—welfare framework.

PECC (1997b), in commenting on the competition policy area of MAPA said:

> The fact that the 18 IAPs show wide variation in the Competition Policy area is no surprise. The Individual Action Plan process is designed to reveal such variation arising from differences in level of economic development; in degree of openness and market orientation; and in other circumstances which characterize member economies.

Bollard and Vautier (1998, Table 6.4) construct an index of similarity between the competition laws of pairs of countries taken from 11 APEC economies, including the US, Japan and China. The index of similarity covers the treatment of mergers, the unilateral behaviour of powerful firms, horizontal agreements, vertical restraints, exceptions and unfair (domestic) trading, as well as judicial and enforcement characteristics. This shows great variation among the indices for different pairs of APEC economies.

Importantly, PECC (1997b) added:

> But where variation reflects a lack of consensus over the objectives and scope of competition policy, and the role which competition policy can play in promoting APEC's overall objectives of trade and investment liberalization, this is more problematic. The present lack of consensus that exists in this regard greatly complicates the task of suggesting improvements to the Individual Action Plans.

For those economies with competition laws, some common elements emerge in the IAPS. For example:

- prohibitions on private anti-competitive conduct;
- competitive neutrality (including as between government and private business operations) through general applicability of rules; and
- utilities/natural monopolies as special cases.

A linkage is drawn between trade liberalization and more competitive domestic economies. Reference is made to securing effective benefits from the globalized economy, through competition policy. This links with the aim of eliminating trade and investment distortions (including those arising from anti-dumping actions).

As with competition policy, there is a range of views on the compass of the deregulation area and its links with competition. More noticeable than any linkage between deregulation and competition is that made between deregulation and trade/market access. Views of and commitments to deregulation seem to depend partly on the stage of economic development. Some IAPs make the link between domestic deregulation and the competitiveness of economies.

Table 9.1: Measures of similarity between country competition laws (scores in %)

	Australia	Canada	China	Chinese Taipei	Japan	Korea	Mexico	New Zealand	Philippines	Thailand	United States	Overall Index
Australia	0											42
Canada	67	0										43
China	17	17	0									19
Chinese Taipei	41	46	17	0								38
Japan	41	47	17	47	0							42
Korea	43	44	17	53	54	0						41
Mexico	47	50	17	31	41	41	0					37
New Zealand	77	70	17	53	53	56	59	0				47
Philippines	20	20	29	21	31	31	14	23	0			25
Thailand	17	16	21	26	29	27	23	14	23	0		23
United States	51	53	17	43	61	46	47	47	36	29	0	43

Note: For a description of the index, see Bollard and Vautier (1998, Table 6.4 notes). Lloyd (1998a, Appendix) provides a multilateral version of the index.

Source: Bollard and Vautier (1998, Table 6.4)

144

New Zealand's IAP outlines principles that in its view govern best practice in regulation. And there are several references, notably by Hong Kong Special Administrative Region (SAR), to evaluation techniques[1] for reviewing regulation. An emerging guideline is the need for least distortion to trade and investment in achieving regulatory goals. Australia's IAP explicitly integrates regulatory review into its competition policy.

In reviewing the competition policy and deregulation areas of the revised (1997) Individual Action Plans, the dominant impression is again the diversity of responses, in terms of the wide range of policy issues included under these two headings.

> This [diversity of responses] lends support to the view that neither of these [policy] areas should be narrowly defined. In turn, this might provide the basis for developing an approach which places less emphasis on policy definitions and more emphasis on an overall competition framework. If consensus could be reached on such a framework in which to address competition issues, this would help to unify the thinking that guides all policy areas in the IAPs, however they are labelled (PECC, 1998).

Competition law, as an instrument for the promotion of competition, is not a focus in all APEC economies but it is often mentioned in the IAPs. Two matters are of particular note. First, the reviews on exemptions from existing laws are in progress. It is hoped that, over time, those exemptions which lack an adequate rationale in the context of APEC's liberalization agenda, and particularly those which cut across competition objectives, will be removed. Secondly, there is an interest in cooperation between different enforcement agencies (including for purposes of technical cooperation); this may well lead to further bilateral arrangements in the enforcement area.

Deregulation is often approached primarily in terms of actual or planned privatization and in relation to key sectors, such as telecommunications, financial services, transportation and energy. It is important to recognize, however, that privatization also needs to be seen in the context of a competition framework which should apply to a broader range of policy actions and business conduct affecting all industries, whether they are publicly or privately owned (PECC, 1998).

Assessment

Constructive dialogue is proceeding among APEC members. Consensus has been achieved on the importance of transparency as a facilitating objective. As PECC has stressed, transparency requires a clear and authoritative statement by each member economy of all relevant laws and regulatory interventions and related procedures. But it also requires an equally clear articulation of the considerations which will guide administrative discretion on all regulatory matters and a clear outline of the reasoning behind those decisions which result from the exercise of that discretion. This is consistent with the business preference for a degree of policy certainty over time.

Overall, the Action Plan process is serving to highlight critical differences in policy perspectives and where the development of some unifying principles could contribute to greater policy coherence and improved policy performance.

While each APEC economy will use its discretion in determining the appropriate role for the market, competition could be a highly relevant and unifying theme for several policy areas identified in the Action Plans, including deregulation, intellectual property and government procurement. Explicit recognition of the competition dimension of a range of policy areas, in addition to the area labelled competition policy, would assist APEC to develop a more comprehensive approach to competition issues.

Given the obvious lack of agreement among APEC governments on the objective(s) of competition policy, and widely divergent views on the scope of this policy area, there is clearly a long way to go before a common approach is achieved, let alone a clear understanding of how competition principles link with deregulation and other policy areas covered by the IAPs and CAP.

The approach of the most open economies — Singapore and Hong Kong SAR — is noticeably different from the other IAPs and represents a legitimate challenge to any interest in having a common approach to the area designated as competition policy. These economies do not have, nor do they wish to develop, a general competition law. They believe that a comprehensive approach to domestic deregulation and trade and investment liberalization will result in competitive markets requiring minimal (but not zero) government intervention.

The authors share PECC's view that much remains to be done in APEC to establish a policy framework which gives full recognition and effect to the importance of competition principles to regional liberalization, while at the same time recognizing the diversity of economic experience and levels of development within the Asia-Pacific region. Because of this, APEC's Collective Action Plan has an important role in encouraging and promoting, *inter alia:*

- information gathering;
- sharing of experiences;
- linkages between policies, particularly those with a competition dimension;
- institutional capacity building, including relevant training in competition analysis;
- identification of areas of consensus.

But in addition the CAP has an especially important role in encouraging APEC members to cooperate in the development of non-binding competition and regulatory principles as the foundation for a more integrated policy response to competition and regulatory issues in the region.

The CTI's 1997 Annual Report (APEC, 1997b) made no reference to progress on competition principles. Undoubtedly, this was because APEC economies were still engaged in a major learning process, not least in relation to competition law. In fact, a special study on the advantages and disadvantages of competition laws for developing economies is underway, following approval by the CTI early in 1998. The intention of the project, due for completion mid-1999, is to consider the following issues:

- whether competition laws are essential to attaining competition policy objectives, especially for developing members with open economies;
- how the introduction of competition laws will affect the international competitiveness of their domestic firms;
- how the enactment of competition laws will affect their ability to compete for foreign investment *vis-à-vis* developing economies that have not enacted competition laws;
- the social impact of competition laws;
- what are the limits and downside risks of enacting a competition law within a society; and
- the difficulties in obtaining support for the enactment of a competition law within a society.

PECC's Competition Principles Project

APEC reports reflect the fact that PECC is working particularly closely with APEC in the competition and deregulation areas and that PECC's Trade Policy Forum is presently developing a set of (non-binding) competition principles which it hopes will be adopted by APEC economies.

PECC's Trade Policy Forum has had 'competition policy' on its agenda since 1993. In 1997 it resolved to advance its thinking about what (non-binding) *principles* — as distinct from specific competition *rules* and *minimum standards* — might guide the development of an international competition policy framework (including but not confined to competition law) in the short, medium and long term (PECC, 1997a).

The themes of comprehensiveness and coherence have become central to this exercise, and competition and efficiency are emerging as umbrella (rather than ancillary) concepts. The emphasis of PECC's competition principles project is on:

- principles, not rules or standards;
- developing a competition-based policy framework, not policy prescriptions for individual economies;

- promoting a convergence of intentions, not necessarily policy conformity; ultimately, the question of how to operationalize the principles has to be addressed at the individual economy level — through unilateral initiative.

The principled policy framework would apply to:

- public as well as private actions;
- financial as well as other services and goods markets;
- trade as well as other policy instruments;
- developed as well as developing economies;
- large as well as small economies.

Some fundamental points are already emerging from PECC's work. For example:

(a)   the need to foster greater reliance in APEC economies upon market mechanisms and the role of competition in efficiently allocating and employing scarce resources;

(b)   the need to facilitate the competitive process by eliminating progressively government regulations that create or maintain (efficiency-reducing) barriers to market entry;

(c)   the importance of appropriate criteria for future government interventions in globalizing markets, that is, in order to minimize regulatory distortions to the competitive process;[2]

(d)   the importance of competitive neutrality in the sense that the same competition principles should apply to the different modes of domestic/international supply;

(e)   the importance of ensuring that government efforts to make markets more open and contestable, through deregulation and the lowering of barriers, are not replaced or impeded by anti-competitive business conduct.

The Individual and Collective Action Plans of APEC members provide excellent and transparent vehicles for bringing competition (and regulatory) principles to bear on a range of agreed areas of policy development. However, and this seems crucial, APEC Economic Leaders will need to lead by signalling clearly their support for the primacy of the competitive process and for the role that competition principles could play in strengthening the contribution of domestic policies to the realization of APEC's collective liberalization, growth and welfare goals. Such leadership would give impetus to the development of the competition dimension of APEC's work programmes and also to developing a common reference point for assessing unilateral responses to APEC's overall agenda. The point is worth remaking: explicit leadership from APEC Economic Leaders will be pivotal in promoting throughout APEC the value of a competition-driven policy framework as a central element in the realization of APEC's vision for the Asia-Pacific region.

ABAC's Views

In 1995, APEC established an APEC Business Advisory Council (ABAC). If APEC economies are to give less weight to special protection for business and more weight to the roles of competition in allocating resources and of efficiency in business success, ABAC and other business leaders in APEC economies will also need to demonstrate credible support for more open, contestable and efficient markets, that is, for themselves as well as for others.

ABAC (1997) lends support to the view that government regulation (as well as private restrictions) of domestic commercial activity can unduly restrict competition in international trade and investment. Business in the region has already widely signalled that if governments in developing economies want to be in the running to attract private capital into major infrastructure investments, their regulatory and investment regimes will have to respond accordingly.

ABAC supports continuing consensus-building within APEC in respect of competition policy — having special regard to the objectives of competition, deregulation and trade policies, as well as to the linkages between these policies. It has put APEC on notice that it particularly wishes to provide input on:

- the forms of private-sector conduct which should be prohibited on the grounds that they work against the competitive process and have no redeeming features;
- the treatment of utilities and natural monopolies;
- the relationship between competition policy and anti-dumping;
- the constitution of adequate and effective competition law; and
- the identification of key regulatory and other barriers to effective competition.

At the same time there is currently a substantial appetite, including in ABAC, for prioritizing individual sectors for voluntary early liberalization. This strategy reinforces, and does not substitute for, the need for appropriate competition (and regulatory) principles as a modality for guiding policy preferences and performance in relation to nominated sectors. Competition-driven policies are relevant to government and business activities in all sectors:

- whether agriculture, fishing, industrial goods, or services (including financial services);

- whether a sector is judged to be in the 'easy' or 'hard' reform basket; or
- whether sector-specific issues are to be targeted sooner or later.

The breadth of ABAC's interest in competition-related issues further reinforces the suggestion that generally applicable competition principles would better enable cohesive and competition-driven policy development to evolve within APEC.

Support for SMEs is seen by ABAC and APEC as an essential element for economic development. It is interesting to note that of APEC's 12 public—private sector dialogues conducted in 1997, half involved the SME Policy Level Group (APEC, 1997b). Policies targeted specifically at SMEs should also be assessed in a competition framework.

Final Observations

APEC is providing an interesting model for liberalization and economic integration in a region. As a forum it is a consensus-building rather than a rules-based organization. In part this reflects the diversity of its member economies and in particular their different stages of economic development. As far as 'competition policy' and deregulation are concerned, one benefit of the discussions to date has been that members have come to understand better the objectives and scope of policies of other members.

The Collective Action Plan for 'competition policy' together with PECC's Competition Principles Project are leading APEC economies in the direction of a principles-based approach to competition issues in globalizing markets. While we believe this would provide a sound foundation for welfare-enhancing policy in the region, it is too early to tell whether member governments will adopt these principles and apply them in practice.

Notes

1. Cost/benefit, including the cost of both enforcement and compliance, and risk analysis.
2. The prospect of regulatory responsibility legislation in New Zealand is an interesting development in this context. Its purpose would be to impose a legislative discipline on the regulation-making process through establishing principles relating to efficiency, effectiveness, transparency, clarity and equity, to guide good quality regulation. (New Zealand Cabinet Papers released under the Official Information Act.)

PART FIVE

Developments at the Multilateral Level

10. The World Trade Organization

Historically, there has been no multilateral competition authority or organization and no substantial multilateral rules explicitly relating to competition. Under the GATT, the rules of the international trade system ignore private conduct which affects competition, with the exceptions of dumping and subsidized trade, trading by state-owned enterprises and enterprises with exclusive or special rights. Apart from these exceptions, private actions which raise questions of anti-competitive cross-border conduct are not subject to international trade law.

Nevertheless, the World Trade Organization (WTO) is increasingly important for several reasons. Many government measures affect competition in markets and the role of the WTO in relation to competition aspects of international trade measures needs to be worked out. There is some pressure on the WTO to become involved in the resolution of private actions through its dispute settlement procedures. Some economists and lawyers have recommended that the WTO be extended to incorporate a multilateral competition authority which could address all aspects of cross-border business conduct. The most notable of these are the working group of academics and practitioners who, during the negotiations of the Uruguay Round, proposed an International Antitrust Draft Code (International Antitrust Draft Code Working Group, 1993) and the Group of Experts commissioned by the European Commission in the lead-up to the Singapore Ministerial Conference of the WTO (European Commission DG IV, 1996).

After looking generally at the multilateral option and surveying briefly the competition provisions in the WTO, we examine the proposals to develop the WTO into a multilateral competition authority and the proposals for it to act as a multilateral enforcement agency. The final two sections deal with the specific issues of the treatment of dumping and subsidized trade in the WTO, and the activities of the Working Group on the Interaction between International Trade and Competition.

The Multilateral Option for Competition Rules

First, we must consider the reasons put forward for a *multilateral* approach as the preferred form of multi-national action; then we can consider the institution which might be responsible for multilateral competition rules.

Several reasons have been advanced for multilateral competition rules. The most common argument is, in effect, that they are required to take into account Type 1 policy failures which give rise to international competition distortions. Other arguments concern the nullification and impairment through anti-competitive conduct of GATT/WTO trade liberalization and the reduction of frictions within the WTO trading system (see, for example, Petersmann, 1998).

The best-developed argument for a multilateral approach is that put forward by the WTO Annual Report 1997 based on distortions in national competition authorities' actions. Bacchetta, Horn and Mavroidis (1997) and the WTO (1997a) found that multilateral agreement based on the maximization of global welfare was superior to other options: it could eliminate distortions in the world economy. From the point of view of Type 1 and Type 2 failures, the action of a multilateral authority could be based on the maximization of world welfare and it could automatically consider both Type 1 and Type 2 failures; indeed, there is no distinction between these two types within a global economy. This is the meaning of the intuition from the thought experiment described in Chapter 2 above. (Recall from Chapter 4 that the subsidiarity principle in the EU too is based on recognition of these spillover effects at the regional level.)   A multilateral agreement has the second major advantage that it would cover all countries which signed the agreement. If it were part of the WTO, this would comprise most of the world's trading nations.

We can now compare the option of multilateral rules based on the pursuit of global welfare with other options.   Extraterritoriality involves conflict with the interests of other nations, and comity and bilateral cooperation proceed generally on the assumption that the action is taken in the interests of the residents of the nation. We have seen in Chapters 2 and 3 that these actions could lead to the perpetuation of distortions as described by the WTO.

Bacchetta, Horn and Mavroidis (1997) pointed out that bilateral agreements may even create new distortions. This can arise if the agreement is between two countries but the negative spillover is in a third country. They consider a case in which there are three countries, A, B and C, where A and B have a competition law agreement. The authority of country A is to make a decision on a practice by a firm of country B which exploits consumers in country C. Presumably the authority of country A will rule on this because the practice also lowers the welfare of consumers in A. If the harm imposed on the consumers of A and C is greater than the gain in profits to the firm of country B, but the harm imposed on the consumers of country A is less than the gain in profits, the bilateral agreement would result in a lowering of global welfare.

If a national competition authority has an objective function which interprets the national interest as the interests of the producers of the nation, a global competition authority which acts to maximize global welfare including consumer interests would yield an additional gain. Conversely, a global authority which acted to maximize some objective function other than global welfare could result in a loss of welfare.

The case for a global or international competition authority has been received coolly. In particular, the proposal for an international anti-trust code has been severely criticized (for example, Gifford, 1997). The main objection is loss of national sovereignty. The Chairman of the US Federal Trade Commission stated that a world anti-trust code 'is not going to happen in the near future' (Pitofsky, 1996). Another US author, Graham (1995, p. 112), states even more strongly:

> The opinion of this author is that it is highly unlikely that countries will agree in my own lifetime to the creation of an EU-like mechanism in the domain of competition policy at the level of the WTO, i.e., one where an agency along the lines of DG [Directorate-General] IV is given powers to implement and enforce competition applicable to all WTO member nations.

The objection of loss of national sovereignty needs examination. National sovereignty is a fluid concept. The areas of national policymaking and control which are regarded as nationally sovereign have clearly changed over time, with countries ceding to some international or supranational body rights of control over policy areas which were previously regarded as sovereign. When they were established, both the GATT and the WTO assumed rights of control over national trade policies which were contentious at the time. In the case of the WTO, these included GATS and the competition elements in the GATS. Similarly, at the regional level, the EU countries have ceded rights to a supranational body, the European Commission, in many areas including importantly the area of competition law (see Chapter 4); and this is continuing in the area of monetary policies and other areas. An important consideration in determining which areas of policy should remain at the national level is whether there are net economic benefits from establishing some multilateral control over an area of policy. We need, therefore, to examine the substantive case for the creation of a multilateral competition authority.

Two different kinds of proposals have been put forward. One is a full-
169   169
blown multilateral competition authority which would have the power to investigate private conduct and to enforce its decisions. The other is a more limited kind of proposal for the multilateral enforcement of national competition laws.[1] Before considering these proposals we need to consider the extent of the current provisions relating to competition in the WTO.

Competition Provisions in the GATT and the WTO

The law of the GATT, as laid down in the original Articles and subsequent amendments, was incorporated into the WTO when it came into being. This law is known as GATT 1994. It does not address 'competition policy' *per se* and it imposes no obligation on members to have national competition law. But the WTO has a number of specific provisions relating to areas of international competition, general rules relating to non-discrimination and transparency which affect competition in markets, and rules relating to nullification and impairment of negotiated concessions which might in some circumstances be used to enforce national competition laws.

As a part of the Uruguay Round, the General Agreement on Trade in Services (GATS), the Agreement on Trade-Related Investment Measures (TRIMS) and the Agreement on Trade-Related Aspects of Intellectual Property Rights (TRIPS) all contain provisions relating to competition. The First Ministerial Conference, held in Singapore in December 1996, established a Working Group on the Interaction between Trade and Competition Policy (the WTO Working Group);   other activities of the WTO cover some competition issues: these include the Trade Policy Review Mechanism reviews of policies in member countries, and the built-in agenda of items for further negotiation and review from the Uruguay Round. WTO (1997a, sections V.1 and IV.1.c) has a brief but excellent review of the WTO provisions and activities relating to competition law and policy. (The 1960 GATT Decision is a distinct non-binding agreement which is discussed separately in Chapter 7.)

The most important of the specific provisions relating to private conduct are those dealing with anti-dumping and subsidized trade (export subsidies, subsidies and countervailing duties), and with enterprises owned by states or enterprises with import monopolies or exclusive or special trading privileges.   State trading and import monopolies are becoming less important in most countries because of the diminished role of state trading enterprises but they have recently become a major issue in the trade of some transition economies, such as the People's Republic of China and Vietnam, as these economies have opened up to international trade but still have many state trading enterprises. The provisions relating to dumping and subsidized trade are considered later in this chapter.

GATT (1994) does not prohibit or otherwise regulate export or import cartels, which are the most blatant form of anti-competitive conduct based on international trade flows. In the case of import cartels, all it does, under the article dealing with state monopolies, is to require that state monopolies must not operate so as to afford protection in excess of the bound tariff rate (WTO, 1997a, p. 59). It prohibits export restrictions, but there are major limits to this prohibition and it does not apply to cartel activities which raise prices (nor is there any GATT obligation with regard to export taxes). This lack of action against trade cartels is a clear demonstration that the international trade law of the GATT was not concerned with competition issues *per se*.

Articles I and III of the GATT laid down the fundamental principles of most-favoured nation and national treatment. Similar non-discrimination provisions are contained in the GATS, TRIPS and TRIM and other agreements of the Uruguay Round. These provisions apply to all imported goods or services. GATT jurisprudence also makes it clear that Article III applies to enforcement procedures as well as to substantive laws and regulations (WTO, 1997a, p.77).

The GATS has introduced new relationships in the WTO between competition and trade policies. The GATS applies to measures (governmental and some non-governmental) that affect international trade in services; these include direct investment and the movement of natural persons (entrepreneurs, technicians, managers). The goal of the Agreement is the progressive liberalization of trade in services. In pursuit of this goal, the Agreement contains provisions that directly address business practices (Articles VIII and IX). Members of the Agreement recognize that certain business practices of service suppliers may restrain competition and thereby restrict trade in services. Article VIII of GATS contains a general requirement that, where a monopoly supplier of a WTO member competes in the supply of a service outside its monopoly rights, that member shall ensure that the supplier does not abuse its monopoly position to act in a manner which is inconsistent with the MFN obligations and specific commitments made by the member in respect of the service.

An important consideration in the Uruguay Round negotiations on services was the recognition that an offer to provide market access in a specific service area (for example, financial services) could be nullified by the failure of a member country to offer to provide for access to a public telecommunications network that is necessary to sell the service. To be offered market access in financial services but denied access to leased lines or facilities may totally undermine the value of the offer. A Telecommunications Annex to the General Agreement on Trade in Services was added to ensure that 'any other Member is accorded access to and the use of public telecommunications transport networks and services on reasonable and non-discriminatory terms and conditions, for the supply of the service', and similar provisions apply to access to private networks and services. It contains provisions designed to prevent abuse of monopoly power through cross-subsidization and other practices.

The enforcement provisions relating directly to competition are based on positive comity. They provide for consultation among members and the enforcement is by means of national laws and regulations. Each member will, at the request of another member, enter into consultations with a view to the government concerned eliminating these restrictive practices within its territory. When a member is approached to enter into consultations, it is necessary to accord full and sympathetic consideration to such a request. The member is to cooperate through the supply of publicly available non-confidential information of relevance to the matter in question. The member is also to provide other information, subject to its domestic law and to the conclusion of a satisfactory agreement concerning the safeguarding of its confidentiality by the requesting party.

Many other provisions of the GATS address competition concerns. These provisions include transparency, government procurement, the distribution and marketing of services, and subsidies. These are important because services are essential inputs into many production activities.

Since the conclusion of the Uruguay Round, both the Information Technology Agreement reached at the Singapore Ministerial Meeting of the WTO in December 1996 and the Agreement on Basic Telecommunications concluded in 1997 contain provisions relating to competition. The Reference Paper of the Agreement on Basic Telecommunications, which some governments have adhered to, states that any new supplier may interconnect with the existing network of a major supplier on non-discriminatory and reasonable terms. The Reference Paper also specifically refers to the prevention of anti-competitive practices in telecommunications. This goes further than the Annex to the GATS. It states that: 'Appropriate measures shall be maintained for the purpose of preventing suppliers who, alone or together, are a major supplier from engaging in or continuing anti-competitive practices' (WTO Negotiating Group on Basic Telecommunications, 1996). It lists three practices in particular: 'anti-competitive cross-subsidization', 'using information obtained from competitors with anti-competitive results', and 'not making available to other service suppliers on a timely basis technical information about essential facilities and commercially relevant information which are necessary for them to provide services'.

The GATS and later agreements on trade in services are the major occurrences in the WTO of the new dimensions of policy at the interface of international trade and competition policy. Viewed in this light, the fundamental importance of the GATS is that, in the area of services, the WTO has already integrated some instruments of international trade, competition and foreign investment policies.

The TRIPS contains two articles which relate to aspects of competition: these concern 'effective protection against certain competition' (Article 39) and control of 'anti-competitive practices' (Article 40). As with the GATS, they incorporate positive comity. Enforcement of these provisions is by means of civil and administrative procedures and remedies under national laws. More broadly, however, the whole TRIPS Agreement is essentially concerned with fair trade in intellectual property. Much of it concerns issues of pricing for the use of intellectual property, which is a classic competition issue. The WTO will oversee trade-related aspects of intellectual property via the Council for Trade-Related Aspects of Intellectual Property Rights as a part of the WTO; and the Dispute Settlement Understanding applies to the Agreement. The Agreement will inject a substantial new element of multilateral regulation and enforcement of intellectual property rights, including competition aspects. Intellectual property transactions too are an increasingly important part of the international trade in technologies and goods.

The TRIMS Agreement is intended to discipline trade-related investment measures which had hitherto escaped any international regulation. In particular, it prohibits TRIMS which are inconsistent with the WTO

Articles relating to National Treatment or the General Elimination of Quantitative Restrictions. In the context of a competition framework, the importance of TRIMS is that, for the first time, it involves the multilateral body responsible for the management of the world system for trade in goods in the regulation of aspects of investment. The Preamble to the Agreement notes that it desires 'to facilitate investment across international frontiers so as to increase the economic growth of all trading partners' as well as to promote the expansion and progressive liberalization of world trade. Article 9 provides for a review of the Agreement within five years: 'In the course of this review, the Council for Trade in Goods shall consider whether it should be complemented with provisions on investment policy and competition policy.'

We can use the analytical framework outlined in Chapter 2 to assess these elements bearing on competition in the WTO. The WTO does not deal with foreign direct investment and capital markets. With respect to the markets covered, the WTO covers all goods and services markets, though the treatment of services is separate from and different in some ways from that of goods. With respect to the list of business conduct which is covered, the WTO still addresses only a small fraction of the conduct and competition problems which might be addressed by international competition law, although that fraction is much greater than under the former GATT. There are no provisions at all in the WTO that relate to horizontal restraints involving collusion (such as price-fixing or bid-rigging), abuse of dominance, vertical restraints or mergers. With respect to the objectives of the WTO (formally, the objective function), the primary concern of the WTO is with international trade in goods and service, not with competition. To adapt the terminology of the WTO itself, one could say that the GATT 1994 and the GATS, as well as TRIMS and TRIPS, are concerned basically with *trade-related* competition problems only. These limitations on the coverage of the competition law in the WTO are the consequence of the elements of competition issues in the WTO that have arisen as a part of international trade law.

The WTO as a Multilateral Competition Authority

If there were a multilateral authority, there would be a choice of type of organization in which to locate it: the first is an independent multilateral authority whose functions would be confined to international competition law, such as the International Competition Policy Unit suggested by Jacquemin et al. (1998); the second is the WTO. Each of the two options has its advantages and disadvantages.

There is an argument that in order to be effective competition law and international law should be linked in one organization. This view seems implicit in some of the literature and is sometimes stated explicitly

(Petersmann, 1996 and 1998). Indeed, the Director-General of the WTO has suggested that competition and trade law be linked in the WTO:

> As successive rounds of trade negotiations have increasingly limited the scope for government measures that restrict or distort the conditions of international competition, attention inevitably is more focused on private sector measures which have a similar effect but are not subject to international rules.   (Ruggiero, 1995)

In February 1996, he noted that 'the need to integrate questions of trade, competition policy and investment was already recognized in the stillborn Havana Charter' and has similarly been recognized in regional trading arrangements. He concludes:

> In fact, it is inevitable that the WTO will become increasingly involved with questions of competition policy, whether or not this matter is formally put on the agenda at Singapore. The question is whether the WTO should only deal with competition policy-related issues in an *ad hoc* manner in the context of specific trade policy questions, or whether an overall examination of the links between trade and competition should be initiated with a view to developing a coherent multilateral vision of how trade and competition policy can be mutually supportive.   (Ruggiero, 1996)

The rationale for a link between competition and trade policies in the WTO is not, however, the presence of interactions between international trade and competition policies, though these do exist and are important, as we noted in Chapter 2. Rather, the argument is that it is more efficient to pursue the two sets of policies jointly. A link is essential in the WTO only if interactions mean that the multilateral management of international trade in goods and services and, in particular, the multilateral negotiation of further trade liberalization were jeopardized by anti-competitive behaviour or, conversely, if implementation of competition-driven policy depended upon the rules of international trade.

This requirement for a link between competition and trade policies could arise, for example, if international trade policies had negative effects on international competition or vice versa. This negative form of interaction does not seem to be present. International trade liberalization and policies to promote competition reinforce each other. Trade liberalization generally makes markets more competitive. In addition, the liberalization of international capital flows has increased international trade in goods and services and made some markets more competitive. Conversely, the application of policy which removes barriers to competition does not undermine international trade policies.

Non-negativity of the interactions between competition and international trade policies is not, however, sufficient for separate management of the policies to be desirable. If there were mutually positive interactions, the separation of the policies could result in the under-achievement of the objective of efficiency because, typically, international trade policy does not take account of the beneficial effect of trade liberalization on greater competition (as distinct from market access) and vice versa.

What is required for the separation of these policies is the ability of policymakers in each area to pursue their objectives by means of the instruments in one area independently of the actions of policymakers in the other area. In practice, national competition policies seem to have been able to operate independently of national trade policies, and competition laws have been enforced, even though in some markets restrictions on international trade reduce foreign competition.

Conversely, from the point of view of the WTO, if anti-competitive practices limit the benefits of trade liberalization, there are provisions for dealing with these practices in so far as they arise from government measures. Article XXIII (Nullification and Impairment) of the GATT (1947) permits a complaint against government measures when it is alleged that some government measures nullify or impair some condition of market access that has been negotiated under the GATT. This Article could be applied to anti-competitive measures. These provisions must satisfy certain requirements, such as that the measures could not have been reasonably anticipated at the time of the negotiations and they do not apply to export. Most of the complaints under Article XXIII have involved nullification or impairment of a negotiated tariff concession by the introduction of a subsidy. If these nullification or impairment provisions under GATT (1994) are inadequate, they should be strengthened.

Thus, competition-driven policy and international trade policy can be pursued separately without one undermining the other. The WTO recently reached the same conclusion in its survey of trade and competition policy: 'competition policy is generally the most appropriate instrument for combating enterprise practices that restrict or distort international trade' (WTO, 1997a, p. 32). This delinking does not deny the effects which international trade policy has on international competition.

We need, therefore, to consider the argument in favour of the WTO on other grounds. There are some advantages in the choice of the WTO as a multilateral competition authority. The obvious advantages of the WTO are that it exists and comprises almost all of the world's major trading nations (the only notable exceptions are Russia and China which have applied to accede to the WTO). The Marrakesh Agreement establishing the WTO is an international treaty. International treaties signed by member countries and ratified by national legislation are binding upon the members. The WTO has effective dispute settlement procedures (DSP) which enable it to enforce its rules. The WTO could take a world welfare view of competition problems, as the GATT/WTO has a long tradition of taking a world view of trade problems.

With regard to the location of a multilateral authority, most of those who have advocated a multilateral competition law have assumed that it would be incorporated in the WTO; for example, the International Antitrust Code Working Group (1993), the Group of Experts who proposed the International Antitrust Code, Scherer (1994), Nicolaides (1996) and Petersmann (a member of the International Antitrust Code Working Group) (1998).

There are, however, major difficulties in having the WTO as the multilateral body which might be responsible for a multilateral competition law, if one were developed. The first relates to the coverage of anti-competitive conduct currently covered by the WTO, as noted earlier. The law of the WTO in relation to elements of competition law has arisen as a part of international trade law. We have noted that it still addresses only a small fraction of the problems which might be addressed by international competition law, although that fraction is much greater than that of the former GATT. The WTO is a system which deals almost exclusively with the actions of national governments whereas competition law deals primarily with private conduct. In the GATT, GATS and TRIPS, there are no obligations on members to take competition law actions, and these agreements rely on consultation and cooperation among governments. The only provisions relating to business practices are those concerning dumping, state trading enterprises and enterprises enjoying special and exclusive privileges, and some provisions relating to private monopolies in the GATS and the recent Agreement on Basic Telecommunications Services.

The second relates to the coverage of members who have competition laws. Although the number of countries with competition laws is rapidly increasing, a majority of the members still do not have comprehensive laws. A multilateral authority could not operate effectively if members of the organization did not have relevant national laws and the means to enforce them within their own territories.

There are, moreover, strong practical objections. A multilateral system with the WTO acting as an international competition authority would need to investigate private actions in markets. Competition law in this form, by comparison with international trade law, is extremely intensive in its requirement of facts relating to the nature of competition, entry conditions and so on. These vary from case to case and require detailed investigations. When the markets concerned in a case are international, this investigation would require information from different countries. There must be doubts about the ability of a centralized multilateral authority to understand behaviour in markets, and in markets located in different countries to boot.

It would be an enormous change to have the WTO investigating and prosecuting private parties in all goods and services markets. It has no powers to obtain information from private parties; further, under the existing WTO rules, private litigation is not possible (though private parties can make submissions to WTO Panels). The WTO has no remedies which might be applied to private parties, apart from anti-dumping and countervailing duties in the case of dumping and subsidization which affects trade. Indeed, it has no provision to impose penalties or other measures on member governments. It can only require that they change government policies.

There is also a basic difference in approach between the law of the WTO and national competition laws. In respect of the latter, there has in recent years been a movement away from the *per se* prohibition of certain practices towards the rule of reason approach. This reflects the fact that the effects of business conduct on competition and consumer welfare are frequently unclear. Further, the relevant economic framework and analysis continue to be the subject of vigorous debate amongst economists. By contrast, the WTO rules contain outright prohibitions on specified government measures. More fundamentally, the WTO is the body regulating the world trading system and is, as a consequence, primarily concerned with market access. Market access should not be the goal of policies to promote competition.

These practical difficulties are enormous. In our view, the WTO, as presently constituted, cannot operate as an international authority for the investigation and prosecution of private anti-competitive conduct.

Operating under its present constitution, the WTO could do more to foster competition. Perhaps the most important contribution the WTO can make is to continue with the liberalization of border measures which restrict trade in goods and services, and the enforcement of non-discrimination in this trade. If the WTO is to have credibility as a body which is promoting competition (as distinct from trade) then it must recognize that some trade instruments can restrict competition; for example, export cartels and anti-dumping actions, both of which are permitted under the WTO Articles.

There is an alternative form of organization of competition law in the WTO which is not subject to these difficulties. Scherer (1994) argued that competition law could be developed under the umbrella of a single world organization but as a body of law which is separate from and administered separately from international trade law. One possible form is a stand-alone division or directorate for trade which could cover the existing trade law and a stand-alone division or directorate for competition which would cover new competition law, and both would be of equal standing. There is an analogy with the European Union, which has separate Directorates-General for Trade Policy and Competition Policy: Directorates-General II and IV respectively. Moreover, this device could also accommodate other areas, such as the proposed Multilateral Agreement on Investment, as separate divisions or directorates. If this proposal were pursued it would be necessary to ensure that it contributed to rather than distracted from the coherence of the various policy areas relevant to competition and efficiency in markets.

Recently, Jacquemin et al. (1998) argued that because the investigation of private business conduct across borders and the enforcement of international law is so different from the international trade law administered and enforced by the WTO, an International Policy Unit separate from the

WTO was called for. Its mandate would be to help the development and convergence of competition policy standards.

The WTO as a Multilateral Competition Enforcement Agency

Some of the proposals for a multilateral approach to competition are limited to the WTO acting as an agency to enforce national competition laws through the use of existing or of extended dispute settlement procedures.

The existing procedures, under Article XXIII (Nullification and Impairment), apply only to government measures which nullify or impair agreed market access or the attainment of the objectives of the Agreement. They apply only to government trade measures because the dispute settlement procedures are a part of the system which regulates what governments can do.

The most relevant of the procedures is the so-called 'non-violation' clause which applies to cases where it is alleged that benefits accruing to a member are being nullified or impaired or the attainment of an objective of the Agreement is being impeded by a government measure even if it does not conflict with the provisions of the WTO Agreement. The WTO (1997a, p. 79) observes: 'There has been considerable discussion as to whether the failure of a Member to enforce its competition laws to prevent enterprise practices that are impeding market access to trading partners could be successfully challenged under this provision.'

There are severe limitations to the use of the WTO enforcement procedures in cases of private conduct. The private conduct has to be attributed to a government measure; thus, private conduct that was not subject to any government involvement would be outside the scope of the provision. Proof of nullification or impairment is required and other hurdles have to be passed. If a Panel upheld a complaint under this provision, it could only recommend that the parties agree on a mutually satisfactory adjustment. There is doubt as to whether a WTO Panel would be bound by the precedents of earlier Panels (Bacchetta, Horn and Mavroidis, 1997) and, therefore, as to whether any consistent law could emerge.

In fact, only one case concerning the role of government laws and regulations relating to private anti-competitive conduct has been brought to the WTO. This is the case concerning Measures Affecting Consumer Photographic Film and Paper, the so-called *Kodak/Fuji* case (see Chapter 11).

The Agreement on Basic Telecommunications may have broken new ground in relation to the WTO regulation of private conduct. We noted above that the Reference Paper of this Agreement, which some governments have adhered to, specifically refers to the prevention of anti-competitive practices in telecommunications. It lists some practices such as cross-subsidization and not making available to other service suppliers on a timely basis technical information about essential facilities. This may prove to be an important change in WTO law but it is limited to the telecommunications sector at present and is mainly concerned with interconnection. The enforcement is through the agency in the member country which regulates the industry, or failing that, the competition authority. It is untried. It is possible that a similar approach might be incorporated in other service industry agreements that are being negotiated in the WTO, such as that on shipping, which would extend its importance.

A second multilateral method of overcoming cross-border enforcement problems within the WTO has been suggested by Mattoo and Subramanian (1997). They argue that a fully fledged multilateral authority is neither feasible nor necessary. Most of the trade disputes in the competition area have been related to enforcement issues. They advocate a multilateral agreement under which nations would give a commitment on national enforcement of existing national competition laws. The key advance would be for countries to provide rights of action to foreign private parties. The Agreement would include standards of enforcement by national authorities and standards of performance by these authorities. Disputes would be subject to the existing WTO dispute settlement procedures. Given the obligations of national governments under the Agreement, the complaints would take place under 'violation' rather than 'non-violation causes'.

This is an interesting proposal. In principle, this method of enforcement by individual nations could cover all conduct, since Type 2 conduct by producers in one country is, from the point of view of the other country whose residents are harmed, Type 1 conduct. However, universal coverage would require that all countries have competition laws and that these laws were similar. To overcome the present limited coverage of national laws, it would be necessary for all countries to develop competition laws and for these laws to converge. In addition, a world welfare view would be required of the national authorities; otherwise, they would not consider the interests of foreign parties. Unless all these conditions are met, the residents of a complainant country would not regard the mechanism as satisfactory.

A third possibility is to have the WTO act as a multilateral competition enforcement authority with new enforcement procedures which are appropriate for resolving cross-border enforcement problems. Chapter 11 highlights the problems encountered in the *Kodak/Fuji* case in using present dispute settlement procedures.

Dumping and Subsidized Trade in the WTO

Article VI of GATT (1994) concerns specifically dumping and subsidization of goods traded internationally and it provides for remedies in the form of anti-dumping duties, price undertakings and countervailing duties. Neither dumping nor subsidization is an important part of competition law in general. Under the Agreement on Subsidies and Countervailing Measures, which entered into force on 1 January 1995, all members have to notify the WTO annually of anti-dumping actions and countervailing duties; WTO (1997a, Tables V.2 and V.4) shows that the US, the EU, Canada, Mexico and Australia have been the main users of anti-dumping actions and the US, Australia and Mexico the main users of countervailing duties. Only a small number of WTO member countries have frequent recourse to these remedies, but the number of members of the WTO with anti-dumping and countervailing laws is increasing.

These remedies warrant separate attention because of concern over both dumping and anti-dumping actions in the current debate about international trade and competition. Countries which are subject to anti-dumping actions in particular, and to a lesser extent countervailing duties, complain of the high, arbitrary and unpredictable levels of duties which are imposed under these provisions. This applies especially to developing countries, whose exporters are most frequently subject to these action and which as a group make little use of these actions (see WTO, 1997a, Table V). Both anti-dumping actions and countervailing duties have been the subject of a number of complaints to the dispute settlement procedures of the WTO in the last two years.

Dumping

Dumping illustrates differences in regulation under international trade and competition law regimes and the importance of the choice of policy objective in these two areas.

Dumping entered the set of international trade policies subject to GATT regulation in 1947 because it was perceived as unfair to domestic competitors and therefore a practice which tends to undermine respect for the rules of the international trading system and the willingness of countries to liberalize international trade (Jackson, 1989, Chapter 10). The GATT rules were tightened in the Anti-dumping Code which was agreed to as a part of the Tokyo Round. The Uruguay Round Agreement on the Implementation of Article VI made some changes to the GATT administration of anti-dumping actions (see Hoekman and Kostecki, 1995, Chapter 7.4; Grimwade, 1996; and Palmeter, 1996, for a discussion of these) but it retained all the central features of the system.

From a competition perspective, dumping is an act of price discrimination or selling below cost which might or might not be judged conduct restricting competition.[2] Dumping is regarded by the OECD and by many of its members as a major part of cross-border competition problems.

However, international trade economists have taken a very different view from international trade officials at the national and international levels. From the time of the classic study of dumping by Viner (1926), international trade economists have regarded dumping as a form of price discrimination and most have been opposed to the application of anti-dumping actions by governments. In recent years, the definition of dumping has been broadened to include sales below average cost, even though these sales are not necessarily discriminatory. There has been a proliferation of models of dumping which offer new explanations of this behaviour; for example, demand uncertainty or strategic dumping to discourage firms in the dumped markets from reaching a scale of output that would make them competitive in the exporting country (see the article by Ethier, 1987, in the *Dictionary of Economics*, and the papers by Tharakan, 1995, and Messerlin and Reed, 1995). Only the cases of predatory and strategic dumping are regarded by international economists as harmful to the competition process and welfare of the country in which the goods are 'dumped'. International trade economists today remain widely opposed to government anti-dumping action under Article VI of GATT (1994).

International trade economists regard most anti-dumping action as a form of contingent protection which is intended to provide a margin of protection for domestic producers without regard to the costs imposed on consumers or users of the imported goods. Dumping actions are taken predominantly by the industrialized countries. As voluntary export restraints and other non-tariff barriers have been curtailed by the GATT and WTO, anti-dumping action (including price undertakings as well as the imposition of anti-dumping duties) is being used as a substitute form of non-tariff barrier which is still permissible under the WTO rules. The protective dumping margins in the US and the EU are on average two to three times higher than the substantive rates of tariffs (Messerlin and Reed, 1995, Table 2). Calculations of dumping in Australia (see Vautier and Lloyd, 1997, Appendix I) provide similar results. A review by Messerlin and Reed (1995) of anti-dumping cases handled by the US and EU authorities revealed that at most 10 per cent and most probably only 5 per cent of cases involve predatory dumping and the only country which was in a position to practise strategic dumping was Japan (cf. the views of the OECD CLP Committee which has found that claims of predatory pricing are often unfounded and recommended that governments apply a market structure test to find if the conduct should be challenged; WTO, 1997f, III (c)).

Green (1996) neatly expressed the difference between anti-dumping laws and true competition law in the following terms:

> Unlike competition laws, which seek to protect competition itself, anti-dumping laws protect domestic competitors at the expense of importers and generally result in higher costs to consumers.

Anti-dumping action should take account of the interests of final consumer or the buyers of intermediate goods. However, anti-dumping provisions in the WTO and in the legislation of most nations that take anti-dumping actions ignore the interests of consumers or buyers.

The problems of anti-dumping actions are getting worse. More countries are taking actions; more developing countries are introducing legislation providing for anti-dumping duties, though there is no obligation for them to do so under the Anti-Dumping Agreement.

With the experience of four years of application of the Uruguay Round amendments, one feature can now be seen as a change for the worse, namely, the introduction of cumulation across countries. Before the Uruguay Round Agreement on Dumping, the practice was used on a limited scale and it was doubtful that it conformed to the GATT law. The Uruguay Round Agreement made the practice WTO-legal. This has increased the coverage of complaints and their likelihood of success in countries which use this provision (see the NAFTA section in Chapter 6 and Chapter 4 on the EU).

Pricing behaviour is appropriately examined under a competition law regime. First, competition law typically does not prohibit selling below cost *per se* although prohibitions on the abuse of a dominant position might catch some below cost pricing. One consequence of the co-existence of competition law and international trade law is that conduct when it is not actionable for a domestic seller in the home market of the importing country is actionable, under dumping legislation, when the seller is outside the country. This is discrimination and it evidently causes inefficiency in the global economy.

Secondly, there is growing evidence that some anti-dumping actions are themselves anti-competitive in effect (for the EU, see Chapter 4 above, and, for Australia, see Industry Commission, 1995, Appendix E). Domestic producers sometimes use anti-dumping complaints as a means of restricting foreign competition and thereby reinforcing price-fixing agreements in the domestic markets. In developing countries which export to markets where anti-dumping action is increasing, producers see these actions as attempts to restrict their exports. The 1986 OECD Recommendations relating to cooperation between member countries in areas of potential conflict between competition and trade policies specifically enjoin member countries to take care that the exercise of proceedings under laws dealing with international unfair trade practices is not misused for anti-competitive purposes (WTO, 1997f, Annex IV).

The present provisions of the GATT need to be reviewed as anti-dumping action itself is becoming a major barrier to international trade and a cause of friction in the international trading system. Article VI differs from other articles in the GATT in that it is concerned with 'unfair trade' whereas the other articles are concerned with border barriers, which is an aspect of the objective of efficiency in the world economy. The provisions for anti-dumping (and countervailing) action also differ in that they do not prescribe what governments may do but they permit them, at their individual discretion and subject to the rules laid down in the Article, to take action.

There are several options. First, logically, it would be best to remove anti-dumping regulation altogether from the WTO.[3] To international economists, dumping is not an international trade problem. International pricing may be a competition problem and as such it should, in principle, be addressed as a part of competition laws. The EU, CER and Canada—

Chile Agreements have taken this view for intra-area dumping (see Chapters 4, 5 and 6 above). In fact, in the US and some other countries, dumping arose as a part of anti-trust legislation and it is only in recent decades that it has come to be regarded increasingly as a problem of international trade rather than of competition. If provision for anti-dumping action were removed from the WTO, countries would have no remedy readily available to deal with cases which did involve cross-border price predation. This pricing practice is likely to become less frequent as globalizing goods markets become more competitive. In any event, there is a question of appropriate remedies. There is unlikely to be support for removing anti-dumping provisions from the WTO.

Secondly, economists have begun to ask whether competition objectives and standards could be used within the WTO to guide the applications of anti-dumping actions (see Hoekman and Kostecki, 1995, p. 258; Hoekman and Mavroidis, 1996; and American Bar Association, 1994, Chapter 6). As noted in Chapter 6 above, Canadian anti-dumping law allows competition considerations to be taken into account in the determination of both the dumping margin and injury. Hoekman and Kostecki (1995, p. 258) suggested that allegations of dumping be investigated by the competition authority of the exporter's home country and a finding of anti-competitive behaviour be required before anti-dumping duties are imposed by the importing country. In effect, this would add a competition test to the existing dumping and injury tests. This would make an anti-dumping action consistent with the competition law of the exporting country but it would mean that, in the importing country, an anti-dumping action would vary with the competition standards applied by the competition authority in the exporting country, assuming that one existed. Alternatively, the alleged dumping could be investigated by the competition authority of the importing country, assuming it had one. To obtain consistency of standards across importing countries, there would have to be WTO negotiations to adopt a common competition standard for all members. This would be extremely difficult, as OECD attempts to devise common competition standards have shown.

Many of the anti-dumping actions currently taken would not be taken if the objectives and standards of competition law were substituted for those of international trade law. This would lead to an improvement in the regulation of anti-dumping actions and consistency with competition law relating to other anti-competitive behaviour.

It would, however, be peculiar to subject one set of WTO policies deriving from only one article of GATT (1974) to competition objectives and standards whereas all other WTO rules continued to follow traditional international trade objectives and tests. Furthermore, dumping is only one form of price discrimination or pricing below cost; all forms of price discrimination and other practices which potentially reduce competition need to be considered together.

Thirdly, the WTO could negotiate amendment of Article VI to replace the (producer) injury test by a national (or international) economic welfare test. (An international welfare test would actually be more permissive as it would take account of the benefit to the exporter of dumping.) This would obligate countries investigating alleged dumping to offset consumer/user gains against producer losses. Such a reform could go a long way, if enforced, to removing the use of anti-dumping action as a form of contingent protection.

Subsidized trade

Subsidies provide another illustration of an instrument of government policy which is sometimes regarded as a part of trade law and sometimes as a part of competition law, or both.

Most countries regard subsidies as a part of international trade policy and law because they distort production and international trade (and, it should be added, sometimes as a part of industrial policy) and they fall within the purview of the WTO. Under the GATT, countervailing (or anti-subsidy) duties are permitted to offset the effects of subsidies on international trade. In international trade law, the subsidy provisions originated with concern over the fairness of trade and competition. This is why countervailing duties are permitted under Article VI, the same article that permits anti-dumping duties.

As with anti-dumping, there is no justification for countervailing duties on efficiency grounds. For a small competitive economy, it is optimal to take no action when foreign countries subsidize their production. If the foreign markets in which goods are subsidized are imperfectly competitive, a partial counter-subsidy may improve welfare but in this case the optimal policy for the importing country and the world as a whole is to make world markets more competitive.

The Uruguay Round Agreement introduced a definition of subsidies; members must notify the WTO annually of all subsidies, but the WTO discipline on their use by members is still weak. The emphasis under the WTO rules is on the countervailing of subsidies by other members when goods cross national borders, and this is at the discretion of the importing countries. (There are separate rules for agricultural subsidies, and other provisions which prevent the use of subsidies that nullify and impair concessions made in the multilateral negotiations.) Subsidies which are not prohibited (export subsidies or domestic subsidies not extended to imports) or non-actionable (such as non-industry-specific subsidies or industry-specific R&D subsidies) are actionable if they meet certain criteria. For example, if the rate of subsidy in *ad valorem* terms exceeds 5 per cent, it may be countervailed. In effect, although it addresses them differently, the WTO regards actionable subsidies similarly to border interventions.

All production-based subsidies discriminate among the producers of different nations and reduce the efficiency of production in the world economy in a manner similar to tariffs. The relationship between subsidies and tariffs is made clear by a standard equivalence relation in international economics: an *ad valorem* tariff is equivalent to an *ad valorem* subsidy on production plus an *ad valorem* tax on domestic consumption, with both the production subsidy and the consumption tax levied at the same rate. Subsidies stop at the border and distort international trade in much the same manner as tariffs and other border policies, though they do not have the element of a tax on buyers. This equivalence indicates that subsidies should be considered alongside tariffs as a set of instruments which distort trade and be the subject of trade policy.[4]

Subsidies may come under the purview of competition law. The notable example is the European Union. Competition law in most countries, however, does not cover subsidies.

From the point of view of competition, there are two quite distinct types of subsidies, one of which raises competition concerns and one of which does not. Subsidies and state aids are sometimes intended to start an industry or to drive out foreign producers. In recent years, some governments have granted subsidies to high-technology industries for these reasons. In such cases subsidies can certainly restrict competition (see, for example, Siebert, 1997). In other cases, however, subsidies may have little effect on the nature or degree of competition on international markets. Only the former type of subsidies are the legitimate concern of competition-driven policy and competition laws. This division is recognized in two regional trading agreements, the EU and CER; the EU prohibits those state aids which distort the Single Market and the CER Agreement similarly bans all subsidies and bounties which distort area trade.

There is no question of overlap and possible conflict between competition law and trade law with subsidies, as there is with dumping, because subsidies are not a part of competition law except in the EU. The countervailing duty provisions of GATT (1994) have no bearing on competition law regarding subsidies as the international trade law remedy is at the discretion of the importing country and is only intended to prevent injury to the importing country, not to promote competition.

Those subsidies which are used for anti-competitive purposes should be addressed by national competition laws, supplemented where necessary by cooperation among national competition authorities. With regard to those subsidies which are used for protective purposes, the WTO would make a major contribution to reducing the distortions of world trade and thereby to the improvement of efficiency in the world economy if it introduced discipline on the use of these subsidies and negotiated reductions in their use by members of the WTO.

The Working Group on the Interaction between International Trade and Competition

The interface between international trade and competition had arisen again as an issue in the Uruguay Round negotiations but it was not included in the agreements and decisions of the Round. At the first Ministerial Conference of the WTO in Singapore in December 1996, it was agreed

> to establish a working group to study issues raised by members relating to the interaction between trade and competition policy, including anti-competitive practices, in order to identify any areas that may merit further consideration in the WTO framework.

The decision stresses the importance of cooperation with UNCTAD and other appropriate intergovernmental fora. The Singapore Declaration states clearly that future negotiations in this area, if any, will take place only after an explicit consensus decision is reached among WTO members. The Working Group is to report to the General Council of the WTO, which will determine after two years how its work should proceed.

The Working Group has become the most important forum for debating the issues involved in the interface between trade and competition policies and multi-national competition law. It has held a number of meetings: the IMF, World Bank, OECD and APEC have observer status at these meetings. The work programme of the Working Group has been guided to date by the checklist of issues suggested for study, prepared by the chairman after the initial meetings in the light of suggestions made by delegations. The first item deals with the relationship between the objectives, principles, concepts, scope and instruments of trade and competition policy, and their relationship to development and economic growth. The second item deals with a stocktaking and analysis of existing instruments, standards and activities regarding trade and competition policy. These are divided into national competition policies, laws and instruments as they relate to trade, existing WTO provisions, and bilateral, regional, plurilateral and multilateral agreements and initiatives. The third item concerns interaction between trade and competition policy, and the fourth is identification of any areas that may merit further consideration in the WTO framework. This agenda is similar to that of the OECD CLP Committee.

In the Working Group there has been a vigorous debate about which matters fall within the Group's terms of reference. In particular, the US and the EU argue that anti-dumping measures are authorized under Article VI of the GATT and are not trade-and-competition matters. Developing countries argue to the contrary that they are one of the most important matters at the interface between trade and competition.

Under the first item of the checklist, almost all countries accept the usefulness of competition law; only China, Hong Kong SAR and Singapore have expressed strong reservations about the development of national competition laws within their jurisdictions. Under the third and fourth items there is an opportunity to develop a new multilateral mechanism for dealing with cross-border competition problems. There are, however, in the WTO (as in the OECD and other fora) major differences of view among the members. The EU in particular is pressing for a binding agreement on a set of competition rules. In a speech in Geneva in April 1998 the European Competition Commissioner Karel Van Miert urged the WTO to adopt an agreement which commits all members to develop competition laws, lay down common basic rules and common principles on harmful practices with an international dimension (Van Miert, 1998). The WTO would not have investigative powers in the area but the agreement would be enforceable through the WTO dispute settlement procedures. On the other hand, the US prefers to see the development of a network of bilateral agreements. More than one-half of the members of the WTO do not have comprehensive national competition laws.

The WTO Working Group needs to consider the views of developing economies too. ASEAN is an example of a group of developing countries; because none of its members is a member of the OECD, they have not been involved in those plurilateral discussions. In its Communication to the Working Group (WTO, 1997e) ASEAN refers to 'the lack of a common understanding of competition policy among [ASEAN] members'. The Communication adopts a broad approach to the scope of 'competition policy', that is including foreign trade regimes, deregulation, privatization and intellectual property rights. It makes clear that 'competition policy' also includes anti-dumping duties, quantitative restrictions and all other government measures that impact on market conduct. It comments that the absence of legal instruments or competition laws need not mean that a country is not generally promoting competition and 'the decision whether or not to enact law, in the final analysis, rests on the judgment of the responsible authorities'.

ASEAN also makes the point that, as a whole, WTO provisions do not have consumer welfare or the public interest as central obligations. And it goes on to highlight the potential conflict that exists between trade and competition policy, particularly if individual governments use their discretion to permit competition-restraining measures in respect of services or investment, for example, or in protecting concentrated market structures considered to be of strategic importance. However, the ASEAN Free Trade Agreement (AFTA), which is the regional trading arrangement covering nine members, has not yet taken up the issue of 'competition policy'.

Thus, some submissions to the Working Group have recognized the broad nature of competition policy extending beyond competition law but, in the tradition of the GATT and the WTO, the WTO is primarily concerned with the interface between competition policy and international trade policy. The terms of reference of the Ministerial Conference adopted a cautious approach to the development of competition policies and law in the WTO. It is too early to know if the Working Group will develop any major multilateral initiatives regarding principles or standards or rules.

Notes

1. The proposals of the International Antitrust Draft Working Code Group are a hybrid of the two kinds. They envisage the negotiation of commitments on competition law and minimum or harmonized standards. Enforcement, however, would be by national authorities with national treatment for foreigners wishing to bring an action, positive comity and a multilateral dispute settlement procedure to resolve disputes between nations. Membership of the Code was to be on a WTO—plurilateral basis, that is, a country could opt whether or not to join. Some members of the Group supported a less ambitious proposal.
2. Border restrictions are important indirectly because dumping across national borders can occur only if markets are segmented. Border restrictions are a means of segmenting world markets.
3. Individual countries with anti-dumping legislation could unilaterally remove it but this is a politically unrealistic option at present.
4. The equivalence also indicates that the GATT view of subsidies as a matter for policy subject only to countervailing action is inadequate. One possibility would be for international negotiations to reduce subsidy levels multilaterally in the same way as the GATT has liberalized tariffs and other non-tariff restrictions on international trade. But this is a matter of multilateral trade policy, not multilateral competition policy.

11.   An Historic Case: the *Kodak/Fuji* Dispute

Introduction

The WTO is a multilateral body designed to regulate government behaviour through agreed obligations. Its rules do not cover the conduct of private firms and there is no provision for rule-of-reason assessment of the market impact of private business conduct (see WTO, 1998b, p. 173) nor of market structures themselves, although private actions may be deemed to be affected by government measures (WTO, 1998b, p. 387). Even if there were such provisions, the WTO operates within a market access/trade framework and not a competition framework. Essentially it is governed by *market access* objectives and concerns about the impact of *government* measures on *trade* and its possible nullification or impairment.

As the result of a trade dispute between the US and Japan, the US took a complaint to the WTO relating to its exports to Japan of photographic film and paper. This has become known as the *Kodak/Fuji* dispute but the full name of the case adjudicated by the WTO Panel was *Japan — Measures Affecting Consumer Photographic Film and Paper*. This is a major case which illustrates the procedures and the problems of dispute settlement in relation to *competition* matters in the WTO.

Kodak and Fuji Film are private firms. A WTO panel could not therefore be asked to rule on the conduct of those firms nor on the impact of their conduct on *competition* in the relevant market. More specifically, a panel could not determine whether or not Fuji's practice of exclusive dealing in Japan was restricting Kodak's access to that market (as distinct from access to established distribution chains) and/or was undermining competition in that market. Rather, in order for the US *Government* to bring a case involving private firms to the WTO, which it requested in September 1996 pursuant to the Dispute Settlement Understanding, it had to attribute responsibility for the alleged violation of market access/trade rules (and for non-violation nullification/impairment) to measures[1] supported or implemented by the Japanese Government. The context was trade rules, not competition rules.

The Case

Nullification or impairment claim

The essential claim of the US related to systematic and deliberate intentions on the part of the Japanese government to nullify or impair[2] its Kennedy/Tokyo/Uruguay Round tariff concessions[3] through protection to production in Japan and less-favourable treatment to imported compared with national products. Allegedly this protection and discriminatory treatment resulted from certain non-transparent Japanese laws, regulations and requirements which affected the distribution, offering for sale and internal sale of imported consumer photographic film and paper ('the measures' or, as the US termed them, 'liberalization countermeasures', which in combination violated various Articles of the GATT and also caused non-violation nullification or impairment).

The term 'distribution measures' was used by the US to cover 'Japan's policy of restructuring the distribution system for photographic materials into exclusionary distribution channels' (WTO, 1998b, p. 42). The Large Stores Law has allegedly been restricting the growth of an alternative film distribution channel and has worked to ensure that Japan's manufacturer-dominated distribution system would not be undermined; and the Premiums Law has allegedly restricted sales promotions and been disadvantageous to imports. Overall, the relationship between imports and domestic products in the Japanese market was 'upset' (WTO, 1998b, p. 226).

Japan questioned the link made by the US between 'measures' (including administrative guidance) and private decisions (not covered by GATT's dispute settlement system) affecting single-brand distribution and hence market structure (WTO, 1998b, p. 201). It argued that marketplace conditions or trade flows, which reflect multiple influences, were an inappropriate basis from which to infer nullification or impairment. Rather, it argued, the Panel should determine whether the provisions (rather than the consequences) of the measures themselves 'are inherently less favourable to imports of the [tariff] bound product than to domestic products' (WTO, 1998b, p. 230). It regarded any possibility of a remedy requiring that primary wholesalers be forced to deal with Kodak as 'extraordinary', as it would radically expand the Panel's authority to the restructuring of Japan's distribution sector (WTO, 1998b, p. 175).

Japanese Cabinet decision, 1967

The US relied heavily on a 1967 Japanese Cabinet decision relating to liberalization of inward direct investment, which highlighted the perceived risk that the offer of premiums and large-scale advertising and publicity and other 'disorderly activities by foreign capital' might qualify as 'unfair trade practices' (WTO, 1998b, p. 6). Order in domestic industries might be disturbed if foreign enterprises used 'the strength of their superior power'. Countermeasures would be established 'for strengthening the capacity of [Japanese] enterprises for international competition and for preventing foreign enterprises from disturbing order in [Japanese] industries and market'. The ability to resist the influence of foreign capital in the distribution sector in particular was seen as weak, with adverse impact on the production sector. It was considered necessary, therefore, 'to implement countermeasures in support of the efforts of industry with the objectives of modernizing the distribution structure, fundamentally strengthening the enterprises in this sector, and establishing a mass sales system' (WTO, 1998b, p. 8).

While Japan submitted that in 1980 it had formally repealed the 1967 Cabinet decision that had become the focus of US (and now WTO) attention, the US maintained that the repeal only affected controls on international investment in Japan and not the 'liberalization countermeasures'.

Large Stores Law

The US also placed much reliance on Japan's Large Scale Retail Store Law which currently requires notification of proposed large stores to MITI (if floor area is 3,000 square metres or above, or 6,000 square metres in large cities) or to a prefectural governor (if floor area is between 500 and 3,000 square metres). As one of a number of procedures, both the floor area and planned opening date of the new or expanded store must be notified at least 12 months before the proposed opening (WTO, 1998b, p. 18). The authority determines 'whether the proposed store poses a probability of a significant effect on nearby small and medium business retail activities'[4] and may recommend a reduction in sales floorspace and/or a delay in the opening date. This recommendation passes to the appropriate Large Store Council, which in turn advises MITI or the prefectural governors, who then can recommend or order the large store investors to delay the store opening or reduce the floorspace.

The US contended that large stores more frequently carry imported products including film and, if permitted to proliferate, would allow circumvention of the wholesale 'bottleneck'.

The Premiums Law

US attention was also focused on both the Antimonopoly Law and Premiums (that is, economic benefits attached to goods or services transactions) Law, enforced by Japan's Fair Trade Commission (JFTC). The Premiums Law enables the JFTC to restrict the value or form or method of offer of premiums or to prohibit such an offer on grounds of 'unfair inducement to customers'. The US contended that this law, at least in part, was intended to protect local producers from anticipated aggressive import competition as trade became liberalized.

Japan's response

Japan's broad response was that as markets liberalized MITI's distribution policies (which said nothing about single-brand distribution) were aimed at Japan's distribution inefficiency; they were not aimed at blocking imports through protective vertical integration. The so-called liberalization countermeasures did not discriminate against imported film or paper by creating or facilitating an exclusionary market structure. The practice of single-brand distribution in Japan, based on economic incentives, preceded implementation of the alleged measures.

The Large Stores Law reflected a long-standing policy of preserving a diversity of small, medium and large retail competitors. Japan submitted that the law did not regulate product composition and that no correlation existed between store size and the likelihood of stocking imported film brands.

As far as the Premiums Law was concerned, Japan submitted that this was part of consumer protection, it did not distinguish between imported or domestic product, and it only targeted unfair/excessive inducements or deceptive and misleading representations.

Further, Japan denied the existence of any distribution 'bottleneck':

> [I]f a foreign manufacturer is dissatisifed with the quality of its distribution system for film and paper in Japan, there is nothing that would prevent it from taking steps to improve matters. There are no current government measures preventing the foreign manufacturer from hiring more sales people, offering lower prices, or spending more on advertising. Further, there are no current government measures preventing a foreign manufacturer from acquiring other distributors or photofinishing laboratories if they were for sale. And further, there are no current government measures of any kind that would in any way stop a foreign manufacturer from expanding or improving its distribution network . . . [I]n particular, there are no government measures that prevent foreign manufacturers from attempting to establish relationships with independent primary wholesalers that currently choose to carry only a single brand . . . Fuji's contracts with its primary wholesalers do not contain any provisions that prohibit or discourage the carrying of other brands . . . [S]ome of Fuji's primary wholesalers do currently sell Kodak products.   (WTO, 1998b, p. 61)

> [The fact that brands are] sold by the manufacturer to single-brand primary wholesalers . . . does not mean that imports lack access to the primary wholesaler distribution channel. Rather, the different brands simply utilize different primary wholesalers.   (WTO, 1998b, p. 65)

> [Kodak sells through] a wholly owned subsidiary [which] was a Japanese company, Nagase, and then a joint venture with Nagase. (WTO, 1998b, p. 268)

> Fuji's primary wholesalers are independent companies. (WTO, 1998b, p. 365).

Japan also pointed to evidence of Kodak's unwillingness to compete on price.

Third parties

Both the EC and Mexico entered arguments as third parties to the dispute. In the EC's view the Panel's focus should be on any GATT/WTO infringement resulting from protection of *domestic production* :

> and not with any other general governmental measure which is aimed at limiting or regulating, at the same time and in the same way, the marketing of both domestic and imported products . . . The dispute settlement procedures have [not] been conceived and structured to . . . compare or harmonise different legal or economic systems applied by WTO Members. (WTO, 1998b, pp. 358—9)

But the EC took the opportunity to register its view that there is a need for an international framework of competition rules within the WTO system. It gave weight to the following factual aspects:

*   the difficulties 'despite intensive efforts' in acquiring a market share in Japan for film/photographic products 'which corresponds to [Europe's] actual overall world market share';
*   the lack of (foreign) brand awareness amongst Japanese consumers. Media advertising and store promotions would provide an additional burden on distribution of imported products;
*   imported film and paper are excluded 'from the best way to reach the Japanese customers'.

The WTO Panel's Findings

The WTO Panel's preliminary legal findings and conclusions, with which the US expressed strong disagreement, were contained in its interim (December 1997) report. None the less, the Panel's final report (WTO, 1998b) concluded unequivocally that the US had not been able to demonstrate benefit nullification or impairment as a result of the alleged measures — whether these measures were viewed individually or together; neither, the Panel found, did the US demonstrate — either in terms of *de jure* or *de facto* discrimination — that the alleged distribution measures accorded treatment to imported photographic film and paper that was less favourable than that accorded to supply of Japanese origin. In respect of the Premiums and Large Stores Laws the alleged violations of Article X were not sustained.

In considering the non-violation nullification or impairment remedy, the Panel accepted the possibility that the national treatment requirement of a competitive relationship between domestic and imported products, that is the competitive market access condition/expectation, could be upset by a WTO member pursuing a sectoral policy to increase efficiency (WTO, 1998b, p. 382). Importantly, it went on to say:

> In this regard, however, we must also bear in mind that tariff concessions have never been viewed as creating a guarantee of trade volumes, but rather, . . . as creating expectations as to competitive relationships.

When later discussing Article III's national treatment requirement (WTO, 1998b, pp. 481—82), the *Kodak/Fuji* Panel made it clear (as had previous Panel reports) that the appropriate emphasis is on 'equality of competitive opportunities' for imported products, in so far as the application of laws and regulations is concerned.

The Panel found that single-brand distribution in Japan appeared to have occurred before and independently of the distribution measures cited by the US; and that the complainant had not demonstrated that the purpose of these measures was vertical integration or single-brand distribution. But also, the Panel said (WTO, 1998b, p. 431) that the US had not explained:

> why the vertically integrated, single-brand distribution structure of the film sector in Japan — a state of affairs that the evidence suggests is similar to that occurring elsewhere in the world (including in the United States) — would have broken down in the absence of continuing government intervention.

It was unclear to the Panel 'why the same economic forces acting to promote single-brand wholesale distribution in the US would not also exist in Japan' (WTO, 1998b, p. 483).

Parties to the dispute did not appeal the Panel's final report, either on factual issues or on legal interpretations developed by the Panel. The report was formally adopted in April 1998 by the WTO's dispute settlement body.

A Brief Review

Underlying the *Kodak/Fuji* dispute taken to the WTO by the US Government was a debate about the role of *market* rules relative to the role of *trade* rules. And a *competition* framework was clearly lacking. The

Panel was bound by the criteria for adjudicating the nullification or impairment of negotiated trade concessions and was constrained (at least in its final report) from giving more attention to such matters as: the economics of vertical integration; the role of economic organization in the competitive process; promoting competition versus protecting competitors; how governments and firms — consistent with competition and efficiency objectives — might respond to the threat of foreign capital and prospects of efficient competition; and Kodak's (among others') approach to investment, promotion and price competition in respect of photographic film and paper in Japan.

The Panel did, however, make the crucial distinction between the *guarantee* (which it dismissed) of trade volumes and the *opportunity* for market share. Only the latter is relevant in trade or competition disputes. Also, national treatment, being an obligation upon member governments, does not impose obligations on market participants to ensure that actual operating conditions are equalized for all-comers.

There is an irony associated with the US Government's role in taking the *Kodak/Fuji* dispute to the WTO. The US is clearly in favour of intergovernment anti-trust cooperation via sound anti-trust enforcement at a national level, together with bilateral cooperation agreements (see Chapter 3, and WTO, 1998a). There are several reasons why the US might not wish to pursue anti-trust objectives or other competition-oriented policies through the WTO: business practices are better covered by anti-trust than by trade law; long-established US anti-trust rules, including extraterritorial provisions, could be diluted in the process of multilateral negotiations; a WTO panel could make rulings about, say, Kodak's exclusive dealing practices within the US, which could conflict with rulings under US anti-trust law; government-condoned private business practices that create trade barriers by restricting parallel importing might come under closer scrutiny; and the competition culture sought in respect of anti-trust at national and bilateral levels might come too close to the anti-dumping rules used disproportionately by the US Government.[5] Anti-dumping intervention is widely recognized as a source of contingent protection from trade and price competition. Government support for parallel importing prohibitions can also be viewed in this way (see Chapter 5). US calls for 'an international culture of competition' and 'a more comprehensive regulatory framework for competition policy' will not resound unless the US itself can demonstrate a more consistent and coherent approach to competition issues in the interests of efficiently functioning markets.

In taking the *Kodak/Fuji* dispute to the WTO, the US — despite its failure to convince the Dispute Settlement Panel of the robustness of its allegations against the Japanese Government — has assisted in focusing attention on two issues of fundamental relevance to a multi-national approach to competition issues. These have become thematic in this book: first, government regulatory or other actions, whether directly or passively supportive of business conduct, can interfere with the competitive process and with legitimate expectations of competitive relationships in a market. A corollary of this is that a range of both government and private actions are an integral part of a competition framework.

Secondly, trade rules are inadequate as a basis for resolving cross-border *competition* disputes. For a start, competition analysis would pay more attention to the distinction between access to a 'market' defined by country and jurisdictional boundaries, and success in a market defined by economic parameters which might cover several countries. It would go well beyond market share measures and frustrated expectations of a trade benefit, and, particularly in distribution disputes, it would or should make a distinction between access to a (properly defined) market and access to established distribution outlets.

Just prior to the Panel's final report, the USTR (1998a) announced a 'new market opening initiative' for imported photographic materials in Japan. The EU (1998) supported the US plan. An inter-agency monitoring and enforcement committee is to 'review implementation of formal representations [i.e. "market access commitments"] made by the Government of Japan [to the WTO Panel] regarding its efforts to ensure the openness of its market to imports of film'. Data to be collected and assessed would include the availability of foreign brands in distribution channels, the number and type of retail stores in Japan carrying photographic products, and the availability by volume of foreign brands in those outlets. No reference was made to relative prices or promotional policies.

Despite the Panel's findings and the fact that these were not appealed, the US Government, on behalf of US companies, is pursuing the film case along the same lines as before, that is, with emphasis on market outcomes rather than on inputs to the competitive process. The USTR has not concealed its disappointment with the WTO's decision, believing that it did not address market realities. On the other hand, Japan has resisted the 'unreasonable' suggestion that its submissions to the WTO Panel be treated as commitments subject to monitoring to ensure their implementation, seeing this as a unilateral attempt by the US to create new future obligations (MITI, 1998). Japan stresses the importance of rule-based criteria in dispute settlement as distinct from result-based criteria and numerical targets. Whatever the merits of the US allegations, the analytical framework for addressing them is still wanting.

Pursuant to the US—Japan Enhanced Initiative on Deregulation and Competition Policy, signed by President Clinton and Prime Minister Hashimoto in June 1997, the Japanese government has agreed *inter alia* to abolish the Large Scale Retail Stores Law, make regulatory decisions more transparent, and to strengthen areas of anti-trust enforcement and compliance monitoring, including in respect of film.

Notes

1. That is, within the meaning of GATT Article XXIII:1(b).
2. That is, within the meaning of GATT Article XXIII:1(b), which provides a right of redress for impairment of any benefit accruing from a reciprocal tariff concession even if there is non-violation of GATT provisions. In practice, this remedy has been used sparingly and in situations where a new or modified GATT-consistent domestic subsidy was involved. A complainant must have regard to three elements: namely, application of a current measure; a currently accruing benefit; and causality.
3. Following the Uruguay Round, bound tariffs on film and paper were zero.
4. Since 1994, stores with retail space not exceeding 1,000 square metres have, in principle, been deemed not to have any such probability.
5. The WTO's Annual Report 1997 (Vol. 1, p. 110) shows that of 900 anti-dumping measures (including undertakings) in force at 31 December 1996, 35 per cent were maintained by the United States; whereas in 1996 their share of world merchandise imports by value was 15.1 per cent (Vol. 11, Table 1.5) or 19.9 per cent if intra-EU trade (for which no anti-dumping remedy applies) is excluded (Vol. 11, Table 1.6).

PART SIX

Emerging Patterns and Principles

12. An Approach to Promoting Competition in Global Markets

As a consequence of globalizing markets, issues of competition increasingly involve more than one country. This gives rise to a basic problem: markets do not stop at national borders and therefore dealing with competition issues cannot be limited to national jurisdictions. In response, there have been numerous national and multi-national approaches to this basic problem. Some nations have sought to make extraterritorial use of their powers and a variety of multi-national approaches is evolving.

Some positive initiatives have emerged but many of these are untested or have shown a limited capacity to address cross-border competition problems. These initiatives have been hampered generally by a failure to recognize the real nature and scope of the issues and by a confusion of objectives. To advance multi-national initiatives a clear analytical framework is required.

Principles for Promoting Global Competition

There is a consensus in the OECD countries and a growing recognition among other countries that markets should be contestable and more weight attached to efficiency in the allocation of scarce resources. Economic theory shows that efficiency generally requires both competitive markets and free trade among nations. However, most of the multi-national initiatives have been based on the premise that 'competition policy' is a trade-related issue; that is, the central concern has been that barriers to competition, and in particular anti-competitive private business conduct, reduce the benefits from lowering border barriers to international trade. It emphasizes market access in the trade policy sense of border access. This emphasis on market access tends to assume that the appropriate objective here is the maximization of international trade.

Free trade is about opportunities for trade, based on real costs of production; export and other subsidies, for example, over-expand trade. It is distortions of trade that reduce the gains from trade. Similarly, distortions to the competitive process lead to a misallocation of resources amongst both producers and consumers. This leads to a two-track approach to improving efficiency in the world economy: promoting competition and liberalizing trade. A two-track approach is not meant to deny the two-way interactions between trade liberalization and the promotion of competition.

To promote efficient competition in all markets requires comprehensiveness. By this we mean that many areas of government policy and their application impinge upon competition and efficiency in markets. Therefore, policymakers need to create an overall operating environment for businesses that is most conducive to competition among them. For example, the trade policy which would have the greatest effect on the competitive process is to continue with trade liberalization. This environment would minimize the opportunities for business to act anti-competitively. Thus, policies aimed specifically at anti-competitive business conduct should be required to deal only with residual problems of the competitive process. One consequence of a comprehensive approach to the minimization of competition problems would be a reduction in inter-government competition disputes.

Recognizing the comprehensiveness of policies which promote competition, it is important to ensure coherence among the different areas. In the earlier chapters we found a number of examples where a policy or policy instrument in one area conflicts with the promotion of competition. Anti-dumping duties and producer boards/state trading enterprises are two instruments of trade policy that can interfere with the competitive process. The ban on parallel importing under copyright laws also interferes with the competitive process, though it is more commonly seen as a trade-related issue. The exemption of export cartels is an example of inconsistency within the area of competition law. Another type of inconsistency occurs when one jurisdiction treats a particular type of conduct differently depending on whether it occurs within its borders or across the borders, for example, price discrimination. Similarly, some countries are in favour of extraterritoriality when they are applying it but not in favour when it is applied to them. A comprehensive approach to competition issues helps to identify such inconsistencies and potential distortions to the competitive process.

Opinions on how to resolve these inconsistencies depend fundamentally on whether a national view or a global view is taken. The above examples could result in inefficiencies, that is policy-induced distortions (as discussed in Chapter 2), in the world economy. One advantage of a global perspective is that it focuses on aggregate world output and economic welfare. Indeed, distortions can be eliminated only if a global view is taken. In some cases, removing a policy-induced distortion may make an individual nation worse off. But it is short-sighted to dwell on an individual case. Any one nation is affected by many such cases and the elimination of these various distortions is a repeated game, to use the language of game theory. Hence, a global perspective generally serves the interests of individual nations. (Multilateral trade negotiations under the GATT provide another example of a repeated game.)

One objection frequently made to changing policies or their implementation is that national sovereignty is thereby eroded. The set of policies which are regarded as nationally sovereign has changed over time and will inevitably continue to do so. Although national sovereignty will remain a fundamental principle, even with globalization, nations will inevitably be called upon from time to time to judge whether it is in their long-term interests to retain or cede sovereignty in a particular area.

When individual nations consider how to adopt a comprehensive view of policies to promote competition, and how to resolve national or cross-border policy conflicts involving a competition issue, they should be guided by a set of over-arching competition principles. These would be operationalized by individual economies so as to allow economy-specific characteristics and in particular the level of economic development to be accommodated. Obviously, the more countries which can agree on a set of common principles the better. In addition to guiding national policy formation and implementation, the principles would guide multi-national approaches to competition issues. Of itself, this would help to avoid and resolve inter-country policy conflicts.

In Chapter 2 we said that principles embody general characteristics or values which can be used to guide policy formation and application. We have advocated the principles of *comprehensiveness* and *coherence.* Another principle often advanced, and which we endorse, is *non-discrimination*; this principle clearly has several applications: for example, to modes of supply and to foreign/national persons within a jurisdiction.

A complete set of competition principles should be a product of consensus building in major multi-national fora such as the WTO, OECD and APEC. APEC is one forum that is taking an interest in PECC's work in this area, consistent with APEC's Collective Action Plan requirement for member economies to consider developing non-binding principles on competition policy and/or laws.

There is no doubt that competition issues are extremely complex. One area of complexity is that of analysis of an alleged competition problem; in competition law this is recognized by the move away from *per se* prohibitions in favour of a rule-of-reason approach to individual cases of business conduct. Another source of complexity is the diversity among nations in the objectives and in rules and their enforcement in relation to anti-competitive business practices. Much is being done in international fora to gain a better understanding of these complexities. This is helping the evolution of mechanisms for addressing cross-border competition issues in order to improve efficiency in the world economy.

Countries have started to take different positions on their preferred multi-national mechanism(s) for addressing cross-border competition issues. Their preferences depend on, among other things, their own legal systems and policy objectives; their domestic and international experiences; and what they regard as appropriate for the international competition agenda.

As far as the ability of a nation to pursue cross-border enforcement is concerned, there is a choice between two avenues for enforcement: coordination versus centralization. In respect of coordination, the individual nation retains responsibility for enforcement but this depends on cooperation from other countries. By contrast, in respect of centralization, a central or supranational authority assumes enforcement responsibility.

It is already clear from our research that no single mechanism can deal with cross-border competition issues. While each of the multi-national mechanisms studied has some positive features, each also has its limitations. In making choices between different multi-national mechanisms for dealing with cross-border competition issues, it is crucial — as part of the process of determining optimal policies — to understand the limitations of each of the present mechanisms. Our research suggests that the principal limitations of each mechanism are as follows.

Principal Limitations of Multi-National Mechanisms

Bilateral mechanism

The fundamental principle of national autonomy limits a nation's ability to exchange information and to carry out enforcement activities at the request of another nation. This will necessarily limit the extent to which bilateral cooperation agreements on competition law enforcement will evolve.

Despite the breakthrough in developing the concept of positive comity, there is no obligation on one party to act upon a request from another party, and the requested nation is not likely to do so when the outcome could work against its national interest.

A particular limitation on the conflict-management potential of bilateral agreements is the fact that they have not to date contained a provision which excludes extraterritorial action between the parties to the agreement. This exclusion could be added to bilateral agreements which contain positive comity provisions. Of itself, the continued threat of extraterritorial action would seem to undermine the cooperative approach to the resolution of cross-border competition problems.

Regional mechanism

This mechanism is limited by the inherent nature of a region. First, a region is conceived of as a trade liberalization mechanism, and it has generally proven difficult for member countries to take a regional view of competition problems in markets which cover their region. Secondly, regional arrangements do not extend to markets in third countries.

Plurilateral mechanism

This mechanism is by definition confined to non-binding arrangements.

Multilateral mechanism

The WTO is the existing multilateral mechanism. The choice of the WTO as the institutional location for addressing emerging competition issues has considerable appeal. This is because of the breadth of its membership and its positioning as an organization which could, in principle, correct policy distortions affecting globalizing markets.

However, as presently constituted, the WTO's concern is with rules for world trade in goods and services. Thus, it tends to emphasize a market-access/trade-related approach to competition issues, in respect of both its rules and dispute settlement procedures. As an organization which promulgates binding rules, individual members are understandably wary of ceding powers to the WTO in respect of a range of competition issues in globalizing markets. Even if the members were not, it is questionable that the solutions to competition issues and problems lie in a multilateral rules-based organization, given the principle of comprehensiveness, the nature of business conduct in markets, the trend away from *per se* prohibitions of business conduct and the analytical complexities of the rule-of-reason approach. There is the further practical difficulty of securing agreement amongst more than 130 members, especially in view of their different stages of development and institutional capacity.

Positive Features of Multi-National Mechanisms

Yet the evolving mechanisms have several positive features. These include a sharing of policy experiences among countries; a greater awareness of policy options; some recognition of the interconnections between different policy areas; advocacy of policies to promote or defend competition; better management of conflict between jurisdictions; early attempts to develop competition principles and standards; and some convergence towards an efficiency goal for competition law.

There are some specific precedents of multi-national significance which other countries could follow, although not all of these would have universal relevance or acceptance. These include the positive comity features of the 1998 US—EU cooperation agreement; the NAFTA requirement that all members adopt or maintain measures to proscribe anti-competitive business conduct; the EU and CER provisions for removing the anti-dumping remedy in conjunction with other provisions for economic integration; the provision in the Canada—Chile Free Trade Agreement to remove the anti-dumping remedy without giving specific extraterritorial extension to their competition laws; the CER action to eliminate production subsidies affecting trade and competition in the area; the OECD 'hard-core' cartel agreement; the attention paid by ministers of FTAA countries to coherence between interrelated policy areas; and the declared APEC interest in developing (non-binding) principles on 'competition policy' and laws.

National and International Responsibilities

We have concluded that it is not feasible or desirable at present to have a multilateral competition authority and that there is no single multi-national mechanism which provides the solution to all cross-border competition issues. Consequently, nations or groups of nations will have to seek solutions which are most appropriate to their circumstances. But, especially as unilateral extraterritorial action should be used sparingly and bilateral enforcement cooperation arrangements are somewhat limited, a broad conceptual and policy approach which aims to minimize the potential for cross-border competition problems is clearly pivotal. However, even if nations adopt comprehensive and coherent policies to promote competition in all markets (which is what we advocate), there is likely to be a residual of business and government conduct which spills over to other nations and leads to inefficiencies in the world economy. A combination of multi-national mechanisms should therefore continue to develop to ensure that the nations in which such conduct is located take action to eliminate or correct conduct which harms the competitive process in a relevant market. We have identified several valuable precedents above.

This action will require countries, in examining this conduct within their borders, to take a global market and global efficiency view, rather than a national jurisdiction and national interest view. It is this perspective which will be most conducive to the enhancement of global welfare.

Great responsibility thus remains with individual countries to cooperate not only on investigative and enforcement matters but also in the development and application of competition principles at the national and multi-national levels. This could be called positive unilateralism consistent with a multi-national approach.

References

American Bar Association (ABA) (1994), *Report of the Task Force of the ABA Section of Antitrust Law on The Competition Dimension of NAFTA*, Chicago: American Bar Association

APEC Business Advisory Council (ABAC) (1997), *Report to the APEC Economic Leaders*, Singapore: APEC Secretariat

Asia-Pacific Economic Cooperation (APEC) (1997a), *Workshop on Competition Policy and Deregulation,* Quebec City: 18—19 May

Asia-Pacific Economic Cooperation (APEC) (1997b), Committee on Trade and Investment, *Annual Report to Ministers*, Vancouver, Canada: 21—22 November

Australian Department of Foreign Affairs and Trade (1995), *Trade and Competition Policy: A Survey of the Issues*, Mina & Gibbons, International Trade Research Paper Series, Canberra: Australian Government Publishing Service

Baccheta, M., H. Horn and P. Mavroidis (1997), 'Do Negative Spillovers from Nationally Pursued Competition Policies provide a Case for Multilateral Competition Rules?', mimeo, August 14

Baker, D.I., A.N. Campbell, M.J. Reynolds and J.W. Rowley (1997), 'The Harmonization of International Competition Law Enforcement' in L. Waverman, W.S. Comanor and A. Goto (eds), *Competition Policy in the Global Economy: Modalities for Cooperation*, London and New York: Routledge

Baumol, W.J., J.C. Panzar and R.D. Willig (1980), *Contestable Markets and the Theory of Industry Structure*, San Diego: Harcourt, Brace, Jovanovich

Baxt, R. (1990), 'Competition and Securities Law. Institutional Arrangements and Issues', in K.M. Vautier, J. Farmer and R. Baxt (eds), *CER and Business Competition: Australia and New Zealand in a Global Economy,* Auckland: Commerce Clearing House New Zealand Limited

Bhagwati, J.N. (1971), 'The Generalized Theory of Distortions and Welfare' in J.N. Bhagwati *et al., Trade, Balance of Payments and Growth*, Amsterdam: North-Holland

Bollard, A. and K.M. Vautier (1998), 'The Convergence of Competition Law within APEC and the CER Agreement', in Rong-I Wu and Yun-Peng Chu (eds), *Business, Markets and Government in the Asia Pacific*, PAFTAD, London: Routledge

Bourtese, R.B. (1994), *Competition and Integration: What Goals Count?* Deventer-Boston: Kluwer

Brittan, L. (1992), *European Competition Policy: Keeping the Playing Field Level*, London: Brassey's

Brittan, L. (1997), 'Competition Policy and the Trading System: Towards International Rules in the WTO', Washington, DC: Institute of International Economics, 20 November

Buigues, P., A. Jacquemin and A. Sapir (eds) (1995), *European Policies on Competition, Trade and Industry: Conflict and Complementarities*, Aldershot: Edward Elgar

Burdon, Philip (1996), Speech to the Trans-Tasman Tax Conference, Auckland, in New Zealand Ministry of Foreign Affairs and Trade, *CER: Key Documents, Speeches and Statements 1996*, Wellington: Ministry of Foreign Affairs and Trade

Burdon, Philip and Bob McMullan (1995), *Joint Statement*, Review of CER, Wellington: Ministry of Foreign Affairs and Trade

Campbell, A.N. and N. Trebilcock (1997), 'Interjurisdictional Conflict in Merger Review', in L. Waverman, W.S. Comanor and A. Goto (eds), *Competition Policy in the Global Economy: Modalities for Cooperation*, London and New York: Routledge

Canada—Chile Free Trade Agreement (1996), 'Competition Policy, Monopolies and State Enterprises', Chapter J, Ottawa, Ontario: Department of Foreign Affairs and International Trade

Cantwell, J. (1994), 'The Relationship between International Trade and International Production' in D. Greenaway and L.A. Winters (eds), *Surveys in International Trade*, Oxford: Blackwell

Centre for Economic Policy Research (CEPR) (1993), *Making Sense of Subsidiarity: How Much Centralization for Europe?*, London: CEPR

Closer Economic Relations Agreement (CER) Steering Committee of Officials (1990), Memorandum of Understanding between the Government of Australia and the Government of New Zealand on the Harmonisation of Business Law, *Report to Governments on Competition Law*, Wellington

Cocuzza, C. and M. Montini (1998), 'International Antitrust Cooperation in a Global Economy', *European Competition Law Review*, Issue 3, 156—63

Commission of the European Communities (CEC) (1995), *White Paper: Preparation of the Associated Countries of Central and Eastern Europe for Integration into the Internal Market of the Union*, Brussels: CEC

Crampton, P. (1994), 'Alternative Approaches to Competition Law: Consumers' Surplus, Total Welfare and Non-efficiency Goals', *World Competition*, 17, 55—86

Crampton, P. and C.L. Witterick (1996), 'Trade Distorting Private Restraints and Market Access: Learning to Walk before We Run', *International Business Lawyer*, November

Ehlermann, C. (1994), 'The International Dimension of Competition Policy', *Fordham International Law Journal*, 17, 833—45

Estrin, S. and P. Holmes (1998), *Competition and Economic Integration in Europe,* Cheltenham: Edward Elgar

Ethier, W.J. (1987), 'Dumping' in J. Eatwell, M. Milgate and P. Newman (eds), *The New Palgrave Dictionary of Economics*, London: Macmillan

Ethier, W.J. (1994), 'Multinational Firms in the Theory of International Trade' in E. Bacha (ed.), *Economics in a Changing World*, London: Macmillan

European Bank for Reconstruction and Development (EBRD) (1995), *Transition Report*, London: EBRD

European Commission (1995), *Competition Policy in the New Trade Order: Strengthening International Coopeation Rules,* Brussels: EC

European Commission (1996), 'Towards an International Framework of Competition Rules', a communication submitted by Sir Leon Brittan and Karel Van Miert to the European Council, Brussels: European Commission

European Commission (1997), Commission Notice on Cooperation between National Competition Authorities and the Commission in Handling Cases Falling within the Scope of Articles 85 or 86 of the EC Treaty, Brussels: European Commission

European Commission (1998), 'International Cooperation in Antitrust Matters: Making the Point in the Wake of the Boeing/MDD Proceedings', *EC Competition Policy Newsletter*, 4, February

European Commission, Directorate-General IV (1996), *Report of the Group of Experts, Competition Policy in the New Trade Order: Strengthening International Co-operation and Rules*, Brussels: European Union, CM 91-95-124-EN-C

European Commission, Directorate-General IV (1997), *European Community Competition Policy 1997*, Brussels: European Commission

European Commission, Directorate-General for Economic and Financial Affairs (1998), *European Economy*, no.3, Brussels: European Commission

European Union (EU) (1998), Statement (6 February) referred to in *Inside US Trade*, 13 February

Falvey, R. (1998), 'Mergers in Open Economies', *World Economy*, 21, November, 1061—76

Farmer, J. (1990), 'The Harmonisation of Australian and New Zealand Business Laws', in K.M. Vautier, J. Farmer and R. Baxt (eds), *CER and Business Competition: Australia and New Zealand in a Global Economy*, Auckland: Commerce Clearing House New Zealand Limited

Finance Ministers (Australia and New Zealand) (1996), Correspondence, September, Wellington: Treasury

Fox, E.M. and J.A. Ordover (1995), 'The Harmonization of Competition and Trade Law', *World Competition*, 119, December, 5—34

Fox, E.M. and J.A. Ordover (1997), 'The Harmonization of Competition and Trade Law', in L. Waverman, W.S. Comanor and A. Goto,

Competition Policy in the Global Economy: Modalities for Cooperation, London and New York: Routledge

General Agreement on Tariffs and Trade (GATT) (1961), *Basic Instruments and Selected Documents*, Ninth Supplement, Geneva: GATT

Gifford, D.J. (1997), 'The Draft International Antitrust Code Proposed at Munich: Good Intentions Gone Awry', *Minnesota Journal of Global Trade*, 6, 1-30

Goldman, C.S., J.D. Bodrug and M.A.A. Warner (1997), 'Canada' in E.M. Graham and D. Richardson (eds), *Global Competition Policy*, Washington, DC: Institute for International Economics

Graham, E.M. (1995), 'Competition Policy and the New Trade Agenda' in OECD, *New Dimensions of Market Access in a Globalising World*, Paris: OECD

Green, C. (1996), 'Competition Regulation in the Asia-Pacific Region', paper presented to the Asia-Pacific Roundtable Meeting on the Global Contestability of National Markets, Singapore, 26—28 January

Grimwade, N. (1996), 'Anti-dumping Policy after the Uruguay Round: an Appraisal', *National Institute Economic Review*, 1/96, 98—105

Hansen, W.L. and T.J. Prusa (1996), 'Cumulation and ITC Decision-making: the Sum of the Parts is Greater than the Whole', *Economic Inquiry*, 34, 746—69

Hilmer Committee (1993), *National Competition Policy*, Report by the Independent Committee of Inquiry, Canberra: Australian Government Publishing Service

Hoekman, B. (1998), 'Free Trade and Deep Integration: Antidumping and Antitrust in Regional Agreements', mimeo, Washington, DC: World Bank

Hoekman, B. and M. Kostecki (1995), *The Political Economy of the World Trading System: From GATT to WTO*, Oxford: Oxford University Press

Hoekman, B. and P.C. Mavroidis (1996), 'Dumping, Antidumping and Antitrust', *Journal of World Trade Law*, 30, February

Hoekman, B., P. Low and P.C. Mavroidis (1996), 'Antitrust Disciplines and Market Access Negotiations: Lessons from the Telecommunications Sector', mimeo

Hong Kong Government (1996), 'Open Markets as an Approach to Competition Policy', paper presented to the APEC Workshop on Competition Policy and Deregulation, Davao, Philippines, 17—18 August

Independent (1998), 'Parallel Importing: the Battle Has Only Begun', Auckland: 1 July, 31—33

Industry Commission (1995), *Annual Report 1995—96*, Canberra: Australian Government Publishing Service

International Antitrust Code Working Group (1993), 'Draft International Antitrust Code: a GATT—MTO—Plurilateral Trade Agreement', *World Trade Materials*, 5, September, 126—96

Jackson, J.H. (1989), *The World Trading System*, Cambridge, Mass.: MIT Press

Jacquemin, A. (1993), 'The International Dimension of European Competition Policy', *Journal of Common Market Studies*, 31, March, 91—101

Jacquemin, A., P.J. Lloyd, P.K.M. Tharakan and J. Waelbroek (1998), 'The Way Ahead', *World Economy*, 21, November, 1179—83

Jardine, E. (1996), 'An Agreement between Australia and the European Union on Trade Practices: a Proposal', *Trade Practices Law Journal*, June, 67—76

Johnson, J. (1994), *The North American Free Trade Agreement: A Comprehensive Guide*, Aurora, Ontario: Canada Law Book

Keegan, L. (1996), 'The 1991 US/EC Competition Agreement: A Glimpse of the Future Through the United States *v* Microsoft Corp. Window', *International Legal Studies*, 2, 149—79

Klein, J. (1997a), 'The Internationalization of Antitrust: Bilateral and Multilateral Responses', prepared remarks, the European University Institute Conference on Competition, Florence: 13 June

Klein, J. (1997b), 'International Antitrust Enforcement at the End of the Twentieth Century', prepared remarks before Fordham 24 Annual Conference on International Law and Policy, New York: 16 October

Lall, A. (1996), 'Competition Policy in Singapore: There is None', in C.J. Green and D.E. Rosenthal (eds), *Competition Regulation in the Pacific Rim*, New York: Oceana Publications

Lawrence, R.Z. (1996), *Towards Globally Contestable Markets in OECD Market Access after the Uruguay Round: Investment, Competition and Technology Perspectives*, Paris: OECD

Levinsohn, J. (1996), 'Competition Policy and International Trade' in J.N. Bhagwati and R.E. Hudec (eds), *Fair Trade and Harmonization: Prerequisites for Free Trade?*, Cambridge, Mass.: MIT Press

Lloyd, P.J. (1977), *Anti-dumping Actions and the GATT System*, London: Trade Policy Research Centre

Lloyd, P.J. (1998a), 'Competition Policy in APEC: Principles of Harmonisation' in Rong-I Wu and Yun-Peng Chu (eds), *Business, Markets and Government in the Asia Pacific*, PECC, London: Routledge

Lloyd, P.J. (1998b), 'Multilateral Rules for International Competition Law?', *World Economy*, 21, November, 1129—49

Markusen, J.R. (1995), 'The Boundaries of Multinational Enterprises and the Theory of International Trade', *Journal of Economic Perspectives*, 9, Spring, 169—89

Mattoo, A. and A. Subramanian (1997), 'Multilateral Rules on Competition Policy: A Possible Way Forward', *Journal of World Trade*, 31, 95—115

McGowan, F. (1995), 'EC Competition Policy' in El-Agraa (ed.), *The Economics of the European Community*, 4th edn, London: Harvester-Wheatsheaf

Meltz, D. (1996), 'The Extraterritorial Operation of the Trade Practices Act: a Time for Reappraisal?', *Trade Practices Law Journal*, December, 185—205

Messerlin, P.A. and G. Reed (1995), 'The US and EC Antidumping Policies', *Economic Journal*, 105, November, 1565—75

Miller, Russell V. (1998), *Annotated Trade Practices Act*, 19th edn, Sydney: LBC Information Services

Ministerial Declaration of San Jose Summit of the Americas (1998), Fourth Trade Ministerial Meeting, Costa Rica, 19 March, p. 9

Ministry of International Trade and Industry (Japan) (MITI) (1998), *Seventh Annual Report of the Subcommittee on Unfair Trade Policies and Measures under the WTO Committee of the Industrial Structure Council*, Tokyo: MITI

Montagnon, P. (ed.) (1990), *European Competition Policy*, London: Royal Institute of International Affairs

Moussis, N. (1997), *Handbook of European Union*, 4th rev. edn, Rixensart: European Study Service

Neven, D. and P. Seabright (1997), 'Trade Liberalization and the Coordination of Competition Policy' in L. Waverman, W.S. Comanor and A. Goto (eds), *Competition Policy in the Global Economy: Modalities for Cooperation*, London and New York: Routledge

Neven, D., R. Nuttall and P. Seabright (1993), *Merger in the Daylight: The Economics and Politics of European Merger Control*, London: CEPR

New Zealand Commerce Commission (1998a), A Submission in Response to New Zealand Ministry of Commerce, 13 March, Wellington

New Zealand Commerce Commission (1998b), Media Release 1998/52, Wellington

New Zealand Government (1998), Electricity Industry Reform Act, Wellington: 3 July

New Zealand Government Commerce Committee (1998), Electricity Industry Reform Bill Commentary, p. iii, Wellington

New Zealand Herald (1998), 20 May

New Zealand Institute of Economic Research (NZIER) (1998), *Parallel Importing: A Theoretical and Empirical Investigation*, Contract no. 1441, February, Wellington

New Zealand Ministry of Commerce (1989), *Review of the Commerce Act 1986: Reports and Decisions*, Wellington: Ministry of Commerce

New Zealand Ministry of Commerce (1998a), *Penalties, Remedies and Court Processes Under the Commerce Act 1986: A Discussion Document*, Wellington

New Zealand Ministry of Commerce (1998b), *Trade Remedies in New Zealand: A Discussion Paper*, Wellington: February

New Zealand Ministry of Commerce (1998c), *Review of Trade Remedies Policy Analysis of Issues*, Wellington: 30 June

Nicolaides, P. (1996), 'For a World Competition Authority: the Role of Competition Policy in Economic Integration and the Role of Regional

Blocs in Internationalizing Competition Policy', *Journal of World Trade Law*, 30, August, 131—45

North America Free Trade Area (NAFTA) Working Group on Trade and Competition (1997), *Interim Report of the NAFTA Working Group*, Washington, DC

Organization for Economic Cooperation and Development (OECD) (1976), *Declaration on International Investment and Multinational Enterprises*, Paris: OECD

Organization for Economic Cooperation and Development (OECD) (1984a), *Trade and Competition Policy*, Paris: OECD

Organization for Economic Cooperation and Development (OECD) (1984b), *Competition and Trade Policies: Their Interaction*, Paris: OECD

Organization for Economic Cooperation and Development (OECD) (1994), *Interim Report on Convergence of Competition Policy*, Paris: OECD

Organization for Economic Cooperation and Development (OECD) (1995a), *New Dimensions of Market Access in a Globalising World Economy*, Paris: OECD

Organization for Economic Cooperation and Development (OECD) (1995b), *Revised Recommendation of the OECD Council Concerning Cooperation Between Member Countries on Anti-competitive Practices Affecting International Trade*, OECD Document No. C(95) 130/Final, 21 September

Organization for Economic Cooperation and Development (OECD) (1996a), *Antitrust and Market Access: The Scope and Coverage of Competition Laws and Implications for Trade*, Paris: OECD

Organization for Economic Cooperation and Development (OECD) (1996b), *Market Access after the Uruguay Round: Investment, Competition and Technology Perspectives*, Paris: OECD

Organization of American States (OAS) (1997), 'Mechanisms and Measures to Facilitate the Participation of Small Economies in the Free Trade Area of the Americas', Washington, DC: OAS Trade Unit Studies

Organization of American States (OAS) (1998a), FTAA Working Group on Competition Policy 'Peru Report on Developments and Enforcement of Competition Policy and Laws 1995—96', *Report on Developments and Enforcement of Competition Policy and Laws in the Western Hemisphere*, Washington, DC: March

Organization of American States (OAS) (1998b), FTTA Working Group on Competition Policy 'Brazil: Report on Developments and Enforcement of Competition Laws 1994—96', *Report on Developments and Enforcement of Competition Policy and Laws in the Western Hemisphere*, Washington, DC: March

Oxley, A. (1997), 'Parallel Imports and Trade Skirmishing', *Second Annual Conference on Trade Education and Research*, University of Melbourne, December

Pacific Economic Cooperation Council (PECC) (1996) (in collaboration with the Philippine Institute for Development Studies and the Asia

Foundation), *Perspectives on the Manila Action Plan for APEC (MAPA)*, PECC, 1st and 2nd edns

Pacific Economic Cooperation Council (PECC) (1997a), Trade Policy Forum *Conference and Experts Roundtable on Trade and Competition Policy*, Montreal: 13—14 May

Pacific Economic Cooperation Council (PECC) (1997b), 'Comments on Competition Policy Area of MAPA', *APEC Workshop on Competition Policy and Deregulation*, Quebec City: 18—19 May

Pacific Economic Cooperation Council (PECC) (1997c), 'Asia-Pacific and Western Hemisphere Regional Initiatives: Cooperation for Increasing Competition', *Background Paper for PECC's Trade Policy Forum for the PECC XII General Meeting*, Santiago: October

Pacific Economic Cooperation Council (PECC) (1998), 'Comments on Competition Policy and Deregulation Areas of APEC's Collective and Individual Actions Plans' (unpublished)

Padoa-Schioppa, T. *et al.* (1987), *Efficiency, Stability and Equity: A Strategy for the Evolution of the Economic System of the European Community*, Report of a Study Group appointed by the EC Commission, Brussels: European Union

Palmeter, D. (1996), *Anti-dumping, Antitrust and the Inclusion of Competition Laws in the World Trade Organisation*, Washington, DC: Graham and James

Pelkmans, J. (1997), *European Integration: Methods and Economic Analysis*, Heerlen: Netherlands Open University

Petersmann, E.U. (1996), *The Need for Integrating Trade and Competition Rules in the WTO World Trade and Legal System*, Geneva: Program for the Study of International Organizations

Petersmann, E.U. (1998), 'The Need for Integrating Trade and Competition Rules in the WTO World Trade and Legal System' in G. Parry, A. Qureshi and H. Steiner (eds), *The Legal and Moral Aspects of International Trade*, London and New York: Routledge

Pitofsky, R. (1996), 'FTC Chairman says World Competition Rules Currently not Feasible', *Inside US Trade*, 14, 26 April

Prusa, T.J. (1998), 'Cumulation and Antidumping: a Challenge to Competition', *World Economy*, 21, November, 1021—33

Rakovsky, C. (1997), 'The Commission's Cooperation with Third Countries in the Field of Competition', prepared remarks before FIW Conference, Brussels: 18 September

Rose, V. (ed.) (1994), *Common Market Law of Competition*, 4th edn, London: Sweet and Maxwell

Ruggiero, R. (1995), Speech to Conference on Antitrust, Rome, 20 November, Press/30, Geneva: WTO

Ruggiero, R. (1996), Speech to Conference on Future Directions of the Multilateral Trading System, Rome, 22 February, Press/43, Geneva: WTO

Schaub, A. (1996), 'Competition in the Information Society: Multimedia', prepared remarks, Mentor Group, New York: 6 December

Schaub, A. (1998), 'International Cooperation in Antitrust Matters: Making the Point in the Wake of the Boeing/MDD Proceedings', *EC Competition Policy Newsletter*, 4, 1, February

Scherer, F.M. (1994), *Competition Policies for an Integrated World Economy*, Washington, DC: Brookings Institution

Second Summit of the Americas (1998a), Plan of Action signed by the Heads of State and Government, April

Second Summit of the Americas (1998b), Santiago Declaration of the Heads of State and Government, April

Siebert, H. (1997), *Towards a New Global Framework for High-technology Competition*, Tübingen: J.C.B. Mohr

Sleuwaegen, L. (1998), 'Cross-border Mergers and EC Competition Policy', *World Economy*, 21, November, 1077—93

Smith, E. (1998), 'EU Competition Policy without Membership: Lessons from the European Economic Area' in S. Estrin and P. Holmes, *Competition and Economic Integration in Europe*, Cheltenham: Edward Elgar

Smith, Lockwood (1997), 'The International Dairy Trade Environment after the Uruguay Round', *Address to the New Zealand Dairy Expo*, Hamilton: 22 January

Smith, Lockwood (1998), 'Producer Board Reforms', *Address to the Warkworth Rotary Club*, 11 June

Spier, H. (1997), 'The Interaction between Trade and Competition Policy: the Perspective of the Australian Competition and Consumer Commission', prepared remarks, Seminar on International Trade Policies, Taipei: 2 May

Spier, H. and T. Grimwade (1997), 'International Engagement in Competition Law Enforcement: the Future for Australia', *Trade Practices Law Journal*, December, 232—41

Stragier, J. (1993), 'The Competition Rules of the EEA Agreement and Their Implementation', *European Competition Law Review*, 14, 30—38

Swann, D. (1998), *The Economics of the Common Market*, 6th edn, London: Penguin Books

Tavares, J. (1995), *Contestability and Economic Integration in the Western Hemisphere*, Discussion Paper, Washington, DC: OAS Trade Unit

Tavares, J. and L. Tineo (1998), 'Harmonization of Competition Policies among Mercosur Countries', *Antitrust Bulletin*, Spring, 45—70

Tavares, J. and L. Tineo (1999), 'Competition Policy and Regional Trade: NAFTA, Andean Community, MERCOSUR and FTAA', in P. Low, B. Kotschwar and M.R. Mendoza (eds), *Multilateral and Regional Trade Negotiations: Convergence or Conflict?*, Washington, DC: Brookings Institution (forthcoming)

Tharakan, P.K.M. (1995), 'Political Economy and Contingent Protection', *Economic Journal*, 105, November, 1550—64

Tharakan, P.K.M., D. Greenaway and J. Tharakan (1998), 'Cumulation and Injury Determination of the European Community in Antidumping Cases', *Weltwirtschaftliches Archiv*, Band 134, Heft 2, 320—39

Tirole, J. (1990), *The Theory of Industrial Organization*, Cambridge, Mass.: MIT Press

United Nations (1981), *The Set of Multilaterally Agreed Equitable Principles and Rules for the Control of Restrictive Business Practices*, New York: United Nations

United Nations Commission on Transnational Corporations (UNCTC) (1990), *Key Concepts in International Investment Arrangements and their Relevance to Negotiations on International Transactions in Services*, UNCTC Current Series no. 13, NewYork: United Nations

United Nations Conference on Trade and Development (UNCTAD) (1997), *World Investment Report 1997: Transnational Corporations, Market Structure and Competition Policy*, New York: UNCTAD

United States Council of Economic Advisers (1994), *Annual Report*, Washington, DC: United States Council of Economic Advisers

United States Information Service (USIS) (1998), 'The United States Government's Views on New Zealand's Decision to Lift the Ban on Parallel Imports', Wellington

United States Trade Representative (USTR) (1998a), 'USTR and Department of Commerce Announce Next Steps on Improving Access to the Japanese Market for Film', Press Release, Washington, DC: 3 February

United States Trade Representative (USTR) (1998b), Press Release, Washington, DC: 26 May

Valentine, D. (1997), 'Building a Cooperative Framework for Oversight in Mergers: the Answer to Extraterritorial Issues in Merger Review', prepared remarks before George Mason Law Review's Antitrust Symposium, Arlington: 10 October

Van Miert, K. (1998), 'The WTO and Competition Policy: the Need to Consider Negotiations', Address before Ambassadors to the WTO, Geneva: 21 April

Varney, C. (1995), 'Cooperation Between Enforcement Agencies: Building Upon the Past', prepared remarks, APEC Committee on Trade and Investment Conference on Competition Policy and Law, Auckland, New Zealand: 25 July

Vautier, K.M. (1987), 'Competition Policy and Competition Law', in A. Bollard and R. Buckle (eds), *Economic Liberalisation in New Zealand*, London: Allen & Unwin

Vautier, K.M. (1990), 'Trans-Tasman Trade and Competition Law' in K.M. Vautier, J. Farmer and R. Baxt (eds), *CER and Business Competition: Australia and New Zealand in a Global Economy*, Auckland: Commerce Clearing House New Zealand Limited

Vautier, K.M. and P.J. Lloyd (1997), *International Trade and Competition Policy: CER, APEC and the WTO*, Wellington: Institute of Policy Studies

Vautier, K.M., J. Farmer and R. Baxt (eds) (1990), *CER and Business Competition: Australia and New Zealand in a Global Economy*, Auckland: Commerce Clearing House New Zealand Limited

Veugelers, R. and H. Vandenbussche (1998), 'European Anti-dumping Policy and the Profitability of National International Collusion', *European Economic Review*, (forthcoming)

Viner, J. (1926), *Dumping: A Problem in International Trade*, Geneva: League of Nations

Waverman, L., W.S. Comanor and A. Goto (eds) (1997), *Competition Policy in the Global Economy: Modalities for Cooperation*, London and New York: Routledge

Weatherill S. and P. Beaumont (1993), *EC Law*, London: Penguin

Whish, R. and D. Wood (1994), *Merger Cases in the Real World: A Study of Merger Control Procedures*, Paris: OECD

Wood, D. (1992), 'International Competition Policy in a Diverse World: Can One Size Fit All?' in Barry Hawk (ed.), *EC and US Competition Law and Policy*, New York: Fordham Corporation Law Institute

Wood, D. (1995), 'Effective Enforcement of Antitrust Law for International Transactions', prepared remarks before Business Development Associates Inc., Washington, DC: 15 March

Wood, D. (1996), 'Regulation in the Single Global Market: From Anarchy to World Federalism?', *Ohio Northern Law Review*, 23, 297—307

Woodland, A.D. (1982), *International Trade and Resource Allocation*, Amsterdam and New York: North-Holland

World Bank (1997), 'Competition Policy in a Global Economy: a Latin American Perspective', World Bank—OECD Conference

World Bank (1998), 'Competition Policy in a Global Economy: an Interpretive Summary', summary papers from Global Forum for Competition and Trade Policy Conference, New Delhi, India: 17—18 March 1997

World Trade Organization (WTO) (1996), Negotiating Group on Basic Telecommunications, Reference Paper, Geneva: World Trade Organization

World Trade Organization (WTO) (1997a), *Annual Report 1997*, Volume 1, Geneva: World Trade Organization

World Trade Organization (WTO) (1997b), Working Group on the Interaction between Trade and Competition Policy, *Communication from the United States*, Geneva: 15 September

World Trade Organization (WTO) (1997c), Working Group on the Interaction between Trade and Competition Policy, *Communication from New Zealand*, Geneva: 10 September

World Trade Organization (WTO) (1997d), Working Group on the Interaction between Trade and Competition Policy, *Communication from Australia*, Geneva: 19 June

World Trade Organization (WTO) (1997e), Working Group on the Interaction between Trade and Competition Policy, *Communication from ASEAN*, Geneva: 10 September

World Trade Organization (WTO) (1997f), Working Group on the Interaction between Trade and Competition Policy, *Communication from the OECD*, Geneva

World Trade Organization (WTO) (1998a), Working Group on the Interaction between Trade and Competition Policy, *Communication from the United States*, Geneva: 10 March

World Trade Organization (WTO) (1998b), 'Japan: Measures Affecting Consumer Photographic Film and Paper', *Report of the Panel*, Geneva: 20 March

Young, D. and S. Metcalfe (1997), 'Competition Policy' in M.J. Artis and N. Lee (eds), *The Economics of the European Union: Policy and Analysis*, 2nd edn, Oxford: Oxford University Press

Zampetti, A.B. and P. Sauvé (1996), 'Onwards to Singapore: the International Contestability of Markets and the New Trade Agenda', *World Economy*, 19 May, 333—44

Author Index

Subject Index

Hard Core Cartels 135, 191
Patent and Know-how Licensing
  Agreements 135
Recommendations Concerning Action
  Against Restrictive Business
  Practices Affecting International
  Trade 135
Recommendations Concerning
  Cooperation between Member
  States on Anticompetitive
  Practices Affecting International
  Trade 19—20
Recommendations for Bilateral
  Cooperation 132—33
Recommendations for Cooperation
  between Member Countries in
  Areas of Potential Conflict
  between Trade and Competition
  Policies 134
sector-specific work 136—37
Trademarks and Trademark Licences
  135
OECD Committee on Restrictive
  Business Practices 133
OECD Competition Law and Policy
  Committee 15, 131—32, 134, 138
OECD countries, competition laws 7
OECD Trade Committee 133, 136, 138

Pacific Economic Cooperation Council
  see PECC
Paraguay, and MERCOSUR Agreement
  114
parallel importing 92—96, 188
Pareto-efficiency 22
Patent and Know-how Licensing
  Agreements, OECD
  Recommendations 135
PECC's Competition Principles Project
  147—48, 189
Peru, and Andean Community 116
Philippines, Individual Action Plan 142
photographic film and paper *see* Kodak/
  Fuji dispute
plurilateral approaches 18, 19—20
  APEC 139—50
  ECOSOC and UNCTAD 127—30
  GATT 1960 Decision 125, 126—27
  limitations 190
  OECD 131—38

policy analysis
  cross-border merger example 25—28
  framework
    application 28—29
    elements 21—25
policy failures, cross-border competition
  13—15, 20, 64, 108, 154
positive comity 20, 23
  bilateral cooperation agreements 37,
    38, 52—53, 69, 71, 133, 191
positive spillover effects 24, 26
Premiums Law (Japan) 176, 177—78, 180
price discrimination provisions repeal,
  Australia 81—82
price-fixing agreements, domestic
  markets 168
principles, definition 19
private anti-competitive conduct 164
private sector 3
privatization 7, 102, 145
  state-owned enterprises, EU 61
producer boards 96
Project Blue Sky v. Australian
  Broadcasting Authority case 78

redistributive effects 24
regional competition authorities 28
regional trading agreements 19, 28
  Closer Economic Relations 77—98
  European Union 59—76
  limitations 190
  The Americas 101—22
restrictive business practices
  GATT views 126—27
  ITO views 125—26
  multinational enterprises, OECD
    views 20, 135, 137—38
  UNCTAD views 128
Robinson—Patman Act (US) 104
rules, definition 19

'second generation' agreements 37—38,
  69
Sherman Act (US) 104, 105, 107
Singapore
  free trade 10, 12
  Individual Action Plan 146
Single Act (European Union) 59, 62
small and medium-size enterprises *see*
  SMEs